16.95

9+

WITHDRAWN

D1226785

Folklorist of the Coal Fields

George Korson's Life and Work

928
K8448

Folklorist of the Coal Fields

George Korson's Life and Work

Angus K. Gillespie

Foreword by Samuel P. Bayard

The Pennsylvania State University Press

University Park and London

Library of Congress Cataloging in Publication Data

Gillespie, Angus K   1942-
    Folklorist of the coal fields.

    Includes bibliography and index.
    1. Korson, George Gershon, 1899-1967. 2. Folk-
lorists—United States—Biography. 3. Folk-lore of
mines—United States. I. Title.
GR55.K48G54   398'092'4 [B]   79-25839
ISBN 0-271-00255-7

Copyright © 1980 The Pennsylvania State University
All rights reserved
Designed by Glenn Ruby
Printed in the United States of America

For Rae R. Korson, HH.D.

Anyone who reads this work will be convinced, as I am, of the loyalty and support of Rae Rosenblatt Korson. Few women would have had the patience to find happiness with a man who simultaneously worked at a full-time occupation and at a full-time avocation. I also salute her courage in giving me so much material and then leaving me alone with it, to tell the story as I saw it. My aim was to write the truth about George Korson, and I would not have come near it if Rae Korson had not been so honest and so courageous.

CAT Aug 24 '81

G. Henderson

ML 3 14.14

8-10-81

81-1003

18'45'81

Contents

Foreword

George Korson, whom I knew for more years than I am able to count, was a man for whom I have always entertained the highest respect. Like a number of other American folklorists, he was self-taught—or, rather, taught by experience and exposure. Thrust by the circumstances of his calling into a situation where he was confronted by a specialized group's culture that included a mass of folklore, he showed remarkable insight in recognizing the material for what it was and great intelligence in equipping himself to recover it. His timely interest in this material, and in the humanity of the people who preserved it, resulted in the rescue of a large mass of song, verse, music, and other lore that would now be impossible to find. His work, carried on in surroundings different from those in which most contemporary folklore collectors pursued their activities, entitles him to be ranked as a pioneer in the gathering of what we now call "industrial folklore."

Korson was a man of integrity and generosity. He was outgoing and friendly, treating his miner friends and all other helpers with scrupulous fairness, giving unstinted credit and thanks to all who assisted him, and presenting his material with a sympathy and accuracy with which it would be hard to find fault. As a writer, he possessed a vivid, rapid, ongoing prose style that made all his books readable.

As an American folklorist who (wittingly or unwittingly) broke new ground and opened up new prospects to his contemporaries, Korson certainly deserves a study of his life and work, and I am extremely glad that Angus Gillespie has chosen to write such a study.

Samuel P. Bayard

Acknowledgments

First of all, I am grateful to Don Yoder and Kenneth Goldstein for introducing me to the folk culture of the anthracite miners and the work of George Korson. Many of the ideas here were initially prompted in discussion with them. I also wish to thank Archie Green, who gave generously of his time and constantly helped me to appreciate the ideas raised by Korson's work. At several key junctures he was able to steer me to just the right book or just the right person. When I was most in need of direction, he stepped forward with helpful suggestions and clarifications. His discernment, analytical intelligence, and commitment to the labor movement were a constant source of inspiration.

I wish to express my gratitude to Mary Barrett and Judith Tierney of the D. Leonard Corgan Library of King's College in Wilkes-Barre, Pennsylvania. As noted in the text, it was through Mary Barrett's foresight that the importance of the Korson papers was recognized very early, in time to preserve them carefully. Judith Tierney did the actual work of cataloguing and indexing the papers. The resulting George Korson Folklore Archive is a boon to folklorists. Her meticulous work saved me at least a year of research time, and her detailed knowledge of Korson's achievements enabled me to try out most of the ideas in this biography with her before casting them into final form.

I am delighted to acknowledge the enthusiastic cooperation of the following individuals who contributed to the completeness of this work: Catherine H. Bryan, Richard Dorson, Henry Glassie, Betsy Korson Glazier, Harold Glazier, Nancy Joan Glazier, Wayland Hand, Bess Lomax Hawes, Frank Hoffman, Pandora Hopkins, Charles McCarthy, John M. Pickering, Warren E. Roberts, and Fran Korson Wruble. My thanks also to colleagues in the American Studies Department at Douglass College of Rutgers University for their comments and suggestions. I benefited from the help of a number of associates who read portions of earlier drafts: Louise Duus, Susan Dwyer-Shick, Leslie Fishbein, Amy Richlin, Michael Aaron Rockland, and Paul Schiffer.

Many of my students in American folklore at Douglass College have been helpful along the way, but I owe special thanks to Marjorie Kraus, who read and categorized 1,115 of Korson's letters according to the McBee Keysort System of classification. Thanks are also due Neal Mowry and Hedy Goller for their advice on folk song material. I could not have completed this book on schedule without a leave of absence granted by the administration of Douglass College. It was very helpful to have this uninterrupted time.

Preface

What a wee part of a person's life are his acts and his words. His real life is led in his head, and is known to none but himself.[1]

—Mark Twain

Born into a poor working-class Jewish family in the Ukraine in 1899, George Korson grew up in Wilkes-Barre, Pennsylvania, where he became a newspaperman and later a folklorist with a national reputation for his pioneer work collecting the stories and songs of coal miners. Following his death in 1967 a number of laudatory obituaries appeared, but to date there has been no complete assessment of George Korson's contribution to American intellectual life. In the 1970s several folkloristic publications paid tribute to Korson. The most important of these was Archie Green's *Only a Miner* (1972). Because Green's work expanded Korson's inquiry, he made his debt to Korson explicit in that book. In the first chapter, called "Folksong and Folk Society," Green presents a balanced account of Korson's work. He points out Korson's magnificent efforts to establish a chapter in American industrial folklore, but notes Korson's blurring of analytic distinctions and his neglect of some peripheral material.[2]

In addition to Green's book, several periodicals are of special interest. The "George Korson Memorial Issue" of the *Keystone Folklore Quarterly* appeared in the summer of 1971. This issue helped to spur my own interest in writing Korson's biography. Other periodicals, not dedicated to George Korson, dealt with occupational folklore. Articles in these journals acknowledged Korson, criticized him, broadened his definitions, and recognized his accomplishments. One such periodical was *Folklore Forum* for Spring 1978, called "Occupational Folklore and the Folklore of Working," with articles by Philip Nusbaum, Catherine Swanson, and Richard March, all of whom dealt in some degree with Korson's contribution. Another such periodical was *Western Folklore* for July 1978, called "Working Americans: Contemporary

Approaches to Occupational Folklife," with articles by Robert S. McCarl, Jr., Roger D. Abrahams, and Archie Green, all of whom explicitly acknowledged Korson's contributions. In spite of all this interest there still has been no full-length investigation of Korson's work.

At one point Archie Green writes, "Eventually we must go through Korson's books and ephemeral material to formalize his theoretical position—weak or strong—if only to advance industrial folklore as a sub-area within American Studies."[3] This is what I have attempted to do. To begin with, this is not a definitive biography, or a swollen catchall. There are a great deal of data available on the life of George Korson; I defined my task as giving order, shape, and coherent meaning to this information. By the selection and arrangement of this material, I have tried to communicate my view of Korson's essential contributions to American intellectual life.[4] In short, this is an intellectual, not a personal, biography.

My work was made possible chiefly by two circumstances. In 1965 Korson donated to the library of King's College in Wilkes-Barre all the books, periodicals, discs, tapes, and papers that he had accumulated over a lifetime of research and writing. With the kind permission of his wife, Rae Korson, I have gone through this material. Though Korson kept no journal or diary, he was a habitual writer of letters. Fortunately he saved nearly all the letters he received and made carbons of those he sent. Korson was a good correspondent. He answered his mail promptly and spoke to the issues that had been raised. He not only wrote to professional collaborators, he also wrote numerous letters to his family and his old pals. Since nearly all of this material is carefully dated, the correspondence provides a reliable baseline to monitor his activities. Fortunately this archive is accessible and usable because Judith Tierney, Special Collections Librarian, spent nearly a year arranging and cataloging the material.

Even the best archive of documentary materials has gaps and leaves many unanswered questions. From a historical point of view, working with a twentieth-century figure like George Korson affords a unique advantage. Although most of his informants are now dead, his family and many of his colleagues are still alive and eager to help. I am especially obliged to George Korson's wife, Rae Korson, and his daughter, Betsy Korson Glazier, for their help in rounding out my account. I made an effort to interview as many of

Korson's professional colleagues as possible, but I did not speak with them all. For example, I was especially disappointed not to interview Benjamin Albert Botkin, Korson's lifelong friend, who died on July 30, 1975, just as I was planning to visit him.

It is evident from even a casual survey of the literature that George Korson was a very productive writer. But how important was his contribution to American intellectual life? After the biographer has gone through Korson's books, articles, and ephemeral material, it is possible to reach one of two conclusions. We may conclude that George Korson was a typical self-educated folklorist, neither stronger nor weaker than most of the others. Under this interpretation he would be shown as illuminating an obscure corner of Pennsylvania—a sort of regional journalist interested in local color. Or we may conclude that Korson was a pioneer in the collection of American industrial folklore.

Without wishing to prejudice the case, I would like to take this dichotomy a bit further. Paradoxically, Korson's weaknesses are also his strengths. For example, consider the matter of self-education. Although Korson attended Columbia University for one year and read widely as an adult, as a folklorist he was largely self-educated. His family was simply too poor to send him through college. Because he was the oldest of six brothers and sisters, the family depended on him to support the younger siblings. Yet in some ways Korson's lack of formal credentials was an asset. Without formal training in folklore, Korson had not absorbed the prevailing bias toward rural lore. Industrial folklorist Archie Green points out that Korson might have easily overlooked the lore of coal miners in northeast Pennsylvania, just as Cecil Sharp had in southern Appalachia, if he had absorbed the usual prejudices. Also, because of his position in the community as a working newspaperman, Korson's rapport with the miners was usually good.[5]

Another weakness that proved a strength was his background in journalism. Although gradually Korson's principal professional interest became folklore scholarship, all his life he worked as a journalist to support himself and his family. He worked for various newspapers in Pennsylvania and New Jersey and as an editor for the American Red Cross National Headquarters in Washington, D.C., for some fifteen years. This necessary time spent as a journalist may have been the highest price he paid for his lack of an advanced academic degree. He never enjoyed the time for research that would have been afforded by summer vacations and sabbaticals, and he never enjoyed the security of tenure. Korson compensated for these handicaps with unusual strength and vigor, despite suffering from angina in his later years. As a veteran newspaperman he was proud of his ability to meet deadlines.

Leaving aside the question of quality for a moment, it should be pointed out that Korson's work of salvaging coal miner lore is unique. During the 1920s machinery was changing the nature of the trades, the crafts, and industry. At the same time isolated communities were drawn into the mass culture by the automobile, the radio, the movies, and the phonograph record. The important thing is that during the 1920s no one undertook parallel work in metal mining, steel, textiles, or printing. At least part of the credit for the early work in the collection of coal miner folklore must be given to John L. Lewis, then president of the United Mine Workers of America, who early on recognized the value of what Korson was doing, and who supported some of Korson's later research. Korson's work was unique; folklorist Archie Green says that there were at least a dozen other occupations that could have been investigated while the old-timers were still alive.[6] It is a little surprising that there was no George Korson of steel. Though it is a vast industry, almost nothing in folklore has been done except by Jacob Evanson.[7]

Another intriguing aspect of Korson's work is that almost from the very beginning he intuitively understood that folklore is best presented in the context of the entire way of life of a small community. Long before this holistic folklife approach became a formalized academic position, Korson took it for granted that the miners' lore had to be set in context. Green points out that Korson assumed that the miners were "folk" for two basic reasons. First, their songs behaved like folksongs in their origin and transmission. Second, miners were isolated in remote villages set apart by dangerous work and a homogeneous lifestyle.[8] Thus Korson, without benefit of formal definition, was really very close to the perspective of folklife scholarship developed in Scandinavia and espoused in this country by Robert Redfield and Don Yoder.[9]

But even granting that Korson's work was both unique and holistic, further definition is necessary. Perhaps his work *was* unique and holistic, but is it really folklore? Korson has been called a social historian, a historian-folklorist, and a writer of informal history. In this book I attempt to clarify the nature of his work.

The introduction to this biography, "The Folklorist's Image of the World," erects a theoretical scaffolding. With this system of ideas in mind, I have dealt with Korson's work in terms of his contributions to American intellectual life. While the ensuing chronological chapters do touch upon Korson's life and times, the focus is on the ideas generated by his work. My model for this approach was Ruth Michaelis-Jena's *The Brothers Grimm*.[10] Except for his folklore field work, the life of George Korson was relatively uneventful, even colorless. There are very few anecdotes or legends about George Korson, as there are about his contemporaries Ernest Hemingway and Scott Fitzgerald. He did not go on speaking tours across the nation; his face did not appear on the cover of *Life* or *Time*.[11] Korson was very much a private person. Although he clearly had strong feelings about many matters and succeeded in conveying these feelings where he felt they mattered, his impulse to remain a private person often led him to tone down his utterances for the sake of maintaining correct behavior. Korson kept his private thoughts to himself. As far as I know, he never poured his soul into any confessional writing.

In the first chapter, "Korson's Early Life," I begin the chronological account with his boyhood in Wilkes-Barre and his apprenticeship in journalism in the 1920s. The last four chapters are organized by decades. Chapter 2, "The Anthracite Years," deals with the 1930s, chapter 3, "The Bituminous Years," deals with the 1940s, and so on. Although these are not watertight compartments, they are helpful subdivisions that allow us to handle the various strands of concurrent events—Korson's public life, his private life, the mood of the times, and his intellectual development. My aim as a biographer was to extract the significant themes from the welter of surrounding circumstances.[12]

George Korson is a fascinating figure to the student of American civilization because he defies ready categorization. We cannot easily drop him into a prearranged pigeonhole. Korson is a bundle of contradictions. He is somewhere between the amateur gentleman collector of the nineteenth century and the scientific, analytically minded scholar of the twentieth century. At first glance it might appear that this would be an easy way to sum up his career. *Songs and Ballads of the Anthracite Miner*, which appeared in 1927, was written in the spare time that he could snatch from a full-time job on a newspaper. Korson himself saw this book as a salvage attempt. *Black Rock*, which appeared in 1960, was the last scholarly book written by Korson. He was urged to write it by the Pennsylvania German Society. A Guggenheim Foundation fellowship helped in the writing of it, and a grant from the Ford Foundation brought it to publication. Thus at the close of his career Korson received a good deal of official and professional recognition. The comparison of these two books, spanning more than thirty years, seems to show a neat pattern of straight-line professional growth. Like most simple generalizations, this notion has a kernel of truth, but Korson's career is not really such a simple matter.

Korson was an amateur folklorist, but a professional writer. He was a rigorous scholar, but not a college graduate. He was a labor sympathizer, but not a radical. Korson had no doctorate, yet he was a Fellow of the American Folklore Society. He never bothered to learn to drive a car, yet his field work stands as a model. He could not transcribe music, yet he is recognized as an authority on folksongs. He enjoyed quiet moments of reflection and writing, but he spent a large part of his life in organizational and administrative work.

In the course of this biography I attempt to explain and resolve some of these contradictions. One important clue is that Korson's motives were nearly completely pure. By this I mean that Korson was not writing because of academic motivation. Professors of folklore, or any other discipline, must write. The motivation in such cases may be the desire for tenure or promotion or professional recognition as well as the innate love of learning. But Korson was working outside the academy. To be sure, he was not immune to the attractions that publishing holds for all writers—the pride and pleasure of seeing one's name in print or of seeing one's work appear between two covers. But the point is that Korson wrote and continued to write mainly because he wanted to do it, not because he had to do it. Certainly money was never his motivation. None of his books was a tremendous commercial success. It was not money that drove Korson; it was not a case of a scholar needing his academic meal ticket punched; in a genuine human sense it was enthusiasm about coal miners' folk culture—their life-style, their anecdotes, and their songs—which drove Korson. He had the newspaperman's instinct for a good story. Even later in life, when he was very attentive to all the fine points of academic convention and precise citation, he never completely lost his early habits of writing readable and lively prose. Another good habit that Korson picked up early in his life as a newspaperman was industry—sheer hard work. Over a lifetime he had eleven major publications. Nine of these were written by Korson himself; the other two were edited or co-edited by him. He also edited two phonograph records issued by the Library of Congress. In addition to these major publications there were, of course, many articles and speeches.

It is difficult to reconstruct Korson's years of childhood and adolescence. Documents are scarce, almost nonexistent. For years, his younger brother Meyer Korson had kept a trunk of Korson juvenilia in his basement. In time this material probably would have been donated to the George Korson Folklore Archive at King's College. But on June 21, 1972, tremendous rains triggered by Hurricane Agnes caused the Susquehanna River to overflow its banks, resulting in the worst flood of the century. The Great Disaster, as it is now known, caused many losses in the Wyoming Valley, among them the trunk with Korson's work as a schoolboy and his letters written home when he was in the British Army. Ironically, it was in the summer of 1972 that my research on this biography began. Had I begun work a year earlier, I might have seen these documents before they were lost.

One bright note in this dark picture is that the bulk of the Korson Collection came through the flood intact. This was due to the fortunate circumstance that the Korson Collection was housed on the third floor of the D. Leonard Corgan Library. Had it been housed in the basement, it would have been nearly a total loss. That summer I recall remarking to Mary Barrett, director of the King's College Library, how brilliant the architect had been to place the special collections on the third floor where they would be out of harm's way in any possible flood. Of course, I was simply mistaken. Neither the architect nor anyone else had ever expected a flood of such magnitude. The real reason for placing the archives on the top floor had nothing to do with flooding. Mary Barrett told me that she herself had planned to have the Korson Archives on the top floor so that George could have a desk there from which he could look out over the valley he loved and see the breakers and culm banks.[13]

An additional problem in reconstructing Korson's childhood is that I never met or interviewed him. Korson died in 1967, when I was still in my first year of graduate school, just beginning to take a serious interest in folklore. Even allowing for the untrustworthiness of memory after some sixty years, it would have been wonderful to have Korson's own construction of his childhood. A further difficulty is that Korson was the oldest child. He had three younger sisters, Fran, Sue, and Ann, plus two younger brothers, Selig and Meyer; but none of them is in a good position to recall George's childhood.

We do know, however, that George Korson acquired from Wilkes-Barre not only a sense of family but also a sense of place. Though it was a town smudged with coal dust and dotted about with unsightly culm banks, Korson remembered it fondly. As a biographer, my having spent the better part of three summers in Wilkes-Barre heightens my feeling of closeness and understanding of George Korson. When I walk on the River Common and look at the Susquehanna, I know that George Korson has been there. Landmarks that are now familiar to me, like the Hotel Sterling and Public Square, were also familiar to him. In 1917, when Korson graduated from Wilkes-Barre (now James M. Coughlin) High School, the coal mining industry had reached its peak in the Wyoming Valley. In that year there were more than 156,000 men engaged in anthracite mining in Luzerne and surrounding counties, extracting more than 100 million tons of coal a year. Coal mining operations were so extensive in the area that it was possible to travel from Nanticoke to Carbondale through underground mines without ever coming to the surface. Fifty years later, in 1967, the year of Korson's death, the coal industry had faded. By then only about 11 million tons of coal were mined yearly in the total anthracite field covering about ten counties.[14] The constant falling off of the anthracite industry over Korson's adult life undoubtedly contributed to the tone of nostalgia that has been identified with his work.

In 1965 the Mid-America Conference of Literature, History, Popular Culture, and Folklore was held at Purdue University to demonstrate the need for closer alliance among the disciplines. At that conference Ray B. Browne called for closer association between American studies and American folklore. He said that American studies as a coherent discipline with momentum could make a real contribution to American folklore. To be comprehensive, American studies must include the study of folk cultures.[15] In a sense this biography represents a step in that direction. As a discipline the study of American folklore is relatively young, yet as it becomes more mature we can expect more biographies of American folklorists to emerge. During most of the twentieth century it seems that we as folklorists have been so busy gathering data and hammering out theory, that we have scarcely taken a moment for a backward glance at the history of our own field, let alone to consider biographies of individual American folklorists. But already there are signs that this is changing. Two prime examples from the late 1970s will illustrate this trend. In 1977 the University of Illinois Press published Robert Hemenway's full-length biography of Zora Neal Hurston, a sensitive account of America's most prominent black folklorist.[16] Then in 1978 the Folklore Publications Group at Indiana University brought out Peggy Martin's monograph on Stith Thompson.[17]

The research and writing of this book took seven years. Despite occasional frustration, one of the great joys of the work was dealing with the correspondence. Korson's habit of letter writing gives us an excellent point of departure to reconstruct his life. To be sure, most letters are not written to record events for posterity. Even if they contain news, they are written with a particular recipient in mind and are thus colored in a special way. In addition, letters carry more than information. The biographer must also read through displays of rhetoric, reflections of good manners, authorizations for someone to do something, and records of decisions taken.[18] Nevertheless, there is an undeniable delight in reading Korson's original letters, not unlike the thrill experienced by Hart Crane in reading his grandmother's love letters. Crane asked himself:

> Are your fingers long enough to play
> Old keys that are but echoes:
> Is the silence strong enough
> To carry back the music to its source
> And back to you again
> As though to her?[19]

Introduction:
The Folklorist's Image
of the World

George Korson spent his life collecting the stories and songs of American coal miners.[1] Before assessing his contributions to American intellectual life, it is helpful to examine his work in a broad context. Therefore this introduction will outline briefly the perceptions that American intellectuals in general and folklorists in particular have held of workers. The fundamental question is, how do urban middle-class intellectuals and scholars perceive the folk? This problem stems from the earliest stratification of society. It goes back to the time when differences were established between aristocratic or priestly classes and peasants, between patricians and plebeians. The very terms we use in our language—Greek terms, Hebraic terms, Anglo-Saxon terms—suggest how old the problem is. From the beginning of the perception that patricians differed from plebeians, it was the role of patricians to describe plebeians in writing. It is within this tradition that Sir Walter Scott, Cecil Sharp, and others describe "the folk." In the same tradition, George Korson described American coal miners. Korson had to confront the issue of describing the role of workers in American society, and his career illustrates the choices and dilemmas open to folklorists of his generation. Such ideas and ideologies are important because they govern the folklorist's selection of materials and ultimately his analysis of them.

Folklorists often do not express their views on this topic explicitly. The relationship between intellectuals and workers in America has always been difficult. The mere recognition of a working class seems somehow out of step with a democracy, because admitting the existence of a class structure seems opposed to the egalitarian spirit. In Europe a man's place was determined by birth. In America one could get ahead through diligence and thrift; this was the American Dream. Political scientists and economists have to write about these issues; folklorists do not. Thus it requires hard work to find ideological statements. Such statements are often implicit, buried in other things. Folklorists typically do not write on political theory; instead they go out and collect material. Nonetheless, at the risk of oversimplification, I suggest that folklorists in America before the 1930s generally held one of two views of workers: either an aristocratic view that workers were distasteful clods, or a Jeffersonian view that workers were honest yeomen. Consciously or unconsciously, most folklorists have shaped their work in response to these ideas.

In a literal sense an aristocratic society is one in which governmental control rests with a few wealthy or prominent people. In the original Greek the term meant "rule by the best." The theory of aristocracy is not altogether unconvincing. It holds that the few wealthy or prominent citizens are better qualified by birth and training to govern. Since they are better trained, they are in a good position to serve all of society, rich and poor alike.

The democratic suspicion, of course, is that all too often the aristocrats have used their power to look after themselves. However, it is somewhat simplistic to equate aristocracy with individual selfishness. It takes no special insight to see that the aristocrat's commitment to the existing order will often motivate him to prevent injustice and inequality from becoming deep enough to encourage revolt. In making the best possible case for aristocracy, we should point out that the aristocrat, like the conservative, recognizes the presence of evil in the world. The aristocrat is skeptical about noble deeds and wisdom and virtue. He has a certain doubt and caution about the future and thus a limited faith in the rule of the masses.[2]

Needless to say, in democratic America such a literal view of aristocracy has seldom been accepted, except possibly in colonial times, if we consider the slaveholding plantation owners in the South, the Dutch patroons in the Hudson River valley, and possibly the top merchant class in New England. Some of this aristocratic tradition lasted into the nineteenth century, but the nature of American life was not conducive to the growth of a hereditary wealthy class. Although the nineteenth-century robber barons (or captains of industry) were able to amass and transmit wealth over a number of generations, the American situation makes this difficult, and with the graduated income tax and the inheritance tax, it will probably continue to be difficult. In any event, an aristocracy based on money such as we find in America is less enduring than one based on land ownership, as in Europe.[3]

Although we can readily discount the notion of a permanent moneyed aristocracy in America, there is a more subtle sort of aristocracy that is difficult to ignore. The term may be used to refer to the best of something, such as an aristocracy of brains or skill or talent. This kind of aristocracy intellectuals may find irresistibly attractive. Even the ultraliberal college professor may find himself vulnerable to the charge that snobbery is the Achilles heel of liberalism.[4]

In the late nineteenth century the cultural life of the United States was dominated by a complex of values called the Genteel Tradition. This characteristic world view of the 1890s was generally accepted by Anglo-Saxon Protestant upper-middle-class America. The ideal called for "a well rounded individual of noble purpose and refined intelligence."[5] These people were far more interested in the arts than in labor, since they viewed art as the expression of highest idealism. Representative of this group are such people as Theodore Roosevelt, Henry Cabot Lodge, Owen Wister, and Henry Adams. It was during this period that the American Folklore Society was founded (1888). In the beginning, in America as in England, folklore was a gentleman's activity. MacEdward Leach has described this epoch very effectively:

> The first requisite was a fixed income, or a government or church sinecure, allowing the gentleman scholar to devote his time to the leisurely pursuit of scholarship for its own sake. There was no worry about making books or making academic way. From a pleasant study overlooking an old English garden or cloistered digs at one of the old universities, the gentleman scholar could indulge in the pleasure of collecting and investigating any odd bits of lore that caught his fancy.[6]

Leach does go on, however, to explain that these men were amateurs in the best sense of that word, that they loved what they were doing. Also appearing during this same period toward the end of the century was Francis J. Child's impressive five-volume work, *The English and Scottish Popular Ballads* (1892–1898). In a sense Child was both the last of the gentlemen collectors and the first of the scientific collectors. The book was scholarly and detailed, especially with regard to sources, except that Child completely overlooked the immediate oral tradition around him.[7] Archie Green has pointed out that Child in fact did know a great deal about the world of work, since his father was a Yankee sailmaker, but there was nothing in his adult experience or education that prepared him to collect labor lore.[8]

It was not until 1925 that George Korson began to collect living labor lore, specifically anthracite folklore. We can begin to see that it is precisely because Korson was outside the academic, gentlemanly, university-educated, aristocratic tradition that he was naive enough to consider collecting lore from contemporary industrial workers. Korson was not from a highly cultured or socially exclusive family from old New England. As the son of poor Jewish immigrants living in the anthracite region of northeastern Pennsylvania, he could hardly be considered typical of the social or cultural elite.

In sharp contrast to the aristocratic view is the Jeffersonian view, which points up the social necessity of labor and the moral obligation to work. Work in this sense is honorable and productivity is a virtue. In addition to devoting his life to the public service of his country, Jefferson understood the forces that were developing the political and social structure of the United States. Born near the frontier in colonial Virginia, he was sympathetic to the new sort of society the frontier produced—a society in which aristocracy and heredity counted less than in Europe and less than in Tidewater, Virginia. Class distinction and family prestige existed here, but Jefferson worked against them toward a rural, agricultural democracy.[9]

In his early career Jefferson consistently portrayed agriculture as the foundation of national character. As a young man he admired the poet Horace, who created a nostalgic picture of country life. In his early notebooks he copied a poem from Horace:

Happy is he who far from business,
like the first race of man,
can till inherited lands with his teams,
free from all payment of interest.

He who avoids the market and
the proud thresholds of mighty citizens . . .[10]

Jefferson continued to copy the entire poem, leaving out only the lines that could not possibly apply to a farm in Virginia. In all his writings he presented farm life as satisfying, wholesome, and virtuous.

Jefferson wanted to keep America an agricultural nation. He opposed the introduction of manufacturing plants and the immigration of factory workers. He saw America as an exporter of agricultural products and raw materials and an importer of finished manufactured goods. Factories and cities, he thought, tended to have a corrupting influence and were best left in Europe.

Most American folklorists are, I suspect, Jeffersonians at heart: although they are broadly sympathetic to workers, they share Jefferson's lingering rural bias. There is a distinct ambivalence toward the urban scene and toward the industrial worker. When an American folklorist sets out with notebook and tape recorder, where does he head for? Typically, for forgotten settlements in rural areas:

> Such nooks and byways resist the relentless forces of change and mobility in contemporary American life. In place of mass culture, they represent folk cultures, whose roots and traditions contrast oddly with the standardized glitter of American urban industrial society. In the folk region, people are wedded to the land, and the land holds memories. The people themselves possess identity and ancestry, through continuous occupation of the same soil.[11]

Favorite case studies and textbook examples of American folklore are often drawn from such areas as the Pennsylvania Dutch region, the Ozarks, Spanish New Mexico, the Utah Mormon community, and Maine Coast Yankees.

To be sure, some folklorists have confronted the mass-production and mass-consumption culture found in urban areas. One can point to Roger Abrahams's *Deep Down in the Jungle*, which deals with black narratives in Philadelphia, or to Charles Keil's *Urban Blues*, which deals with the interface between folk music and mass music. In addition there is Archie Green's *Only a Miner*, dealing with recorded coal-mining songs. Nonetheless, the majority of folklorists seem to prefer doing field work in rural, peasant folk cultures—as long as they can continue to find them.

Was George Korson also, in his heart, a Jeffersonian like so many of his friends and associates in folklore? The anthracite mine patch was rural and isolated, but it was not agricultural. The mine patch with its background of colliery buildings and culm banks was an industrial setting. Korson was acutely aware of the fact that industrial civilization in the twentieth century tended to crush and swallow up the earlier agricultural and rural civilization. His last full-length study, *Black Rock* (1960), addressed this very problem. Korson knew that the kind of folklore—industrial folklore—that he had spent his life collecting was not quite the same as that collected by most other folklorists. At the same time he saw these were not rigid categories; there was interpenetration between the two worlds. He wrote in the Preface to *Black Rock*:

> This is a study of the Pennsylvania Dutch in an unfamiliar setting, in which folklore helps us understand these traditionally agricultural people as they became adjusted to an industrial environment. The book is about . . . the period in the latter half of the nineteenth century when the United States emerged as a leading industrial power by using anthracite as its principal metallurgical fuel.[12]

Thus far we have seen that Korson was neither an aristocratic folklorist nor a Jeffersonian folklorist, because he never belonged to the aristocratic tradition, and because he took an interest in the industrial rather than the pastoral landscape. For modern folklorists like Korson there was a different set of questions to deal with. Since 1930 folklorists, especially industrial folklorists like Korson, have had to confront the choice between a Marxist view and a corporate-liberal view of American society, in other words, a choice between revolution and reform. A revolutionist stands intellectually outside of the system, believing that capitalism cannot reform itself. The basic Marxist analysis states that the contradictions within capitalism are so great that they doom the system. Reformists believe that there is enough health in the system for it to be reformed.

In the United States, Marxist class consciousness was at best sporadic. But if ever that spirit were alive, it was during the 1930s and the 1940s, a period of enormous productivity for Korson. As R. Serge Denisoff has pointed out, a good number of intellectuals, artists, academics, bohemians, folklorists, and others really believed that the Depression marked the end of the old order and the beginning of the new. Certainly the Marxist law of immiseration, or inevitably increasing misery, seemed to be true as the banks closed and the soup lines formed. Just as the Great Depression had a strong influence on American writing, giving rise to both Marxist criticism and proletarian fiction, so the thirties are associated with folk music and the American left. [13]

Was there any Marxist folklore in the United States during the thirties? Were there any Marxist tradition bearers or Marxist folklorists? Nearly everyone agrees that there *were* some connections between folk music and the American left. But just how strong were those connections? These questions are pursued at some length by Richard A. Reuss in his thesis "American Folklore and Left-Wing Politics: 1927–1957." In his first chapter, Reuss writes: "In the United States, as in Europe, Marxists of every variety made use of songs of persuasion in waging the class struggle. Anarchists, Socialists, Wobblies, Communists, and later Trotskyists, each developed their own stock of revolutionary lyrics . . ."[14]

In the 1930s and 1940s there were three prominent folklorists touched by Marxism—Charles Seeger, Ben Botkin, and Alan Lomax. In the later 1930s, Charles Seeger, the most scholarly of the three, was employed by the WPA Federal Music Project. In this post he was able to communicate with important people from the worlds of music and politics. Among those with whom he had extensive contact was Alan Lomax. Of course, Charles Seeger passed on his family tradition of political awareness and Jewish social conscience to his son Peter. [15]

Also in this group was Ben Botkin. In 1936 the Folklore Studies section of the Federal Writers Project was established under John A. Lomax. Ben Botkin, the editor of *Folkways* and the author of *Folk Say*, took over this section in 1938. The main idea of the WPA folklore philosophy was not to provide data for scholars but to "giv[e] back to the people what we [collectors] have taken from them and what rightfully belongs to them . . . The WPA looks upon folklore research not as a private but as a public function and folklore as a public, not private property."[16] Botkin's sympathy with Marxism was seldom expressed in writing, and there is nothing resembling a credo or lengthy exposition of his views in his published work. [17] However, he does come close to making a formal statement in his preface to Waldemar Hille's *The People's Song Book* (1948):

> If there was ever any doubt that singing has a direct and reciprocal relation to social, economic, and political issues, attitudes, and action, that doubt should have been removed by two world wars, the great depression between wars, and the crucial fight for security, for

civil liberties, and for world peace and unity that is still going on to-day. Out of the Thirties and the Forties has come a stronger and clearer realization that people must not only speak out but sing out in order to be heard. In this book a swelling chorus of people's voices is raised in old and new songs of faith in freedom and protest against oppression—a contemporary "cry for justice" that is worthy of a place beside the collections of Upton Sinclair and Jack London.[18]

The most outspoken of this group was Alan Lomax, who, according to Reuss, "more than any other scholar or performer of the 1930's shaped the popular outlook on folksong, particularly in left-wing circles, which influenced an entire generation of urban folksingers long after the Old Left had collapsed . . ." Lomax studied at the University of Texas and at Harvard. He accompanied his father, John Lomax, on various folklore field trips and assisted him in editing books on folksongs. He engaged in graduate studies at Harvard and Columbia and by 1937 was hired as the Director of the Archive of American Folk Song in the Library of Congress. Reuss described his difficulties there: "Egoistical, brilliant, impatient with the snail-like actions of plodding bureaucrats and reactionary politicians, his proselytizing in behalf of folksongs and his radical social views constantly had his superiors in the Library of Congress on edge, and ultimately led to the loss of his position at the close of World War II."[19]

As with Botkin, it is difficult to find in Alan Lomax's writing a formal credo to sum up his Marxist idealism and his belief that progressive folksongs could make a difference in American politics. However, he comes close to making such a statement in his foreword to *The People's Songbook:*

> Little people have breathed their unshakeable convictions into this book. I have watched it grow for fifteen years—the songs coming in one at a time from up and down the country—collectors pooling their treasures—balladeers like Woody Guthrie coming on with scores of fine ditties. At first I did not understand how these songs related to the traditional folk songs, such as those you will sing in the section called *Songs that helped build America.* Slowly I began to realize that here was an emerging tradition that represented a new kind of human being, a new folk community composed of *progressives and anti-fascists and union members.* These folk, heritors of the democratic tradition of folklore, were creating for themselves a folk-culture of high moral and political content. These home-made

songs of protest and affirmation shared the permanence of the people's tradition, but were most positive and more sharply critical than the familiar ballads.[20]

Reuss points out that Lomax saw folk music as "both class-oriented and indigenous in origin." His view of music was shaped by the "buoyant nationalist tone of the New Deal and anti-fascist spirit of the Popular Front."[21]

Gradually there was a decline of radicalism among these three folklorists, as there was among American intellectuals in general. Crises at home and abroad in the late 1930s left little time for subtle intellectual arguments about politics. As the country moved from the Depression to World War II, there was a decline of interest in ideology and a rekindled sense of national solidarity. Alan Lomax pulled away from Marxism into cantometrics. Charles Seeger moved into advanced musicology. Ben Botkin reverted to his consensus liberal opinions. But Korson was never touched by Marxism in the 1930s. What held him back was his closeness to the United Mine Workers of America.

Korson was a reformist with a fundamental belief in the corporate-liberal state. Unlike the older aristocratic view, the corporate-liberal state view does not take a position of outright disdain toward workers. Nor does it celebrate the worker as honest yeoman as in the Jeffersonian view. Rather it is a "practical" response to the realities of industrial America, a viewpoint based on resignation and adjustment to prevailing conditions. One might be tempted to say that Korson in opposition to Marxism took a "capitalist" view of American society, but this would be too simplistic and narrow. I prefer to stick with the corporate-liberal label, since the ideological framework that binds Americans together is a blend of parliamentary democracy, certain forms of free enterprise, laissez-faire economics, pragmatism, and worship of success. Most critical political scientists of today use the term corporate liberalism, or the corporate-liberal state, or the secular-liberal state, or Lockean liberalism. These terms bring together empiricism, parliamentary democracy, and the free-enterprise system.[22]

Korson's embrace of the corporate-liberal state grew logically out of his commitment to the United Mine Workers of America. Here we find a recognition of the built-in conflict between labor and capital, but there is also a willingness to accept mechanization and to cooperate to some extent with employers through bargaining and negotiations. Richard N. Goodwin has pointed out that under this system unions must restrict themselves to goals consistent with their power, which is limited by the present industrial structure:

> Of course, union leaders dream different dreams from those of company presidents, shareholders, or pension-fund managers. They do not spend long hours studying ways to improve company earnings. Each component of the modern process of production—managers, shareholders, unions, and creditors—differs from the others in claim and estate. But all are linked by the impermanent interest of the corporation itself—to function, grow, and earn. *The nature of their power and property requires each of them to act in a way that is consistent with the purpose—the inbuilt tropisms—of the economic bureaucracy.*[23]

In essence the corporate-liberal view allows the union activist to pursue his interest within accepted boundaries of dispute. In exchange for this industrial peace, the unions are granted a sort of official recognition in the hope that they will show some responsibility to the community at large as well as their membership. In essence, if labor is to work within the capitalist system, it must not appear to be bent on destroying the system.

Historically there have been profound differences within the labor movement itself. On the one hand we find the anarchists and syndicalists encompassing a spectrum from the I.W.W. to the Molly Maguires. On the other hand we find the craft unions represented by the A.F. of L. under Samuel Gompers, with definite purposes and limited goals. In America in the long run the trend has been toward the craft unions.

With a philosophy closely akin to that of Samuel Gompers, John Mitchell served as president of the United Mine Workers of America from 1898 to 1908. In much the same way as Gompers, Mitchell went after carefully defined short-term goals. He became most famous in the Pennsylvania anthracite strike of 1902, which is discussed in the seventh chapter of Korson's *Minstrels of the Mine Patch.* Korson's account of Mitchell's achievement is sympathetic, as is understandable since most observers agree that Mitchell was very clever and very well organized to have united some 150,000 immigrant miners, winning better wages and shorter hours for them. One significant gesture, not reported by Korson, which grew out of the 1902 confrontation, is described by Thomas R. Brooks:

When operator George F. Baer finished his able presentation of the operator's case before the commission, Mitchell crossed the room and shook the coal operator's hand. "To this day," McAllister Coleman wrote in his history of the union and the industry, *Men and Coal,* "veteran diggers speak of that gesture with perplexment." Possibly, speculates Coleman, Mitchell wearied with warfare, wanted peace with honor. "At all events," Coleman concludes, "from that time on, the course of the President of the UMWA, ran more and more to conciliation."[24]

The point, of course, is that increasingly unions tried to win acceptance from respectable elements of the community. Labor leaders like Samuel Gompers and John Mitchell tried hard to dissociate themselves from socialists, radicals, and other militants. It was a realistic assessment of the American situation in the early twentieth century. I think Korson would have basically agreed with John Mitchell when he said in 1903:

> The average wage earner has made up his mind that he must remain a wage earner. He has given up the hope of a kingdom come, where he himself will be a capitalist, and asks that the reward for his work be given him as a workingman.[25]

Thus, at the dawn of the twentieth century in America, it appeared as if labor would be willing to work with capitalism rather than against it. But the twentieth century was not to unfold in a neat, orderly, and ever-more-prosperous pattern. The Depression sapped the strength of organized labor. As workers lost jobs, union membership fell off. With so many unemployed at the gates, strikes seemed futile and hopeless.

In the 1930s, it is widely agreed, capitalism itself was on trial in America. Writers, critics, intellectuals, and folklorists all found capitalism wanting. During this period radical doctrines had strong appeal. Organized labor was in a slump. However, there came a significant and almost unexpected turning point. Franklin D. Roosevelt, perhaps unwittingly, spurred the rebirth of labor unions with his support of the National Industrial Recovery Act, Section 7A, of 1933. This provision guaranteed the rights of employees to organize and bargain freely. The law itself was complex and ambiguous, but labor leaders found a simple enough interpretation for recruiting posters: "President Roosevelt Wants You to Join the Union." Another important development, of course, was the

Wagner Act of 1935. The Wagner Act, in effect, reaffirmed Section 7A, and established the National Labor Relations Board. The importance of this legislation was described by James MacGregor Burns: "This was the most radical legislation passed during the New Deal, in the sense that it altered fundamentally the nation's politics by vesting massive economic and political power in organized labor."[26] Unionism was now an acceptable part of Americanism. Unions were now legitimized and recognized by the legal structure.

How did folklorists react to this fundamental change in the nation's politics? Where were folklorists in this scene? They were mostly absent. We have to remember the folklorist's predominant bias toward country life. Folklorists had been mostly concerned about rescuing rural folkways from the Industrial Revolution. Archie Green explains that "part of this stems from an inability to cope with grime, noise, or tension."[27] But fortunately, as a young working newspaperman, Korson did not know about this bias. It was a classic case of a gifted amateur who was not blinded by prevailing beliefs. Thus Korson felt free to collect anthracite lore in Pennsylvania and bituminous lore in the South and Midwest. Overall Korson accepted a capitalist world view—complete with labor unions. After all, one of his major works, *Coal Dust on the Fiddle*, was sponsored by the United Mine Workers of America. But unions like the UMWA were not trying for revolution, just a larger slice of the pie.

Clearly George Korson was a partisan of the United Mine Workers of America. His notions of reality were shaped by experiences of mine disaster, of callous exploitation. He was committed to reform of these traumatic ills. Korson identified with the mineworkers. Some critics make the assumption that if the folklorist identifies with any element of society, he loses objectivity. But the fact is that every scholar is the heir to some intellectual tradition. There are no scholars who are value-free. They are Socratics or Platonists, Jeffersonians or Hamiltonians, Marxists or Marcuseans. Scholars have positions. Sometimes the positions are explicit; sometimes they are cloaked; sometimes they are stated in confusing and contradictory terms. But they exist, and inevitably shape the scholar's work.

I have argued that Korson was a reformist with a fundamental belief in the corporate-liberal state; but within his ideological framework, he was a particularly warm and sensitive human being with a tremendous empathy for the coal miners with whom he worked. Very few folklorists demonstrated as much empathy for the folk as Korson. His affection for coal miners was genuine and personal, as shown in his final case study on Tom Hill, "My Sweetheart's the Mule in the Mines," to be discussed in Chapter 5.

Eastern Pennsylvania, showing Korson's main bases of operations. Schuylkill County is outlined.

Drawn by Ruth A. Strohl

1

Korson's Early Life

But those days are gone,
They will come no more.
With a tear in my eye,
Oh, how often I sigh
For those days of yore.[1]

Though George Korson's career was closely tied to Pennsylvania, his life did not begin there.[2] It began in Eastern Europe. The first of six children, he was born on August 8, 1899, in Bobrinets in the southern Ukraine, to Joseph and Rose Korson. George was seven years old in 1906 when his parents brought the family to the United States and settled in Brooklyn, New York.[3]

The family was unhappy with the pace of life and crowding in New York. They had friends and contacts in northeastern Pennsylvania who persuaded them that a small town in the mountains of Pennsylvania was a better environment for bringing up a family. Taking this advice, Joseph and Rose Korson bundled up their children and their modest possessions and set out for Wilkes-Barre. It was a little discouraging to relocate again. The cultural shock of leaving the Ukraine for America had not yet worn off. They had to leave some of their possessions behind, as they had done before, but they did manage to include in the few belongings they took with them their samovar, a little metal urn made of copper, which is still in the family.

George Korson was thirteen in 1912 when his family went to Wilkes-Barre. This gritty but prosperous coal mining city on the east bank of the Susquehanna River slowly became George Korson's hometown. It was a city of ethnic enclaves—Irish, Welsh, and Slav. The focal point of social life was the neighborhood, its horizons limited by the general store, the church, and the saloon.

Korson at about thirteen. *Courtesy Betsy Korson Glazier*

Beyond the city limits was the scenic Wyoming Valley and beyond that were the outlying ranges of the Endless Mountains. No one could foresee that one day Korson would be known as "the man from Wilkes-Barre." According to James J. Corrigan, Wilkes-Barre historian and former newspaperman, this honorary title has been bestowed on only two other native sons: Daniel J. Hart, mayor of Wilkes-Barre for several terms, who was nationally known as a playwright and orator; and George Catlin, painter of American Indians in the first half of the nineteenth century. Catlin's love for his native Wilkes-Barre was described by his biographer Lloyd Haberly: "In his deaf, lonely age, after 30 years abroad, he still signed himself, 'George Catlin of Wilkes-Barre.' "[4]

But the fame Korson shared with Hart and Catlin would come only after years of work. It was in Korson's childhood that he acquired a love of folksongs from his mother, who used to sing songs from the old country to the children. Especially memorable were the lullabies that she sang to the babies. Years later, when his own daughter Betsy was born, Korson taught one of these lullabies to his wife, who in turn sang it to their child. The songs were sad, and they left a profound impression on Korson. From his father, with whom he was very close, young George acquired a love of history. Because his mother was so busy doing the washing, cooking, and sewing for six children, she had very little time for reading. But his father always talked about the Ukraine and their way of life in the old days. From his father Korson acquired a love and respect for books. Of course, he also hoped that he could travel some day and see the countries about which he had read.

Joseph Korson's painting business never really prospered. He was too slow and too careful, and he always used the best quality paint and materials. In a sense he was too much an Old World craftsman; he never learned the Yankee tricks of doing a slap-dash job in a hurry to make money. His wife respected him and his children loved him, but the American dream of success always eluded him. But he did take pride in the ultimate accomplishments of his children—especially his sons. Selig went on to become a physician and then a psychiatrist; George, a writer and folklorist.

While Joseph Korson was a loving father, busy and well-respected, if never especially successful, Rose Korson filled the house with her cheerful presence, baking bread, taking care of her husband, and caring affectionately for her six children. The Korsons' home in the modest Heights section of Wilkes-Barre was a typical working-class home, comfortable but unpretentious. The tastes of the family were simple, and, in the Eastern European tradition, family ties were close. It was a stable and secure environment for the children, with strong connections to orthodox Judaism. The children led a tranquil life, ruled by parents who were loving but strict.

Korson's parents had firm ideas about religious education. Being of extremely Orthodox background, they insisted that young George attend Hebrew school. But for the young man who was assimilating American values and customs, neither the rabbi nor his parents were able to make religion palatable to him. One story that illustrates the problem was told often by Korson in later years. Even after George complained bitterly, his parents continued to insist that he attend Hebrew school. Finally, after many months of boredom and restlessness, Korson one day decided to play hooky. Instead of going to Hebrew school, he wandered off to the park in Wilkes-Barre. He was sitting on the bench, beginning to enjoy himself, feeding the squirrels and watching the passersby. All of a

Breaker Boys

In the early days a breaker boy worked ten hours a day. Before water was used in processing the screen room where he picked slate was so thick with coal dust that he could not see beyond his reach. To keep dust out of his mouth he wore a handkerchief and not infrequently took to chewing tobacco to keep from choking. He sat on a narrow plank astride iron-sheathed chutes crouching over a black stream of clattering coal. His tender little fingers worked fast to pick slate and bony out of the stream and often bled from cuts and bruises.

—*Minstrels of the Mine Patch*, pp. 97-98

Courtesy of Wyoming Historical and Geological Society

---

sudden, who should appear in the park but his mother. Abruptly, she took him straight home, and later his father punished him severely. This kind of experience resulted in his not taking part in any organized religion as an adult.

Because the family was always financially hard-pressed and because George was the oldest son, he found himself working part-time as a newsboy in order to bring in a little extra money. The extra duties of getting up early to cover a newspaper route paid

Slate Pickers

They seemed to give fullest play to their animal instincts during lunch hour at the breaker, where they were full of practical jokes. College hazings are mild compared to some of the weird initiations practised on new boys at the breaker . . . other pastimes were games like Rotten Horses, Kick the Wicket, I Spy the Wolf, and Rounders, a crude form of baseball. They also organized circuses, mock Salvation Army meetings and gang fights.

—*Minstrels of the Mine Patch*, pp. 97-98

Courtesy of Wyoming Historical and Geological Society

---

off in an unforeseen way. As a working boy, Korson was invited to join the B.I.A. (Boy's Industrial Association), which had been founded by Mrs. Ellen W. Palmer in 1891. Appalled by the lack of recreational facilities in the area, Mrs. Palmer started a Saturday night program of entertainment, supplemented with educational activities, for working boys who wanted to better themselves. The movement grew and expanded. After a while, classes were held nightly in the basics—reading, writing, and arithmetic. Through the B.I.A. Korson met many boy colliers—breaker boys, door boys, and mule drivers. The informal contacts and friendships he made with these young workers had a profound influence on

Slate Pickers at Work

It makes me sad and lonely now
   When I think of years gone by,
That I spent at the old breaker
   When I was but a boy.
My youthful days are past and gone,
   Old age is coming fast,
The only thing that is left to me
   Is a picture of the past.

                    —"Bear Patch Ridge"
                    from *Minstrels of the Mine Patch*, p. 25

Courtesy of Wyoming Historical and Geological Society

Korson. He gained an intimate knowledge of how coal was mined and what problems the miners, young and old, suffered. This kind of first-hand experience with the abuses of child labor led to the deep feeling and expression years later in *Minstrels of the Mine Patch*. To this very day, there is a statue on River Common in Wilkes-Barre of Mrs. Palmer; she is depicted standing with two boys, a breaker boy and a newsboy.[5]

   In his years at Wilkes-Barre High School from 1913 to 1917, Korson did well academically. Because he liked to write, he enjoyed English. Because his interest in history had been stirred by his father, he did well in that subject. But he had enormous difficulty with algebra. In high school he became very friendly with one Benjamin Sperling, who was both confidant and rival. They were both on the debating team, and in one important debating contest the two friends were pitted against each other. Korson lost, but the two remained very good friends down through the years. In fact, Ben Sperling was the best man at Korson's wedding in 1926.

Growing up in Wilkes-Barre, Korson's main concern was his school work, but he found the public library far more exciting. He learned much about his adopted hometown by writing a short history of Wilkes-Barre for the school newspaper. He learned that the city was named for the Honorable John Wilkes and Colonel Isaac Barre, members of the British Parliament who spoke out against oppression in America. He also learned about the famous battle of Wyoming of July 3, 1778, in which a small band of patriotic Americans were defeated by a numerically superior British force consisting of Butler's Rangers and some seven hundred Indians.[6]

Young Korson's researches were based on secondary sources and added nothing new to the well-worked historical terrain of the eighteenth century, but the exercise sharpened his writing skills and gave him the opportunity to explore the valley. Through his grappling with the history of the area, Korson could understand and appreciate his surroundings. When he passed through Public Square, as everyone in Wilkes-Barre must, he recognized the monument to the two British statesmen for whom the city was named. He knew about the nearby Old Fell Tavern, where Judge Jesse Fell first successfully burned anthracite on an open grate without the use of an air blast on February 11, 1808, a subject which he would investigate in a more scholarly way many years later.[7]

Korson learned about the Rampart Rocks, the site of one of the battles of the Yankee-Pennamite Wars. He learned about Campbell's Ledge and its legends. He learned about the Nanticoke Indians and the Shawnee Indians. All of this knowledge was valuable background for his subsequent research. He became fascinated with the Wyoming Valley, and in time he would add to the history of the region. Korson's strongest contribution, though, would be to the history of the post-Civil War period, a period still

Gaylord Breaker, 1875

At the colliery operated by the Wilkes-Barre Coal and Iron Company. The breaker was described by Korson as "a struggling hulk of a building . . . the most characteristic feature of the anthracite landscape. It is there that the amorphous lumps which the miner has extracted from the seam are cleansed and cracked into standard sizes for the market. Standing close to the mouth of a mine slope or shaft, it frequently may be found hugging a hillside. Almost from the time that the first breaker cast its shadow, miners have invested it with symbolical significance."

—Editorial notes for record album L 16
"Songs and Ballads of the Anthracite Miners"
Courtesy Wyoming Historical and Geological Society

---

strangely understudied in the region.[8] Symbolically, then, Korson's historical interest in the area would be represented not so much by the Revolutionary War statues in Public Square as by the giant coal breakers found looming up on the landscape.

On April 6, 1917, the United States entered World War I. Two months later, in June, Korson graduated from high school. His immediate impulse was to enlist in the Army and fight for the

United States. But his parents, remembering the hardships of soldiers in Europe, refused to sign their permission. So Korson looked for employment. He capitalized on his work on the high school newspaper and landed a job as a reporter on the *Wilkes-Barre Record*. In the time-honored tradition Korson started at the bottom as a general assignment man, receiving his share of practical jokes and unimportant assignments. But he was eager to learn and had a retentive memory. He learned to work quickly under pressure, and he learned to get the facts straight.

As Korson received more important assignments, he became accustomed to fires and accidents. He had the hardening experience of getting the names and addresses of the injured and the dead, even in the midst of grief and confusion. Korson learned to be very careful to spell names correctly and to get figures exactly. He learned the standard form of a story—short paragraphs with the most important items coming early, the less important material left to the end. His later writing as a folklorist often reflects this same style. He was an able apprentice and he learned his craft well, enabling him to earn his living as a journalist for the rest of his life.

Although Korson was happy in his job, he still had a nagging sense that he was missing out on the biggest adventure opportunity of the century by not going to war. In 1918, when he heard that the Zionists were getting together a group of volunteers in Philadelphia to fight for Palestine, he could not resist. Turning a deaf ear to the protests of his mother, he went to Philadelphia and signed up. Later he was sent to Canada and from there he went to England for army training. It is impossible now to reconstruct the emotions of the nineteen-year-old who left home in search of adventure in the Middle East. But surely Korson must have felt alternately exhilarated and lonely, brave and scared, curious and homesick. Certainly he had left behind him the warm security of home and job and family.

Jewish troops were mobilized by the British to drive the Turks out of Palestine and to occupy the land. In 1917 Chaim Weizmann had persuaded the British government to issue a formal declaration in favor of establishing a Jewish national home state in Palestine. This statement, the Balfour Declaration, was approved by the League of Nations after the war. The campaigns in which Korson participated were successful, and the story now belongs to history. Thousands of Jews came from many different countries to settle in Palestine. The Zionist pioneers, with nationalistic zeal, built up

Korson at about nineteen, while in the Jewish Legion.
Courtesy Betsy Korson Glazier

cities in the desert. Throughout his life Korson took pride in the fact that the success of the campaigns of 1918 in which he participated laid the foundations for the emergence of the State of Israel in 1948.[9]

Korson had hoped that the war would bring adventure, romance, and excitement. But the realities of army life were something else. There were the early morning roll calls, the insipid meals, the smelly latrines, the vulgarity of barracks life, and the inescapable discipline. Years later he candidly reported that one of his chief duties had been to guard the camels, which he said were very tall and smelled bad. But army life was not totally without its compensations. There was the satisfaction of wearing a snappy dress uniform complete with swagger stick. And there was a certain amount of friendship and camaraderie. Nonetheless, when the war was over, Korson wasted no time in getting out of the army. He entered as a private and left as a private, receiving his discharge on September 6, 1919.

The short, boyish-looking soldier returned home and resumed

Korson (front row, right) in Jaffa, Palestine, June 3, 1919.
Courtesy George Korson Folklore Archive

---

working as a reporter for the *Wilkes-Barre Record*. Even though garrison life had been dull, he did come back with some glamour and glory. He had some stories to impress his friends at the *Record* office, but his friends were understandably preoccupied with the news. It was difficult for Korson to realize the full scope of his ambition as a newspaper reporter in Wilkes-Barre. He had a larger plan; he wanted to go to Russia and become a correspondent for an American paper there. He had become interested in the situation of the Jews in Russia, and he wanted to see first-hand the homeland that had been the source of so many stories in the Korson home. To put this plan into action, Korson felt that he needed a first-rate education. In the fall of 1921 he borrowed some money and set off for New York to study at Columbia.

Enrolled in the University Extension Division, Korson found part-time work as a copy boy on a newspaper. He found a roommate, one Isadore Goldstein, who later became an accountant. For many years they were close friends. Predictably, he took both English and history courses, his favorite subjects from high school.

In line with his career plan, he also enrolled for the formal study of Russian, though of course he already had some knowledge of it from home. In English he took courses on the short story and English literature from 1830 to 1890. One of his courses was titled "History of Poland, Czecho-Slovakia (Bohemia), Serbia, and Bulgaria." In the Russian department, he took one grammar course and one literature course.[10]

At Columbia, to alleviate his loneliness at the beginning, Korson threw himself into his studies. He buried himself in his work, attending lectures and taking notes. He read widely, somehow finding money to buy books and spending much of his time in the library. In addition to his studies, he was intensely interested in travel and poetry. He made the most of his experience in New York and viewed the library as a great resource. Though he was still young, he chiefly wished for a quiet life. Social life held no great interest to him. He did well at the university, receiving two A's in Russian.

Unfortunately, in the meantime, the family back in Wilkes-Barre had financial difficulties. Korson had never asked his parents to send him to college, nor was he financially dependent on them. Quite the reverse: while in New York he sent money home to help support the family. As the oldest son, with five younger siblings, he was expected to help. But the pressures became too great. He could not pursue his college studies, work part-time, and still come up with money to send home. So he returned to Wilkes-Barre to look for work. The family was delighted to see him and they enjoyed a few weeks together, but the *Record* had no immediate openings and he was ready for a change. He left Wilkes-Barre and joined the staff of the *Pottsville Republican* as a reporter.

Taking employment in Pottsville was an auspicious event that marked the turning point in Korson's career. The year was 1924. The big news on the national level was that Senator Walsh of Montana had begun investigation of the scandals in the Warren G. Harding administration. The headlines carried stories of Teapot Dome and Elk Hills and the Naval Oil Reserves. But Korson had been covering local news, not national news. In particular he had been assigned to cover miners and their families in Schuylkill County. In his travels he was struck with the simple beauty of their songs and stories. The story of how he got started in folklore has been told often, but bears repeating in Korson's own words:

One evening in 1924 while taking a walk in Pottsville, where I was a newspaper reporter, the question popped in my mind, why had I never heard anthracite miners' songs similar to lumbermen's ballads, cowboy songs, and sailors' chanties? Assuming there was a printed collection, I asked Edith Patterson, the librarian, for a copy. She believed that no such collection existed, and a survey which I subsequently made among other public libraries in the region confirmed her belief. It was then that she asked me, "Why don't you try to collect these songs yourself?"[11]

He did try, and he succeeded. According to his own account, once he got started he could not stop. Each ballad that he found encouraged him to look for others. In retrospect, Korson's accomplishments as a collector are all the more amazing when we stop to realize that he was not a professional folklorist but an amateur.[12] Bringing to the work his training as a journalist, Korson, with keen intelligence and fundamentally sound judgment, carried out work that even today meets the general approval of professionals who have the benefit of university training, fifty additional years of scholarship in the field, and 20/20 hindsight.

Two aspects of Korson's work as a pioneer collector of the 1920s deserve special commendation: his reporting the context of social life of folklore materials and his abiding respect for his informants. His earliest work indicated that he was not satisfied with a scissors-and-paste collection. He was aware of the importance of the milieu in which the item was collected. He was concerned with finding out the meaning that the item had for the members of the folk group. With no formal training in either folklore or anthropology, Korson instinctively used what today we would call an ethnographic approach to field work.[13] More than thirty years later, in a speech before the Folklore Institute of America at Indiana University, Korson recalled the decision he had made to present the entire way of life of the mine patch in his work:

> When I was writing my first book it struck me as common sense to present the mining songs and ballads in the context of the social life from which they had sprung, and I have tried to do the same in my other books. Without this background, folklore loses significance, vitality, and appeal. It's like trying to keep a plant alive without its soil.
>
> Of course, providing a background requires considerable research beyond the collection of folklore. The whole task is made harder and consumes valuable time. Yet it is the price you have to

pay for thoroughness. And your background information must not only be accurate and complete, but also interesting.[14]

Korson's conspicuous success with his informants stemmed in large measure from the fact that he was not a transient collector. As a newspaper reporter he came into the community with a legitimate social role. Furthermore, as a reporter it was perfectly natural for him to take notes on his observations and interviews on the spot. By this kind of full and natural participation in the life of the community he worked toward creating many friendships of deep and lasting value.[15] Again it is interesting to see his own account of how he established rapport with his informants, given in a speech in Indiana some thirty years later:

> Now a word about informants. They are individuals and must be regarded as such. I have always tried to treat them with respect and too I have given my affection. With that kind of approach, your informants cannot help [but] respond in kind. All the techniques in the handbook won't make you a good collector without your ability to win the confidence of the simple people from whom you must obtain your folk fantasy and folk knowledge. As collectors, we invade their privacy, and ask them to share with us, and ultimately with the whole world, their most intimate memories of the past. They will cooperate if they can trust us—if they have confidence in our sincerity and integrity.[16]

Gradually a mass of material piled up on Korson's desk, mostly from Schuylkill County. As his reputation as a collector became known among the people, contacts were made more and more readily. He asked mainly for mining material, excluding other traditional tales and songs that did not bear on the coal industry. Finally the day arrived in 1925 when Edith Patterson assured him that he had enough material for a book. He decided that the best thing to do would be to get a position somewhere and work part-time, so that he could devote more time to the book. A newspaper agency recommended two jobs to him, one in Connecticut and one in New Jersey. He chose New Jersey and found himself working as a reporter for the *Morristown Jerseyman*.

Next door to the *Morristown Jerseyman* was the law office of the firm of King and Vogt. Working in that office under Harold Price in criminal law was a young woman named Rae Rosenblatt. One day there was a little fire in the law office, and some of the people went next door to the *Jerseyman*. The newspaper let that group, which included Rae, use one of their rooms. George saw Rae and asked one of the other reporters who she was. George found out that Rae had a brother Jack, who was a pharmacist, and George asked Jack to arrange an introduction. So Jack invited George to dinner at the Rosenblatt residence. Soon George asked Rae out to an evening lecture at the YMCA, which he had to cover for the paper. During the lecture, Rae was shocked at George's lack of attention to the speaker. As she tells it:

> All the time George was whispering in my ear telling me about the miners and also about how he discovered folk music. I asked him why he wasn't paying attention to the lecture. He said he was listening with one ear and making notes. The next day, when the *Jerseyman* came out, I couldn't believe my eyes. It was the first byline that he got on the *Jerseyman*. There was everything the man had said. George had it verbatim, really. I couldn't believe it. He called me that night and asked what I thought of the story. He kept calling me, then the next thing I knew he began coming down very steadily and everyone liked him.

About a year later they decided to get married. Rae's father Bernard Rosenblatt was at first unenthusiastic about his daughter marrying a mere reporter, but in time he agreed. The wedding took place on December 16, 1926. The best man was his old friend Benjamin Sperling, who was by this time an attorney in New York, and one of the ushers was Rae's brother Jack.[17]

It was a very good match. They were to remain married for some forty years until Korson's death in 1967. Rae made an ideal marriage partner for George Korson in two ways. She was intelligent and sensitive enough to appreciate the value of his work and to encourage him; and she was independent and autonomous enough to have interests of her own, so that she left him alone to carry on his writing with large blocs of uninterrupted time.

Their honeymoon was spent in New York City, where George introduced Rae to the Greenwich Village folklore scene. They went to a little folk theater run by Will Geer. Korson already knew Geer and many of the intellectuals who would later be identified with urban folk consciousness and the proletarian renaissance of the 1930s. Geer, a graduate of the University of Chicago, had attended Columbia and Oxford as a graduate student.[18] Increasingly in the 1930s Geer would become part of the so-called radical scene of New York City, while Korson would drift toward mainstream New Deal liberalism.

Korson at about twenty-seven.
Courtesy Betsy Korson Glazier

Meanwhile, now that Korson was married, he needed more money, and looked for a better job. He left the *Morristown Jerseyman* for the *Elizabeth Times*, accepting more responsibilities along with a larger salary. As the New Year of 1927 came in, the newlywed couple took up residence in Elizabeth, where they were to stay for nearly three years. Korson's job was going very well. His work kept him busy, but whenever he had any time off, the couple would drive up to Wilkes-Barre and Pottsville. George took pride in introducing Rae to the local librarians and historians; she, in turn, was impressed with the high regard in which they held him. The Elizabeth period was marked by three important events—the publication of *Songs and Ballads of the Anthracite Miner* in 1927, his naturalization as a citizen of the United States in 1928, and the birth of his daughter Betsy in 1929.

In assessing George Korson's contributions to American intellectual life of the 1920s, it is important to remember that at the time Korson considered himself principally a writer, not a folklorist. Korson did not write his first book, *Songs and Ballads of the Anthracite Miner,* in a vacuum. As an omnivorous reader, he was very much aware of what was going on in the larger world of letters. In the 1920s the American literary scene was divided into two different camps. On the one hand there were writers who celebrated America and made extensive use of native "folk" materials. On the other hand there were writers who were alienated from America, often to the extent of becoming expatriates.[19]

Korson took his stand with the nativists as a spokesman for the common people. One of the figures whose work Korson admired was Carl Sandburg, who took pride in describing the vigor of the Chicago stockyards. Sandburg perhaps best represents the nativists who expressed confidence in America and her people. He grew up in Galesburg, Illinois, where his father worked on a railroad construction crew. At an early age Sandburg took odd jobs as a cook, dishwasher, roustabout, wheat field worker, theater hand, truck handler, and carpenter's helper. This kind of experience gave him a broad sympathy for the common man, a sympathy that could easily extend to the coal miners Korson was studying. Sandburg's interest in American folklore was displayed by his collection of folksongs, *The American Songbag,* which was published in 1927, the same year Korson's first book was published.[20] Significantly, Sandburg, among the first to review Korson's book at the time, recognized its great importance.[21]

When we look at the names of the places that Korson knew and loved—Pottsville, Minersville, Shenandoah, Tamaqua, Coaldale, Lehighton, Weatherly, Hazleton, Ashland, Locust Gap, Mauch Chunk, Bear Ridge Patch—we realize that he was operating in an old tradition. To be sure, Korson was a folklorist, not a poet. But like Walt Whitman and Vachel Lindsay before him, and Woody Guthrie and Bob Dylan after him, Korson was celebrating and affirming the American land. Like John and Alan Lomax he found ballads where no one else had thought to look for them. But there was an important difference. Unlike the others, Korson's work was first published in a trade union journal. *Songs and Ballads of the Anthracite Miner* ran in serial form in the *United Mine Workers Journal* from November 15, 1926 (Volume 37) through March 15, 1927 (Volume 38).

The editor of the *UMWJ,* Ellis Searle, explained his policy in deciding to accept Korson's work in an announcement carried in the issue for November 1, 1926. Searle took pride in presenting this material to his readers, and his announcement was a landmark event in labor folklore:

> In an early forthcoming issue, the United Mine Workers Journal will begin the serial publication of "Songs and Ballads of the Coal Miner" by George G. Korson, who, for a long time, was a newspaper man in the Anthracite region. This book brings back to life many of the songs and ballads which the Anthracite coal miner sang during the last century . . .
>
> The collection mirrors not only the surface conditions, but reveals the very soul of the old-time miner. It will bring back many memories to you and make you want to preserve these issues as family keepsakes. "Songs and Ballads of the Coal Miner" contains dozens of these old-time songs and ballads and many stories and legends of the old days in the Anthracite region.
>
> The Journal regards itself as fortunate in securing this material for publication. It will be extremely interesting to every miner in America. Most of the songs and stories have never before been published. The material will be published in installments and will run through several issues of the Journal. [22]

Labor historian Archie Green has pointed out the significance of the *UMWJ* publication of Korson's material. It was a unique event at the time, and no other union journal has since followed the *UMWJ*'s lead in opening its pages to collectors of folklore. In 1964, nearly forty years later, Archie Green summed up the importance of this event:

> . . . *Songs and Ballads of the Anthracite Miner,* was first published serially in the *United Mine Workers Journal.* This initial printing has an importance in its own right beyond the author's factual credit line. To my knowledge no American trade union journal published any folkloristic study before 1926. The union press from the Age of Jackson until today has always printed anecdotes, songs, and tales contributed directly by members or reported in secondary form. Many of these items are pure folklore by the severest standards of life in tradition, anonymity, and variation. (They await an anthologist's eye and hand.) But it is one thing to accept a ballad from a working member, and another to accept a whole collection of ballads from a professional writer. [23]

In the spring of 1927 Korson faced a crisis. The book had appeared serially in the *UMWJ* and had been well received. In fact field work was easier than ever because his name was by now well known to nearly every coal miner in the country. But his name was not well known to publishers. For some time he had been going from publisher to publisher all over New York—walking the streets, knocking on doors, and waiting in reception rooms. No one was interested. Years later Korson described how discouraging it was to look for a publisher:

> My first book was published in the twenties. In retrospect, the 1920's were curious years for American folklore. There were not many of us actively collecting, and the struggle for recognition was rather hard. While peddling my first book-length manuscript in New York, I was told by one publisher after another that there was no market for American folklore. One of the editors who rejected my manuscript in 1926 is now the head of his own publishing firm. Several years ago my agent submitted an idea for a folklore book to him and got a quick rejection. His reason? There were *too many* folklore books being published today. Yet back there in 1926 he had complained of a lack of market.
>
> The Twenties were the heyday of the gentlemen collectors with their quantitative approach to folklore. Many concentrated on a sort of numbers game with the prize going to him who collected the most variants of ballads in the Child collection. At the same time some of them looked down their noses at any fresh findings in the field of American Folklore. It was the great Cecil Sharp himself, you will remember, who made an unfavorable comparison between Old John Lomax's songs and the songs he, Sharp, had collected in the Southern Appalachians.[24]

Eager to get his work into print, Korson decided to seek out a subsidy publisher. Through his friend Benjamin Sperling, Korson made contact with the firm of Frederick Hitchcock. Basically Hitchcock agreed that it was a worthwhile book, but because of the risks involved Korson would have to subsidize the publication at a cost of two thousand dollars. Since the conventional publishing houses were not interested, Korson had no choice. Fortunately, his friend Sperling had steered him to a subsidy publisher rather than a vanity press.[25] Korson dug into his savings and told Hitchcock to go ahead. The book came out under the imprint of the Grafton Press. Physically it was unimpressive—196 octavo pages in length, with no index and no illustrations, but it was well printed on good paper. In retrospect, it turned out to be the best investment Korson ever made.

And so Korson's first major work, with forty-two songs, retailing at three dollars a copy, went out to readers. The book was not an overwhelming, block-busting, smash success, but it was a quiet success. Because it was basically a regional book, the publishers wisely decided to launch the selling campaign in northeastern Pennsylvania. The book department of Fowler, Dick, and Walker, the largest department store in Wilkes-Barre, gave the book a gratifying fanfare. The store set up a special window display complete with miniature breaker. Included in the display was the original manuscript of the book, as well as Judge Jesse Fell's iron grate on which anthracite coal was first burned.[26]

The book got off to a good start in Wilkes-Barre, but both Korson and the publisher were eager for the book to receive national attention. An important review came very early from Carl Sandburg in the *Chicago Daily News*. Sandburg placed the book in the tradition of American labor songbooks and compared it with the I.W.W. hip-pocket songster that celebrated "One Big Union." After Sandburg's favorable review of *Songs and Ballads*, national recognition of the book followed quickly. Sympathetic articles appeared in the *Literary Digest, New York World*, the *Newark Evening News*, and *The American Mercury*.[27] Later the *St. Louis Star* named it among the seven outstanding books published in 1927.[28]

One must admit that many of the early reviews, in time-honored fashion, were written hastily and carelessly. Such reviews would typically either repeat the publisher's publicity or simply indicate the contents of the book. But one thoughtful piece appeared in the *Newark Evening News*. The reviewer was clearly familiar with the scholarship of folklore and realized at once the uniqueness of Korson's contribution to industrial folklore:

> Mr. Korson is following in the footsteps of a long line of ballad-fanciers. Percy, Herder, Scott, Child, Lomax and many others have brought to light many hidden treasures of folk poetry, and offhand one might have thought that there was nothing left to be found. The last place in the world to look, indeed, would have been among the coal miners and Mr. Korson is therefore all the more to be complimented that he looked and found so much. He is not only a pioneer in this field, but he is probably a pioneer in so far as industrial laborers generally are concerned. Hitherto, ballad hunters have sought their material among peasants on the field, among sailors, among lumbermen in the forest, among cowboys on ranches, among outdoor workers generally, but it would not have been readily

believed that skilled manual laborers had developed a balladry of their own.[29]

The key phrase in this review is "he is probably a pioneer in so far as industrial laborers generally are concerned." Indeed Korson was the first to look for ballads in the industrial workplace, as the reviewer noted. One only regrets that such keen discernment appeared as an anonymous review in a metropolitan daily newspaper rather than in an academic journal. Unfortunately, it was to take the academic establishment years to recognize the value of Korson's singular achievement. Another key feature of the book, which the Newark reviewer spotted, was Korson's commitment to presenting the folk culture of Pennsylvania's anthracite coal miners:

> Mr. Korson has wisely done more than merely collect and print the ballads. Each bit of verse is preceded by an introduction telling where he found it and providing, where it is necessary, something in the way of a historical or industrial background. The book is, consequently, a picture of life in the hard coal region, and a very vivid picture. Mr. Korson's sympathies are frankly with the miners, in their hard life, their frequent tragedies, their strikes, their economic difficulties generally. He writes smoothly and entertainingly about the people who gave birth to these ballads, and the volume is one that ought to extend understanding of miners.[30]

Despite this well-deserved praise from northern New Jersey, there was one persistent criticism of the book—that the songs appeared with texts but no music. Sigmund Spaeth, writing in the *Philadelphia Inquirer* in an otherwise sympathetic account, complained: "It is a pity that the words alone are given, for most of these ballads cry aloud for their music."[31] This complaint was echoed by Abbe Niles writing in *The Nation*: "Tunes are not given . . ."[32] And again by John J. Niles in the *Chicago Daily News*: "*Songs and Ballads of the Anthracite Miner* is more than a song book. It is, in many ways, a history, and should prove valuable to the investigative minded reader. We regret, however, that the book does not contain the music to any of the songs."[33] Naturally, Korson had been aware of this shortcoming before the book ever went to press, but he felt that the limitations of time and money were just too severe to include music. Nonetheless, the criticism stung. He vowed not to let this happen again.

Korson's predominant political beliefs, as noted in the Introduction, were always those supporting labor unions in the context
of the existing corporate-liberal state. Indeed the critical reception
of *Songs and Ballads of the Anthracite Miner* tends to confirm this
interpretation. Korson had a broad sympathy for the miner's
plight, but this fell short of advocating drastic social, political, or
economic change. Korson's book, though sympathetic to the
UMWA, was not so radical as to be ignored by management. In fact
it was reviewed in *Coal Age*, the mine operator's trade journal, but
the book received a very cool reception there:

> The songs in this book strike a strongly antagonistic note. They were
> written by people who, perhaps, were a little homesick and not by
> men contented with their lot . . . These songs of Mr. Korson's
> gathering are full of the class struggle . . . His attitude of mind
> throughout is evidenced by the fact that the book is reprinted from
> the *United Mine Workers' Journal*. [34]

If Korson had been more radical the book probably would not have
been mentioned at all. The point here is that Korson's moderate
liberalism insured that he would be noticed by both capital and
labor.

In the labor press Korson's book was received very well. For
example, Elsie Gluck, reviewing the book in *Justice*, the official
organ of the International Ladies' Garment Workers' Union, saw
the book in a very favorable light:

> Mr. Korson not only collected the songs and ballads of the anthracite
> miner, but to each set of ballads he has prefaced a most intelligent
> and illuminating picture of the mine workers' lives, their struggles
> with nature and with their oppressive employers, and their hope for
> freedom in the union.
>
>   In a word, Mr. Korson's collection, as well as his editorial
> comments, are a good proof that the struggles for a livelihood, the
> mass movements of the worker are the most vital and universal
> dramatic material which American life today presents. [35]

But whether we look at the management press or the labor press,
the point is much the same. Gluck is praising Korson for
encouraging the miners' "hope for freedom in the union,"
presumably meaning that workers can achieve relative freedom
through the union, by means of the union. Korson's view of the
miners' condition was based on optimism, not on utopianism. The

miners, through the union, could look forward to a future better than the past—not perfect, just better.[36]

The year after the publication of his first book, Korson decided to become a citizen of the United States. There were practical reasons for taking this step. It would ease getting a passport if the need were to arise, and it would please his wife who was anxious about it. Korson went through the usual steps of petition, investigation, interview, and final hearings in court. The whole matter was expedited because of Rae Korson's legal connections. It was easy for Korson to produce two citizen-witnesses to vouch for him. Naturally he had no problem demonstrating familiarity with the history and form of government of the United States.

But it would be a mistake to emphasize Korson's practical reasons for changing his citizenship. It was also a profoundly symbolic act. It was the last step of a trip he had begun some twenty years earlier. Though his parents would never fully recover from the shock of alienation, Korson had in fact become assimilated. Korson was no longer looking back to the Old World. He had abandoned his earlier plan of becoming an American correspondent in Russia. Through his work in folklore he had fully embraced the American experience. Now he was officially an American. And in 1928 America looked like the land of milk and honey.[37]

The following year, 1929, it did not. The Great Crash came on Tuesday, October 29. No time is a good time for a depression, but for Korson the timing could not have been worse. Ever since his marriage three years earlier he had worked hard, taking extra free-lance writing assignments from the Standard News, a wire service, in addition to his regular job. His wife continued working in a law office. Together they saved every penny. When they had finally saved eight thousand dollars, they decided to have a child.

Then everything happened at once. The paper went bankrupt, the bank failed, and the baby was born. The family went to Rae's father, Bernard Rosenblatt, who had a large house on Lafayette Avenue in Morristown. Fortunately, Rosenblatt was well established in the men's clothing business and was able to help financially.

This period was a real test of Korson's character. He tried to save face and keep up appearances by doing free-lance work, writing stories and articles in the vague hope of selling them somewhere. Yet for nearly two years, he could not support Rae and Betsy. How did he feel? Did he curse his fate? Did he weep late at night? We simply do not know the answers. For all his careful record keeping and filing of correspondence, Korson was in many ways a private man. He kept no diary and wrote no confessions, at least none that anyone has found. But we can be sure that the 1930s held no bright promise for him in that exhausting and demoralizing period.

2

Anthracite Years
The 1930s

Fourty [sic] years I worked with pick & drill
Down in the mines against my will,
The Coal King's slave, but now it's passed;
Thanks be to God I am free at last.
                    —Epitaph, Anthracite miner's tombstone.[1]

The 1930s were for Korson years of personal difficulties and
professional growth. There were practical problems in earning a
living as well as disagreements over money at home. Family life
was disrupted as his career required moves from Morristown to
Allentown to Lewisburg and on to Washington. But by the end of
the decade, Korson had a solid record of accomplishments. The
turning point in Korson's career, as we shall see, was his appoint-
ment in 1936 as the director of the Pennsylvania Folk Festival at
Bucknell University. His affiliation with the university gave his
work in folklore the unmistakable stamp of legitimacy and approval, not to mention personal recognition and prestige. He also
had the necessary self-discipline to keep writing. With the country
in the depths of the Depression and his own private life complicated and insecure, George Korson worked quietly at his desk,
polishing and refining his anthracite songs and ballads. What
started as a modest, privately printed volume in 1927 was to
emerge in 1938 as *Minstrels of the Mine Patch,* a vastly expanded
version published by the University of Pennsylvania Press.

For Korson, the 1930s did not begin auspiciously. He felt that
he could not stay on in Morristown, so he went back to Elizabeth
and rented a room. He did some work for the *Newark News* and
the Standard News wire service. There he paid for his own

expenses and commuted back to Morristown on weekends. It must have been emotionally wrenching for him when his baby daughter hardly recognized him. Apparently she had him confused with her uncles, Rae's brothers. Even though Betsy did not greet him warmly at first, still Korson would take her for long walks in the baby carriage.

Finally in 1931 Korson's luck changed. An employment agency for newspapermen gave him a lead for a job with the *Allentown Chronicle and News.* The editor was impressed with his portfolio and invited him up for an interview. Though several capable people applied, Korson got the job. He would not simply be a reporter; he was to be a columnist. Like countless other reporters, Korson had dreamed about this opportunity. Free of the burdensome assignments, the columnist may roam here and there writing at will about anything that strikes his fancy. The column was to be called "A Stranger in Allentown."

At first writing a column was an exciting challenge. Korson discussed many subjects, including the persistence of the Pennsylvania German dialect, old anecdotes and yarns, and prominent visitors to Allentown.[2]

As Korson grew more familiar with the area, the column was changed to "Rambles in Allentown." But writing a column presented problems. The usual column was twelve column inches of type, or about seven hundred words. It was difficult to come up with a coherent and unified expository essay of this length day after day.

In a sense Korson had trained himself too well as an objective journalist. The ideal for reporters of his generation was to be completely objective, so he thought of himself as simply a recorder of events. As a newsman, he tended to minimize the reportorial shaping of events that he recorded, and as a result, his columns were seldom colored by his own feelings and imagination. In retrospect, it appears that the personal column was simply not Korson's best medium. He dealt with reportage, with factual material. He was an alert observer, and he knew how to dig for information. But the quality we most often look for in a columnist —how he feels about what he sees—was missing. He also had trouble mastering the genre in terms of length. Some of his essays were too long and had to be supplied in installments. On other occasions he abandoned unity altogether and simply presented several short anecdotes broken with asterisks. He stayed with the *Allentown Chronicle and News* for three years, but writing a column did not turn out to be a dream come true. It was just a job.

The most important development of the Allentown period was the Pennsylvania Folk Festival in Allentown, which Korson founded and directed. The festival came into being because of a favorable combination of circumstances, which Korson recognized. The year was 1935, a propitious time to take action because the folk festival movement represented the rediscovery of rural virtue in the middle of a demoralizing depression. Intellectuals and writers everywhere in the country were looking for something worthwhile to hold on to from the American past. Cultural historian Richard H. Pells explained it this way:

> It had become desperately important for writers to find something alive and good in the United States despite the breakdown of its modern, complex political and economic system. If they could locate a fundamental stability and resilience in the American people, they might again feel at home in their native land. This search for roots led them to praise not only the past but also the democratic instincts of the common man.[3]

The folk festival movement was a significant part of this "search for roots." No one was better prepared by background or temperament than Korson to launch this enterprise.

The Pennsylvania Folk Festival was not the first folk festival in America, but it was among the first. Lee Udall and Joe Wilson, who have studied the earliest uses of the term *folk festival*, reported: "In 1892 it was used in advertising literature printed by Hampton Institute, Virginia, to describe the performances of musicians traveling with the Hampton Jubilee Singers. In the early 1900s it was used by the Henry Street Settlement House in New York City and by Hull House in Chicago to describe the performances of recent immigrants at settlement house events."[4] But the first festivals, as we now understand the term, seem to have evolved out of traditional "singin' gatherin's." Perhaps the earliest of these was Bascom Lamar Lunsford's Mountain Dance and Folk Festival in Asheville, North Carolina, started in 1927. Also in the earliest group would be the American Folksong Festival at the cabin of Jean Thomas, the "traipsin' woman" on the Mayo Trail, near Ashland, Kentucky, which began in 1930. Another festival originating in this same period was the White Top Festival at Marion, Virginia.[5]

But Korson's idea did not come directly from North Carolina, Kentucky, or Virginia. Instead he got the idea from the National Folk Festival Association, founded by Sarah Gertrude Knott. Miss Knott, a native of Kentucky and a onetime member of the Carolina Playmakers at the University of North Carolina, had long dreamed of an organization to foster regional folk festivals like those already thriving in the South. The source of stimulation would be a nationwide folk "congress." In 1933, while working in St. Louis with a neighborhood theater project, Sarah Gertrude Knott (often called "SGK" for short) joined forces with M. J. Pickering, then manager of the St. Louis Coliseum, to make the National Folk Festival Association a reality. Pickering—known as "the Major" because of his army service—had spent a dozen years managing auditoriums and stadiums. The NFFA was established in 1934, with Paul Green as president, Sarah Gertrude Knott as national director, and M. J. Pickering as executive secretary and business manager. Policymaking was vested in a national committee with members as distinguished as the Carolina playwright who held the presidential chair.[6]

The chief project of the NFFA was an annual gathering of folk performers and students of folklore, first held in St. Louis in May 1934. Morning sessions consisted of papers and demonstrations for serious folklorists, while in the afternoons and evenings folk performers sang, instrumentalized, and danced for each other and the public. SGK was impresario and producer; the Major was fundraiser and stage manager; and the pair were a limitless source of ideas. One of their ideas, after SGK read *Songs and Ballads of the Anthracite Miner*, was to invite George Korson to bring a group of singing miners to perform at the second National Folk Festival, to be held in Chattanooga in the spring of 1935. The Major—being a native Philadelphian and a graduate of the University of Pennsylvania Law School (also a sympathizer with the miners in the 1902 anthracite strike)—went east to put the idea to Korson in the fall of 1934.

Korson approached Thomas Kennedy, a United Mineworkers official, with the proposal. Kennedy took it to John L. Lewis, who approved the plan and agreed to cover all the performing miners' expenses. Why was Lewis willing to subsidize such a venture during a period of economic depression? What role did the UMWA see folk music as playing? John L. Lewis was a tough man schooled in practical politics. It would be naive to portray him as a disinterested patron of the arts. Undoubtedly Lewis saw UMWA participation in the National Folk Festival as a political plus for his own administration. The UMWA was constantly torn by internal factions and occasional revolts against Lewis's autocratic style. Insurgents within the UMWA, fighting for more democracy within the union and a more strident policy toward the operators, often had contested Lewis's presidency in union elections. Lewis knew that his support of the miner folksingers would make good copy to be ballyhooed in the *United Mineworkers Journal*, which was sent to every member of the union. Lining himself squarely with folk tradition would place Lewis on the side of good solid Americanism and place even greater distance between himself and the discredited Communist-led National Miner's Union sponsored by the Trade Union Unity League.[7] Korson handpicked a small group including Daniel Walsh and Jerry Byrnes, making sure some of the men could play the fiddle and dance jigs as well as sing. The NFFA invitation inspired Korson to plan a regional folk festival a few weeks before his projected journey to Chattanooga. Korson discussed the plan with William S. Troxell of the *Allentown Morning Call* and enlisted the support of Irene Welty, Director of the Allentown Recreation Commission.

Inspired by what he had learned about the National Folk Festival, Korson took full advantage of the contacts he had built up over the years as a newspaperman. Patiently he put together a program of music, singing, and dancing. It took all of his powers of persuasion, because basically the festival was run on a minimal budget. No one was paid to perform, but Korson picked up expenses where he had to. The festival attempted to put together folklore from every possible grouping—racial, occupational, and ethnic. This policy was designed partly as a practical means of attracting community support. However, it stemmed mainly from a principle laid down by the National Folk Festival. Both Sarah Gertrude Knott and M. J. Pickering held that folklore was as diverse as the American people, and that no one group should have any exclusive claims on its presentation and performance. The result was an amazingly diverse presentation by Pennsylvania Germans, Indians, coal miners, Moravians, blacks, and river raftsmen. Despite the apparent diversity, however, the focus was inevitably on the Pennsylvania Germans and on the anthracite coal miners.[8]

The First Pennsylvania Folk Festival was to be held on May 3 and 4, 1935. All that winter Korson visited people, made telephone calls, and wrote letters. The plans took shape. The intellectual climate of the mid-1930s undoubtedly encouraged Korson in launching this artistic experiment. Like everyone else Korson was disturbed by widespread poverty and joblessness, but the festival seemed to offer an opportunity to turn from economic anxiety and to enjoy, at least for a moment, some of the positive aspects of the American cultural heritage. His national standing was recognized when he was invited to read a major paper at a morning session of the NFFA in Chattanooga. A few weeks before the festival he received a letter from Sarah Gertrude Knott offering encouragement and confirming his own feelings:

> I just know so well what the success of this "long time dreaming" has meant to you, and I rejoice with you because all of us who are passing through similar things know best how to appreciate the joy as well as the heart-breaks that come in ventures such as ours.
>
> The things we are doing seem so real to me, I believe we are striking right down at the very depths of something. It is a strange thing how we get these ideas and strong urges, which I believe amount to inspiration and how "hell and high water" cannot stop us. We do not make any money out of it, we have all kinds of battles to fight, and nobody sees why we are fighting, but there is something inside of us that pushes us on. When there is accomplishment it is more to us than those on the outside, and so I quite understand the feelings that you have in seeing your dreams come true, and you are truly doing a marvelous thing.[9]

Meanwhile, from within the state, Korson's work was gaining recognition. It must be remembered that none of the participants was paid to perform. All Korson could do for them was to provide a stage for their own self-expression. This noncommercial aspect of the festival gave it the aura of a cooperative enterprise. Korson himself saw the festival as a means of restoring dignity and a sense of community to the participants. Thus he was pleased to receive a warm personal note from Henry W. Shoemaker, then president of the Pennsylvania Folklore Society, offering these words of encouragement:

And the joy and the dignity you have given these people by digging them out of their retirement, and giving them this final opportunity for fame and appreciation, transcends any humanitarian project of the New Deal. If all of these folk activities could have the same recognition, I believe it would result in a spiritual renaissance all over the State.[10]

Finally the weekend of the festival arrived. Because of a driving rain, the program, originally scheduled for the park, had to be moved to the Allentown High School and the Lyric Theatre. The Friday night program featured Pennsylvania Germans. Saturday morning began with the Cornplanter Indians from Warren County. The afternoon program continued with bow zitherists, anthracite coal miners, and raftsmen. Saturday night's final program included Moravian church music, Negro folk songs, and anthracite coal miner folklore as a grand finale.

The next day the *Allentown Morning Call* carried a headline that told the whole story: "First Pennsylvania Folk Festival Proves Great and Glorious Success."[11] Despite the rain a total crowd of some five thousand attended the combined events.[12] Miss Knott was there and asked Korson to join the NFFA national committee.

Korson was understandably proud of the fact that the press called the event a success, but the newspaper coverage of the event raises some interesting questions. How does one measure the success of a folk festival? Typically the newspaper reported the event as successful in terms of the size of the crowd. There are obvious drawbacks in using this kind of yardstick. The sheer size of the crowd is not a reliable index to the artistic success of the event, nor is there a necessary correlation between the popularity of the event and the authenticity with which traditional culture is presented. And even given a large crowd, we would like to know many things that are difficult to establish. Did some people come merely out of curiosity? What kind of people attended? Did the festival draw heavily outside the immediate Allentown community? To what extent did it attract ethnic groups, coal miners, Indians, and other folk groups? Questions such as these are difficult to answer even for a contemporary event.

Later that month Korson received a letter from Homer P. Rainey, president of Bucknell University in Lewisburg.[13] Rainey, then age thirty-nine, had been president of Bucknell since 1931. Originally from Texas and familiar with the cowboy song tradition there, Rainey was sympathetic with what Korson was trying to do in

Pennsylvania. Rainey felt that Bucknell would benefit from playing host to the Pennsylvania Folk Festival the following year. Rainey was enthusiastic about folklore and felt that the small cost of sponsoring the festival would be worthwhile in terms of prestige and public relations. Rainey also hoped that after two years the festival might become self-sustaining. Korson went to Lewisburg and was impressed by Rainey's enthusiasm and sincerity. The two men got along well from the start. Meanwhile, M. J. Pickering, executive secretary of the National Folk Festival, wrote to Rainey in support of Korson.[14] Rainey decided to appoint Korson as director of the Pennsylvania Folk Festival at Bucknell University with a full-time salary. This was the turning point in Korson's career. For the first time, he could devote himself entirely to folklore.

In September of 1935 Korson went to Lewisburg. It was difficult to leave Allentown. For one thing, he had established himself as a leading citizen there. For another, his wife Rae had established a small business of her own, the Allentown Home Made Ice Cream Company, which she was reluctant to abandon. Understandably, Korson was nervous about his new role. Korson the folklore writer was about to become Korson the folk festival administrator. At the Bucknell convocation Korson, putting on an academic gown for the first time in his life, was in the spotlight of attention. He described the experience in a letter to his wife:

> At the solemn convocation exercises in the First Baptist Church President Rainey made his announcement about me. I almost wept tears at the things he said about me and my work—where he got the details I don't know, but he had them. He spoke for more than an hour and devoted at least a third of his address to what Bucknell was going to do with folklore. That address marked the highest peak of my career. I feel very humble about it all and when I think of the big things they expect of me I am a little afraid . . . The way Dr. Rainey talked, the folk festival would be a permanent part of the university as it works in so well with the far-visioned policy of Bucknell. There is no doubt in my mind that they will want to continue it in future years.[15]

Though Korson was understandably flattered by Rainey's address, his perception of the university's commitment to folklore was not accurate. When he described that commitment as "permanent" he may have been hearing what he wanted to hear. The public relations benefits that Rainey envisioned with the general public, state officials, alumni, friends, and donors were long-range and intangible. The costs to a private college in the Depression of running a folk festival were real and immediate. In any event, Korson threw himself into his work. Organizing a festival on the scale that Bucknell wanted would make heavy demands on Korson. It required considerable understanding of human nature to get along with the university administration and faculty on the one hand and with the performers and civic leaders on the other. Staking his career on a single venture like this also required remarkable courage. Korson had to convince himself he had made a wise choice. Equally important, he had to persuade his wife he had made a good decision. She had carved out a comfortable life in Allentown and was less than enthusiastic about depending on Korson's brand new career in folk festival management. George wrote to Rae: "The break that has come to me must certainly prove to you that I was on the right track all the time . . . I am different— the fact that I am the only man in Pennsylvania and of a few in the country who has made folklore a profession should prove to you that I am different."[16] Korson's immediate purpose in writing was to convince his wife that he was indeed "on the right track." But we see also in this letter his single-minded pursuit of folklore as a profession. His wife Rae may have had private doubts about his plans, but she sold the ice cream business and moved to Lewisburg, where they took an apartment in the Sigma Alpha Mu fraternity house. Korson must have known that what he was doing was historically important, because it was during this period that he began to keep complete personal files and records of his accomplishments. Thanks to this foresight, we have a very good picture of what happened in planning the Pennsylvania Folk Festivals of 1936 and 1937.[17]

As a scholar Korson was undoubtedly motivated to use the Festival as a means of preserving and disseminating the traditional lore of Pennsylvania. However, he had to keep in mind the goals of the Bucknell administration, which was itself in the process of change that fall. Homer P. Rainey resigned from Bucknell on October 5, 1935, to become director of the American Youth Commission. Obviously this move left Korson vulnerable. The man who had singled him out and brought him to Bucknell with considerable fanfare in September was now leaving suddenly in early

October. Korson was worried, but the presidency passed to Arnaud C. Marts, who pledged continued support for the Pennsylvania Folk Festival.

Despite this pledge, the shift from Rainey to Marts was significant. Marts might honor his predecessor's commitment for a time, but he was not bound to a program inherited from a previous administration. Like other private colleges in the Depression, Bucknell was experiencing financial difficulties. While Rainey had been a lifelong educator, Marts was a professional fundraiser. During World War I he had served as associate national director of the $18,000,000 campaign of the War Camp Community Service. Later he became president of a firm he had helped to organize, Marts and Lundy, Incorporated, which raised nearly $300,000,000 for colleges, churches, hospitals, and other agencies. One of his clients was Bucknell University. He made such a favorable impression on the Board of Trustees that they invited him to accept the presidency on October 25, 1935. Reluctant to leave his prosperous business, he worked out a compromise: He would maintain his residency in Plainfield, New Jersey, and work at his own firm in New York City four days a week. But he would accept the title of "Acting President" and spend the other three days a week, usually weekends, at Bucknell. His executive assistant, Paul Hightower, would handle routine matters at Bucknell when he was not there.[18]

Like his predecessor, Marts saw the festival mainly as a public service activity that would provide good public relations. Sensitive to the president's wishes, Korson explained in an early memo four of the benefits accruing to Bucknell from the festival:

> SOCIAL: It will provide a common meeting ground for the varied social elements that have gone into the making of Pennsylvania and promote a fuller appreciation of them. It will discover Pennsylvania for Pennsylvanians in a vivid, memorable way. It will awaken pride in the state's customs and achievements, strengthen our people in a deeper loyalty and a stronger faith in their commonwealth.
>
> CULTURAL: It will make available a mass of hitherto undiscovered folklore material for scholars, folklorists and historians, as well as for musicians and other creative artists.
>
> ENTERTAINMENT: The folk festival makes for wholesome, thrilling entertainment. Its charm, quaintness and simplicity combine to make an irresistible appeal to all classes of people.
>
> TOURIST APPEAL: The widespread appeal of the folk festival

is amply demonstrated in the South which annually draws thousands of tourists from all over the country to its folk festivals. Bucknell believes that its Pennsylvania Folk Festival will be equally attractive to tourists from other states. It will be the only major folk festival in the East.[19]

A clever innovation on Korson's part was to hold five regional folk festivals prior to the state folk festival. This tended to legitimize Bucknell's claim to be holding a statewide festival. It also helped in selecting the most representative material and the most competent performers. Korson had hoped that each of these regional festivals would make a few hundred dollars for the purpose of paying the expenses of the participants representing that region to come to Lewisburg for the statewide festival. For the most part, these financial plans did not materialize. The first regional festival took place at Philadelphia on May 3, 4, and 5. It was followed by the Central Pennsylvania Regional Festival held at Altoona on May 15. After that the Anthracite Coal Region Festival was held at Wilkes-Barre on May 25; this was to be the only regional festival that was a major financial success. Then came the Western Pennsylvania Region Festival at Pittsburgh on May 30. Finally the Pennsylvania German Region Festival was held at Allentown on June 26 and 27; though not as successful as the one in Wilkes-Barre, the Allentown Festival also returned some profit.[20] It was a demanding schedule, but Korson had to do things well. In the pursuit of excellence he was unwilling to spare himself. In an article for the *Bucknell Alumni Monthly* Korson explained his policy on regional festivals:

> Preceding the state folk festival in Memorial Stadium, there will be a series of preliminary regional and local festivals in various parts of the state. It is our policy to help build these preliminary events into local traditions in the respective communities. The folk festival has a technique all its own and until local leadership is developed to handle it properly we shall have to continue to give assistance. The preliminary festivals help us uncover hidden sources of material and performers, while providing a means of promotion for the statewide program at Lewisburg which is invaluable.[21]

The Pennsylvania Folk Festival itself was scheduled for July 30 and 31 through August 1 and 2 of 1936 in the Memorial Stadium of Bucknell University in Lewisburg. The choice of Memorial

The miners and the setting are authentic, but the hoedown was staged as publicity for the 1936 Pennsylvania Folk Festival.
Courtesy George Korson Folklore Archive

Stadium as the site had some unforeseen consequences. Using a large concrete horseshoe that was designed for watching football dictated a certain kind of format. Korson made a number of tacit assumptions. For example, it was assumed that the audience would take their seats and watch and listen while "more than 800 performers" performed. This format contrasts vividly with contemporary folk festivals such as the Kutztown Folk Festival.

At Kutztown, Pennsylvania, the festival is held on a fairgrounds rather than in a stadium. The net effect is a loose arrangement rather than a tight one. At Kutztown there is, to be sure, a main stage that spotlights music, singing, auctions and pageantry. But only a small proportion of the people are there at any one time.

Most of them are wandering around talking to craftsmen, playing games, buying things, eating, and taking in the spectacle. The emphasis there, explains Don Yoder, is "on informality—what the visitor saw was not a closed museum exhibit but a living demonstration, with tools he could touch and handle, and a demonstrator with whom he could chat and exchange techniques as well as lore."[22]

The difference between Lewisburg then and Kutztown now is the difference between formality and informality. This difference stems partly from the fact that Lewisburg featured folksong and Kutztown emphasizes folklife. But this is not so much an ideological difference as it is one of style. Though Korson may not have been overtly aware of his own bias, as a newspaperman he shared the values and assumptions of typography. As shown by the official program, the plan of the Pennsylvania Folk Festival was linear, orderly, and sequential. In McLuhan's terminology we would have to say that Korson's festival was "hot," a highly defined event in which much was given and little had to be filled in by the listener. The festival of today tends to be "cool," more like a seminar and less like a lecture. Most contemporary festivals allow the casual participant more freedom to wander and discover the meaning of the festival for himself.[23]

The Pennsylvania Folk Festival was ballyhooed in press releases as "The Greatest Cultural Step in Pennsylvania in half a century," a quotation attributed to Henry W. Shoemaker.[24] Of course, it must be said that Shoemaker was hardly a disinterested observer. Nonetheless, it was an ambitious undertaking. The ardent festival goer could watch six different programs over a four-day period. The festival opened on Thursday night with a program of racial folklore featuring Indian tribal rites, Ukrainian folksongs, and Pennsylvania German folksongs. The second day was given over to a presentation of occupational folklore. Some of the folklore presented reenactments of historical occupations such as river raftsmen, Conestoga wagoners, canal boatmen, and street criers. Other occupational groups such as sailors, farmers, and anthracite coal miners were represented by actual practitioners. Saturday was devoted to contests and features. The university gave a cash award of $100 to the winning square dance team and medals to individual performers, including ballad singers and traditional fiddlers. Finally the program concluded on Sunday with leading choirs of the state singing hymns and sacred music.[25]

After the dust settled and the crowds went home, Korson could bask in the satisfaction of a job well done. The press coverage had been favorable, and President Marts was pleased. There was one dark cloud on the horizon—the financial picture. Expenditures for the festival had come to about $8,000, but receipts totaled only about $5,000. Still, no one was overly concerned about a $3,000 deficit. Ticket prices had been kept deliberately low, and no one expected the festival to make money the first year. Nonetheless, there was hope that the festival could be self-supporting in 1937.[26]

Planning for the 1937 festival started immediately. One criticism of the 1936 festival had been that the folklore material needed to be given a more dramatic presentation. Korson's handling of this objection is a good example of both his integrity and his diplomacy. At Arnaud Marts' suggestion, the university had employed the professional public relations firm of Lawn and Wendt in New York City. Marts recommended this firm because they were especially experienced in tourist publicity. The fact that Paul Wendt was a Bucknell alumnus may have been a plus. They handled routine publicity and gave advice on how to get the most favorable press coverage. Both Victor H. Lawn and Paul R. Wendt pressed for more professional presentation. It is to Korson's credit that he accepted criticism of the mechanics of production, but he held out against excessive popularization. Thus Korson became one of the pioneer guardians of the integrity of folklore as opposed to "fakelore."[27] Of course, he did not call it "fakelore"; he called it "showmanship," but his judgment in the matter was fundamentally sound, as shown in one of his reports:

> Let us first examine the suggestions of Lawn and Wendt. Theirs is a plan for more showmanship and less folklore. Now staging a folk festival in a large open-air theatre like Memorial Stadium does compel the use of some showmanship. But it can be applied to the production without either impairing the integrity of the material or cramping the spontaneity of the performers. The platform should be moved close to the stands which would promote an atmosphere of intimacy between audience and performers which is one of the charms of a folk festival. Costuming, bright lights, and perhaps a judicious use of colored lights, and perfect amplification would cer-

tainly improve the performances. Further improvement lies in getting the performers on and off the stage expeditiously. The "acts" themselves can be arranged in an effective order but we must be prepared to sacrifice such an arrangement for the sake of a nation-wide radio broadcast.

These, in my opinion, are sound technical devices that can be applied to the festival effectively without sacrificing or compromising its intrinsic qualities. Showmanship that would take us beyond these bounds should be carefully considered.[28]

Korson resisted suggestions to stress entertainment and to minimize folklore. He realized that part of the attraction of the festival was that the performers were close to the soil and to the customs and traditions that they reflected. However, in one important dimension Korson had to compromise. To hold down costs, the program was drastically shortened. Instead of six performances, there were three—Friday evening, Saturday afternoon, and Saturday evening. This abridgment may have been a blessing in disguise, because it did force a greater degree of selectivity of material and performers.[29]

The 1937 festival ran into bad luck. Because of heavy rain on both nights, the festival had to be moved from the stadium to the Lewisburg High School Auditorium.[30] The program, a good balance of different genres from different ethnic groups, went on; but the expected crowd never showed up. Bravely the festival opened on Friday evening, July 30, with a program of "Folk Expressions of Pennsylvania Races." This included Indian dances, Welsh folksongs, Ukrainian folk dances, and a Pennsylvania-German schnitzin (apple-paring) party. In addition, there were the songs of Stephen Foster, a native of Pennsylvania, English folksongs, Scottish folksongs and dances, and finally a reenactment of a Scandinavian Mid-Summer Fest. Saturday, July 31, was billed as "Nanticoke Day." In addition to Nanticoke Indian dances, there were statewide contests in fiddling, clog dancing, ballad singing, country auctioneering, and tall story telling. Finally that evening a program was held featuring "Occupational Folk Expressions of Pennsylvania." The program began with the State Square Dancing Championship Contest with the five regional teams in competition. The square dancing was followed by street cries, canal boatmen's songs, lumberjacks' songs, sea chanteys, anthracite miners' songs, and Conestoga wagoners' songs.[31]

Despite the well-organized program, the festival again lost money. It is impossible to reconstruct the exact chain of events here, but the fact of having lost money two years in a row put a strain on Korson's relations with Bucknell. There were complaints about Korson's handling of the food and lodging for the participants as well as complaints about his business sense. In a memorandum to Marts, his assistant Paul Hightower complained:

> As for my own reactions, I tried to pick up all the pieces of what was going wrong and put them in their proper places, with the result that he apparently is blaming me for the whole thing because since Saturday night he is not speaking to me, praise God. If the Festival is put on next year, it would be wise to have a Business Manager, let Mr. Korson contact the people and then turn all arrangements over to the Business Manager from then on. Mr. Korson can still be Program Director, but when it comes to handling people, he is a complete flop, and when it comes to looking after details, his mind disappears . . .
>
> Had I been told that I would be responsible for looking after the Festival, I would have been prepared, but to try to pick it up where I had to with no notification before hand made it doubly difficult and nerve-wracking without the annoyance of having to do it with Korson in the saddle.
>
> He took the attitude that the whole University should drop whatever they were doing and wait on him hand and foot, and he could only think of one detail at a time. When that was out of the way, he would think of the next, not being able to see the picture as a whole and trying to make it as easy on everyone as possible. I do not care to pass through another week like the last.[32]

Despite Hightower's complaints, Marts continued to support Korson and to seek outside funding from the Pennsylvania Publicity Commission. But as time passed without getting outside help, Bucknell lost interest, and the search for a new sponsor for 1938 was initiated. The search was concentrated in the Philadelphia area, since it was the center of the American Swedish Tercentenary Celebration that year. After considerable negotiation it was decided that the Fourth Annual Pennsylvania Folk Festival would be sponsored jointly by Beaver College and the Pennsylvania Arts and Sciences Society. It was to be held at the Grey Towers estate campus of Beaver College in Jenkintown. Walter B. Greenway, president of Beaver College, and Louis Walton Sipley, director of the society, agreed to collaborate on the presentation of the program on an even basis regarding the risks incurred or profits accrued.[33]

The 1938 festival was limited to a single day—June 18, a Saturday. Though some items had to be cut out, the format remained much the same as in previous years. There were songs and dances of the Swedes, the English, the Scottish, the Welsh, the Pennsylvania Germans, the Slavs, and the blacks. In addition, there were ballads of the anthracite miners, Conestoga wagoners, and lumberjacks. Finally there were the usual contests in auctioneering, ballad singing, fiddling, and dancing.[34]

As it turned out, 1938 was to be the last Pennsylvania Folk Festival for a long time. Again the festival was more of an artistic success than a financial success. In addition, Korson and Sipley had a number of disagreements in managing the festival.[35] President Marts of Bucknell offered to transfer the festival to Beaver College; President Greenway of Beaver was interested, but the executive committee of the Board of Trustees at Beaver decided not to go ahead. Later Korson approached the University of Pennsylvania concerning sponsorship, but its trustees, too, declined.[36] By this time Korson himself was working on new plans for research in the bituminous coal fields.

It seems unfortunate that the Pennsylvania Folk Festival was allowed to wither away. In addition to the problem of bad luck with the weather, there was the more basic problem that educational institutions in Pennsylvania like Bucknell University and Beaver College in the late thirties did not have enough money to sponsor the festival long enough to make it self-supporting.

Though preoccupied with the problems of putting on four folk festivals in the thirties, Korson managed to produce three publications—two short song books and his major work, *Minstrels of the Mine Patch*. It is a tribute to Korson's energy and commitment that he carried through with his publishing projects. Managing a folk festival tends to be an all-consuming task. Like a producer in a theater, the folk festival director has to deal with hundreds of small details that clutter both the mind and the desk. It is difficult to focus one's mind on a manuscript when hounded with the pressing chores of organizing a festival.

Korson had not been hired at Bucknell as a professor, but as the Festival director. Therefore his motivation to produce stemmed from a personal commitment. Korson's position at Bucknell, while not totally secure, simply was not tied to the publication of scholarly books or articles in professional journals as evidence of research activity. His collaborator on the two song books, however, was Melvin LeMon, an assistant professor of music, who of course was under some pressure to publish.

The first book in this period to be published was *The Miner Sings: A Collection of Folk-Songs and Ballads of the Anthracite Miner*, published in 1936 in New York by J. Fischer and Brother. The transcriptions and musical arrangements were by Melvin LeMon. This short book of some forty-two pages contained the words and music for ten songs and ballads. Each musical number was accompanied by extensive editorial notes, written by Korson, giving the background of the song. For example, the first song is "When the Breaker Starts Up Full Time." The breaker, of course, is the large wooden building on the surface containing machinery for sorting out the coal from the rock and slate and other foreign matter that comes up from the mine. Therefore, when the breaker starts up full time, there will be full employment for the miners. Hence it is a happy song. The words of the songs were mostly from his first book; the advantage of this book was that the music was provided. Apparently LeMon at this stage was desperate for a publication, for he wrote the publisher asking that his name precede Korson's on the title page. Korson, not caught up in the back-stabbing way of life in academe, let this affront pass.[37]

The second book in this period was to be published as *Pennsylvania Folk Songs and Ballads for School, Camp, and Playground*, published by the Pennsylvania Folk Festival in 1937 at Lewisburg, as a public service. This thirteen-page book had a different audience from the song book of the previous year. Altogether there were eight songs in this collection, with only one coal mining song, "Down in a Coal Mine." Designed for wide distribution, the book contained other occupational songs such as "The Conestoga Wagoner's Lament" and "The Jolly Lumbermen." There were also Pennsylvania German folksongs in translation such as "The Poplar Tree," "The Hole in the Jug," and "Spin, Spin, My Dearest Daughter." Copies of the publication were distributed free among the state's camps, schools, playgrounds, and Granges. The demand exceeded the supply, and the first edition of two thousand copies was exhausted in two weeks. Unfortunately, there were no funds to bring out a second edition.[38]

By far the most important book Korson produced in the thirties was *Minstrels of the Mine Patch: Songs and Stories of the Anthracite Industry*, published in 1938 by the University of Pennsylvania Press at Philadelphia. Many scholars consider this to be Korson's finest work. Basically it was an expanded version of his first book, *Songs and Ballads of the Anthracite Miner*, which had appeared in 1927. This book was much more polished. It contained biographical sketches of informants, a glossary of technical terms, a bibliography, and an index. Also added was a decorative frontispiece, an etching by Nicholas Bervinchak, as well as several musical transcriptions by Melvin LeMon. In addition to the songs and ballads of the first book, Korson supplied stories, superstitions, and legends, and an entire chapter on Slavs as miners, which appeared for the first time.

The book was brought up to date with new material from the Depression; specifically, the song "My Wee Coal Hole," which deals with coal bootlegging, was added. Historically and sociologically this book represents a major step in the development of industrial folklore as a field of study. Because of its great importance, we will look at the book in some detail.

Minstrels was at least eleven years in the making. All the years of sifting and sorting and rearranging resulted in a first-rate book. Much of this work was done in the period from 1936 to 1938 when Korson worked closely with Phelps Soule, manager of the University of Pennsylvania Press, in revising the manuscript. Though Korson's negotiations with his editor did not reach the same legendary proportions as those between, for example, Thomas Wolfe and Maxwell Perkins, nonetheless the final product did represent considerable effort on both sides to bring shape and unity to the work. Some of Soule's suggestions revealed his lack of knowledge of folklore and were unfortunate. For example, he discouraged Korson from giving three or four versions of the same ballad, though from the standpoint of folklore studies such comparisons are very helpful. Other criticisms made by Soule were often quite constructive. For example, he opposed Korson's early proposed title, *The Saga of the Anthracite Industry*, on the sensible grounds that such a title gave the impression of an epic poem instead of a collection of tales and ballads.[39] On the whole, we must conclude that Korson's work benefited by all this careful revision. The correspondence with Phelps Soule was to continue for many years. They kept exchanging news on common interests both literary and folkloristic.

After two years of rewriting and polishing, the book was ready for publication and release in the fall of 1938, in time for the Christmas trade. No one awaited the finished product more eagerly than Bill Keating, one of Korson's key informants, who wrote:

> Your Book is off the Press, you say:
> Please send me One, without delay.
> I'm surely hungering for a look
> At your "Minstrels of the Mine Patch" Book.
> I live in "The Patch" again, and so
> My *address* is: Seltzer City P.O.;
> By adding *Schuylkill County*, Pa.
> "My" *Minstrels* can NOT go astray.
>
> I know you labored like a Turk.
> I appreciate your earnest Work.
> (Tho your Book may aid me little, or less?)
> I'm wishing *You* complete Success. [40]

In physical appearance the 332-page book was striking. The black cloth binding was specially stamped to resemble anthracite coal. It had a convincing gleam that reflected the light differently as the angle was shifted, as would a vein of anthracite coal. On the dust jacket and on the title page appeared a vignette of a fiddling miner done by artist Nick Bervinchak, whose brother posed as the fiddler. In addition, Bervinchak did an etching, "Home to the Mine Patch," for the frontispiece. It portrayed four miners, lunch buckets in hand, leaving the elevator of the mine shaft for home after a long day's work—presumably to go home, clean up, eat dinner, and start singing. [41]

As mentioned before, one of the most intriguing aspects of Korson's work is that almost from the very beginning he intuitively understood that folklore is best presented in the context of the entire way of life of a small community. In his introduction to *Minstrels* Korson identifies five specific settings where folklore occurred in a natural context: the green, part of every mine patch, and a center of community life; the barroom, which Korson described as a poor man's club; within the mines themselves, during a lull in work and nearly always at lunch time; general stores, the best known of which was Mackin Brothers' store in Wilkes-Barre; and wakes, social occasions with gossip and storytelling.[42]

Long before the holistic folklife approach became a formalized academic position, Korson placed the miners' lore in the context of their entire way of life. As mentioned in the preface, Green has pointed out that Korson assumed that the miners were folk for two basic reasons—the behavior of the songs in terms of their origin and transmission and also the relative isolation of the mine patch communities.[43] Thus we have argued that Korson was really very close—parallel, but independent—to the concept of folklife scholarship developed in Scandinavia and practiced in the United States by Robert Redfield and Don Yoder.

At this point it is worthwhile to quote Redfield's description of a little community, since the qualities he describes are realized to a high degree in the mine patches examined by Korson in his field work:

> What, then, do we mean more particularly by a little community? I put forward, first, the quality of distinctiveness: where the community begins and where it ends is apparent. The distinctiveness is apparent to the outside observer and is expressed in the group-consciousness of the people of the community.
>
> Second, the community we are here concerned with is small, so small that either it itself is the unit of personal observation or else, being somewhat larger and yet homogeneous, it provides in some part of it a unit of personal observation fully representative of the whole . . .
>
> Third, the community to which we are to look in these chapters is homogeneous. Activities and states of mind are much alike for all persons in corresponding sex and age positions; and the career of one generation repeats that of the preceding . . .
>
> As a fourth defining quality it may be said the community we have here in mind is self-sufficient and provides for all or most of the activities and needs of the people in it. The little community is a cradle-to-the-grave arrangement.[44]

In terms of style, Korson's writing was quite different from Redfield's. Korson used vivid imagery to paint a picture in words to create a human interest story, while Redfield's prose is more general and scientific. Nonetheless, these qualities—distinctiveness, smallness, homogeneity, and self-sufficiency—do emerge in Korson's picture of the way of life in the mine patch.

Mine Patch Life

Life was stark, bleak, and semi-primitive. The wretched company houses kept out neither rain, heat, nor cold. They had no plumbing. Water was obtained from a well or from outdoor community hydrants which froze in the winter. Lighting was by tallow candles or kerosene lamps, and streets were dark.

—*Minstrels of the Mine Patch*, p. 14

Erskine Solomon photo, courtesy Wyoming Historical and Geological Society

As a fierce UMWA partisan, Korson recognized the bleakness of mine patch existence. He was interested in efforts to improve the working and living conditions of the miners. But he was writing neither a political essay nor a sociological study, and he knew that telling about the plumbing, the lighting, and the heating—all terribly inadequate—did not tell the whole story. Even in the face of the worse imaginable conditions, Korson knew that the miners had produced many lovely songs and stories. Paradoxically, he realized that many of his informants were nostalgic for the old mine patch days. Korson reported, "Time has softened their bitterness

Homes of the Miners

It was on a summer's day in the coal fields far away
  That I chanced upon a miner's lonely cot;
And I marveled much to see how contented he could be,
  For it seemed that he was happy with his lot.
Roses bloomed around the door and a baby on the floor
  Lent a sunshine to that lonely mountainside,
And I said, "Though fate's unkind you are happy here, I find . . ."

                    —Charles E. Baer and George W. Thornton,
                    "A Miner's Home Sweet Home"
                    from *Minstrels of the Mine Patch*, p. 34

Courtesy Wyoming Historical and Geological Society

---

but has not effaced from their memory the sentimental side of patch life—the communal sings and dances, the neighborliness and friendships."[45]

One of the reasons that this book was Korson's greatest success was that he made his readers feel a human bond with his informants. In the Introduction Korson discusses the method he used.

Though Korson's statement is informal, it is clear that he has given priority to first-hand information and to field work:

> The editorial matter in each chapter whose object is to orient the songs and ballads, legends and stories, is derived chiefly from personal observation and from interviews with hundreds of mine workers, many of them old-timers, and others connected with the anthracite industry; also local historians. Some of it is the result of deliberate effort, but more came to me casually as I listened hour after hour to old men and women recall the days of their youth in the anthracite region. In some cases, reminiscences were the ore which brought forth precious ballads.[46]

This statement is revealing in a number of ways. Korson modestly refers to his own writing as "editorial matter" with the connotation of journalism and the direct message that his own writing is by way of explanation of the folklore items. In other words, he is making clear his own identity as a collector. He is deliberately subordinating his own views and opinions to the "precious ballads." Much of what he learned came to him "casually"; we know that this happened as a result of having spent years and years in the area. It never would have happened in a single short field trip. The statement is also significant for what it does not say. There is no theoretical commitment; his book did not set forth a hypothesis as such. This was once explained by Wayland D. Hand: "I'm not sure there was too much theory as such. Through it ran the notion that they were human beings, they produce folklore, they do it for certain very practical social needs and in some cases physical and spiritual needs. He was not a theoretician."[47] Why was Korson not a theoretician? I think Archie Green supplied the answer when he wrote: "Morally, Korson valued mining society and its members above folklore as a scientific discipline."[48]

Though Korson's book broke no new theoretical ground, it has been widely acclaimed for several reasons. One of these was Korson's willingness to look for folklore in the industrial workplace. As suggested earlier, Korson's was the classic case of a gifted amateur who was not blinded by prevailing beliefs. Formal training in folklore might have given Korson the folklorist's predominant bias toward country life. Among the early reviewers only Constance Rourke, whose book *The Roots of American Culture* (1942) was to achieve prominence in the next decade, seemed to appreciate this important point. In her review in the *Nation* she immediately identified what Green was later to call "the dichotomy between rural and industrial lore."[49] With vivid imagery and considerable insight she wrote:

> Earth magic is so closely associated with folksong and folklore that we are likely to think of it as an essential element, but in these ballads and stories of the anthracite miners of eastern Pennsylvania there are no green leaves a-fallin, no sprig of yew, no whitethorn bough, not even a branch of native willow or white oak.[50]

What Constance Rourke is describing here is nothing less than a tradition-shattering shift in the folkloristic point of view. If Korson's definition of folklore were accepted, then rural subject matter would no longer be an "essential element." The unspoken assumption that folklore was strictly a rural phenomenon shared by the folkloristic community had been challenged. Korson's work was so unprecedented that it was completely overlooked by the *Journal of American Folklore*.[51] Actually this oversight is not surprising because the *JAF* was still interested in further exploration of normal and acceptable, that is, rural, problems. The study of folklore was not heavily theoretical in the thirties, nor is the history of the study of folklore generally considered part of the history of science; however, many concepts from the history of science work well in looking at folkloristics. For example, Thomas Kuhn in his landmark study, *The Structure of Scientific Revolutions*, argues that most normal research problems do not aim to produce major novelties. In this light, it is not surprising that the folklore establishment was slow to recognize Korson's achievement. Assimilating a new viewpoint like his demands more than just an additive adjustment of theory. Until that adjustment is completed—until the folklorist has learned to see his world in a different way—the new viewpoint is either ignored or resisted. As we shall see in the next chapter, it was not until 1944 that the *JAF* took note of Korson's work; and the reaction of the reviewer—if not of the profession in general—was predictably hostile.[52] If Korson's vision was accurate, then previously "completed work" in folklore field trips and publications would have to be done again. To take one example, the work of Cecil Sharp in southern Appalachia had failed to recognize any industrial lore, such as that from textile mills. In effect, the implications of Korson's findings would force changes in books that were already published. Thus it should not surprise us that there was resistance to change. Indeed, following our analogy

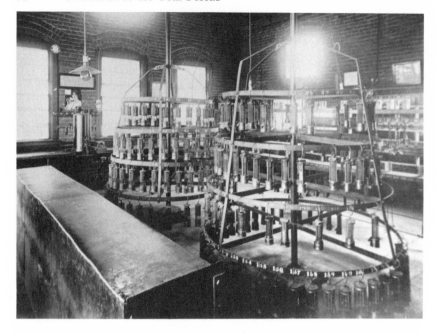

Safety Lamp Room

The lamp man he squints through the window at me,
"What's your name? What's your age? What your number?" says he.
"Bill Keatin', I'm thirty, number twenty-three,
Mark that down, down, down."

—William Keating, "Down, Down, Down,"
from *Minstrels of the Mine Patch*, p. 49.

Erskine Solomon photo, courtesy Wyoming Historical and Geological Society

to the history of science, we can see that Korson's discovery of industrial lore is not unlike the discovery of oxygen, x-rays, or the Leyden jar.[53]

But there was more to Korson's success than his choice of the industrial setting, revolutionary though that choice was. A collector cannot succeed without informants. Through tactfulness and persistence, Korson found some remarkable tradition bearers. With the passage of time it is difficult to say exactly what personal qualities and skills were needed for Korson to locate and draw out his informants. In his *Guide to Fieldworkers in Folklore* Kenneth Goldstein suggests: "The intelligent, personable, sociable, and sensitive person will find his own way to establish the relationships necessary for him to achieve his goal."[54] Indeed Korson did find his own way. Apparently he felt that the proper stance of the folklorist toward the folksinger should be that of devoted scribe rather than austere analyst.[55] The miners, in turn, valued Korson as a friend and opened their hearts to him. Korson at one point in his introduction said simply: "It was a pleasure to hear them talk."[56]

One of his finest informants and a lifelong friend was William Keating. Born on March 31, 1886, at Mount Laffe Patch, Keating was one of the third generation of Irish miners. Not until he was thirty-two years old did Keating learn to write. Korson recruited Keating for both the Pennsylvania and National Folk Festivals, where he appeared with "patched faded blue overalls tucked inside high-laced boots, his work shirt open at the collar, a dinner pail suspended from one shoulder and a canteen from the other, his teapot shaped open-flame lamp protruding from his miner's cap, and a long braided leather whip slung carelessly around his neck."[57] Keating's most memorable ballad was "Down, Down, Down."[58] It was a favorite among folk festival audiences, and it is perhaps the most entertaining item in Korson's entire collection. Even casual readers of *Minstrels* are often able to recite whole verses of the ballad. The only thing funnier than the ballad itself is Keating's story of how it was written.

The ballad can be read on several levels of meaning. On the first level, it is a vivid word picture that describes typical steps in the miner's everyday work experience. For example, almost like a textbook of mining engineering, it tells of checking out a safety lamp:

> The lamp man he squints through the window at me,
> "What's your name? What your age? What your number?" says he.
> "Bill Keatin', I'm thirty, number twenty-three,
> Mark that down, down, down."

It goes on to describe miners being lowered through the mine shaft by elevator:

> "All aboard for the bottom!" the top-man did yell,
> We stepped on the cage, he ding-donged a bell;

Miners Wait to be Lowered

"All aboard for the bottom!" the top-man did yell,
We stepped on the cage, he ding-donged a bell;
Through that hole in Oak Hill, like a bat out o'hell
We went down, down, down.

—William Keating, "Down, Down, Down,"
from *Minstrels of the Mine Patch*, p. 51

Erskine Solomon photo, courtesy Wyoming Historical and Geological Society

Through that hole in Oak Hill, like a bat out o'hell
We went down, down, down.

Another verse describes the principal tool used by the miners:

I asked Sam what tools would I need in the place.
"Very few," said the boss with a grin on his face.
"One seven-size scoop in a coop-stoopy space
Away down, down, down."

On a second level of meaning, we realize that every stanza is

Miners Loading Coal Car

I asked Sam what tools would I need in the place.
"Very few," said the boss with a grin on his face.
"One seven-size scoop in a coop-stoopy space
Away down, down, down."

—William Keating, "Down, Down, Down,"
from *Minstrels of the Mine Patch*, p. 50

Courtesy Wyoming Historical and Geological Society

---

elaborately set up to create a pun with the words "down, down, down." Part of our delight in hearing it is watching Keating's nimble mind driving again and again toward the inevitable pun. Each pun is a gratifying fulfillment of our expectations. On a third level of meaning, we realize that the ballad tells the story of a miner who is reporting for work with a hangover. The reason that he is so impertinent to the lamp man and the boss is that he is suffering from a terrible headache. We realize that this is a barroom ballad, and that virtually every stanza constitutes another invitation to pour another drink "down, down, down," as Keating himself described:

In the days when I was hittin' the booze the drinks would come up, up, up when I sang "Down, Down, Down." She was too long to sing straight through, so I broke her up into groups of verses corresponding to levels in a mine. When I got through singing one level, the boys alongside the bar would yell, "Time out for drinks." Then the drinks would go round and Billy Keating would have a drink on the house or on whoever was payin' at the time. As the ballad has about forty verses, you can imagine in what condition the singer and the customers were by the time I got to the end. The barroom floor was me stage for thirty years and, be jabbers, I done it up brown when I was at it. But I'm off the hard stuff for life. I've got it licked now.[59]

Minstrels of the Mine Patch gives further support to the view that, regarding labor and society, Korson was perhaps a reformer, but certainly not a revolutionary. The book does have a pro-union slant, but it does not attempt to arouse readers against the evils of capitalism. It does not suggest any alteration of institutional arrangements or class relationships. Indeed Korson goes out of his way—perhaps too far out of his way—to soften his tone. Partly Korson spoke quietly because in gathering his songs he was more interested in art than in politics. Partly the cutting edge of Korson's outrage was somewhat dulled by nostalgia. But mainly he did not believe that the Depression, bad as it was, called for a change in the country's institutions. A close reading of *Minstrels* reveals numerous instances where Korson moderates controversial material. For example, in discussing the concluding days of the bitter and protracted coal strike of 1902 he wrote: "Public opinion was with the strikers, and most of the country's newspapers supported them. One of the breaks came late in the strike when George F. Baer, operators' spokesman, wrote a letter, duly printed and derided in the newspapers, in which he intimated that the operators were doing God's work."[60] Baer's tone had actually been more offensive than Korson indicated: he had shown outright contempt for his starving employees. Baer's actual words (not quoted by Korson) were: "The rights and interests of the laboring men will be protected and cared for . . . by the Christian men to whom God in his infinite wisdom has given the control of the property interests of the country."[61]

Not only did Korson moderate and temper the issues he chose to deal with, he also simply left out some of the more inflammatory characters. This omission of radical material has already been pointed out by Archie Green. Because this point is so central to my argument, it is worthwhile to consider Green's analysis:

> Korson was the first American folklorist to present any labor lore to the public; nevertheless, he too rejected some data, for he did not include in his books the contributions of communists to union tradition. He knew intimately the internecine conflict which wracked miner's organizations during the 1920's and 1930's, for he had observed the radical movement directly and understood clearly the use by dual unionists of folkloric material. It was not easy to write objectively about Communist party members when they were perceived as union wreckers, aliens, and subversives. Yet Korson's views on a red song or singer would have been most helpful in sketching the little-known relationships of polemical to industrial material.
>
> I am concerned at this point only with the role of such bards as Aunt Molly Jackson . . . Korson chose to overlook her. He wrote to me that in his collecting he distinguished between "the 'folk,' the workers themselves and union organizers from the outside . . . When I found that a ballad had been written by an outsider I didn't use it . . . I had to be especially careful because in the 1920's and 1930's the Communists were making a determined effort to capture the United Mine Workers of America, and some of the songs were composed by their organizers. When I was sure of this source—and I had ways of finding out—I just didn't use the song in my collection."
>
> Obviously, there exists a hierarchy of "the folk": peasant, worker, miner, unionist, radical, communist. Spargo drew the line at one end of the scale and Korson at the other. Korson himself recognized the great difficulty in distinguishing between "organizers from the outside" and those who "were miners first, most of them since they were nine or ten years old, which made them acceptable." Such scholastic hair-splitting breaks down when the life histories of particular miner organizers are pursued. Some UMWA old hands came from a Knights of Labor or Socialist party tradition; some highly conservative Appalachian miners, inheritors of Jeffersonian and Jacksonian values, became Marxists in the Depression. The difference between Knights of Labor songs, which Korson accepted, and Communist party songs, which he rejected, was frequently but a distinction in chronology.[62]

One radical group that Korson could not avoid dealing with was the Molly Maguires, to whom he devoted an entire chapter in *Minstrels*. The Molly Maguires were a secret organization of Irish mine workers who fought back against the operators and bosses through intimidation, violence, and occasionally murder. They were overturned by a Pinkerton detective who infiltrated the organization and revealed their secrets and their plots. Subsequent generations of historians and folklorists from Arthur H. Lewis to Richard Dorson have wrestled with the controversies regarding whether they were indigenous or foreign radicals and regarding their attitude toward, and use of, violence.

The Mollies are so controversial that they provide an excellent political litmus test for any author. No responsible writer, even a mainstream consensus historian, can avoid dealing with the central questions they raise. Do the ends justify the means? Is capitalism inherently evil? Is revolution justified in the face of oppression? Basically Korson was distrustful of ideology. His training in journalism taught him to be "objective." In the Molly Maguire chapter he tried desperately to present both sides of the story. Through the use of carefully chosen words and skillful rhetoric, he tried to avoid taking a stand, but a close reading of the chapter reveals his point of view. Korson believed that the ends did *not* justify the means; the Mollies were not justified in their terrorism. Korson's judgment on the matter was given in a very low-key manner: "The general opinion expressed was that the Mollies found fertile ground for a reign of terror because of the weaknesses of the miners' union to cope with the powerful buccaneers who ran the industry in those early days."[63] Despite Korson's use of the passive voice and the "general opinion" device, his meaning is clear—the Mollies were wrong. If there had only been a strong union, there would have been no need for extreme measures. The underlying sentiment, then, is that strong labor unions are socially desirable as a countervailing force against the excesses of capitalism. Again, this is the position of a liberal reformer, not of a revolutionary.

In view of Korson's pro-union position, it is a little surprising to note the reaction of his friend Thomas Kennedy, Secretary-Treasurer of the UMWA, who after reading the manuscript suggested suppression of the whole affair:

> As to the Molly Maguires proposition in the manuscript, it is my judgment that it might probably be better if some other subject were substituted for that chapter because as a rule, a great many people in the anthracite region do not like this subject to be retold. There are so many different interpretations of the matter, that no matter what

way one would write on the subject it is bound to raise controversy and revive old sores that have long since been healed.[64]

One can only guess at Kennedy's motives here. Perhaps he felt that any mention of former labor strife and violence would somehow hurt labor's image as a responsible component of the corporate-liberal state. It is to Korson's credit that he did not follow Kennedy's suggestion.

When *Minstrels of the Mine Patch* was published in 1938, reviewers in politically oriented periodicals tended to seize on the colorful and controversial Molly Maguire chapter in order to dramatize their reviews. The reviewer for *Time* magazine virtually ignored the central content of the book—the collection of ballads and stories—in order to give his opinion of the Molly Maguires, quite different from Korson's view:

> In some of the mine patches of northeastern Pennsylvania June 21, 1877 is still remembered as Black Thursday. That was the day the Molly Maguires—ten of them—were hanged. Far from sissies, the Molly Maguires were a gang of Irish plug-uglies who for two decades had terrorized miners' families, taken pot shots at bosses, and made things generally hot for law-abiding mine folks. "Mollies" had been as much of a nuisance to the coal fields' feeble labor organizations as to the mine owners. When they were finally dispersed with the aid of Pinkerton detectives and the hangman's rope, all the soberer citizens of Pennsylvania's mining towns sighed with relief.[65]

In vivid contrast to the hostility toward the Mollies shown by *Time* magazine's reviewer is David Silver's review of the book in *The New Masses*, a weekly magazine with an editorial viewpoint in accordance with the policies of the Communist party. Silver wrote a generally sympathetic and thoughtful review with well-chosen examples to make his points. However, once again the Molly Maguire chapter caused trouble. Predictably, Korson's even-handed treatment was not well received. Silver's review shows that an even-handed treatment is not necessarily an accurate one:

> It is a pity that Mr. Korson's section on the Molly Maguires has more the character of "folklore" than actual history. As in his earlier volume, *Songs and Ballads of the Anthracite Miner*, he tends to portray the Pinkerton spy McKenna (MacParland) sympathetically and to accept all the stories of Molly Maguire outrages without

question. . . . The testimony of the ballads commemorating the prosecution and hanging of the framed leaders of the miners whose union had been driven underground by the operators flatly contradicts the slanders against them.[66]

Taken together, the review from *Time* magazine and the review from *The New Masses* show the difficulties of Korson's position. As a mainstream liberal reformer he found himself under fire from both the right and the left. Korson sought reforms in the economic system, but he did not argue against the existing system. Perhaps naively, Korson's objection was never to the private enterprise system, but to the irresponsibility of the big business coal operators—"the powerful buccaneers."[67] He was content to make the operators the villains in the story. Of course, it is doubtful that the businessmen could have made the same level of profits in safe mines with modern equipment while paying the miners a living wage. But Korson did not see, or did not care to explain, the relationship between the private enterprise system and the villainy of the operators.

3

Bituminous Years
The 1940s

Oh, it's hard to hear the hungry children crying
  While I have two hands that want to do their share,
Oh, you rich men in the city, won't you have a little pity,
  And just listen to a miner's prayer?
  —"A Miner's Prayer"[1]

For George Korson the decade of the 1940s was a period of consolidation. He was able to apply his talent to projects that grew logically out of his work of the 1930s. In this period he produced two major publications. The first was *Coal Dust on the Fiddle* (1943), a study of the folklore of the bituminous industry, which was in effect a sequel to the earlier work on the anthracite industry. The second major work was *Pennsylvania Songs and Legends* (1949), an original collection of related essays on Pennsylvania folklore that he edited. In a sense this book grew out of the 1930s, since it was through the role of festival director at Bucknell that he made his reputation as a statewide folklore authority. Also it was in this capacity that he made the many personal contacts necessary to assemble a list of distinguished contributors.

Korson also produced two juvenile publications in the 1940s. The first was *Black Land: The Way of Life in the Coal Fields* (1941), one in a series of junior high school texts on occupations in their geographic settings. The second juvenile work he co-edited with Marion Vallat Emrich. It was an anthology titled *The Child's Book of Folklore* (1947), and it became very popular. Throughout most of the 1940s Korson was employed full-time as a writer and editor for various American Red Cross publications. It is a tribute to his competence and efficiency that he was able to make major contributions to American folklore while earning his living and supporting his family as a working journalist. To do this required an unusual combination of skill and energy along with a family willing to sacrifice some of their demands on his time. Korson was so dedicated to his work that at times his family had to tempt him away from his typewriter. And there were unavoidable conflicts at times between the demands of Korson's dual career as journalist and folklorist and his family obligations. He did not always resolve these conflicts to the full satisfaction of his family or himself.

In the late 1930s Korson faced a major crossroad in his career. It was becoming increasingly difficult to find a suitable sponsor for the Pennsylvania Folk Festival. Both Bucknell and Beaver were losing interest in it. Korson approached the University of Pennsylvania, but the trustees there were cool to the idea. At this crucial point President John L. Lewis of the UMWA stepped forward with the proposal that Korson come to Washington, D.C., to write a book on the bituminous miners similar to *Minstrels of the Mine Patch*, which had greatly impressed Lewis.

The proposal came at a good moment. Though Korson had outgrown conventional newspaper work, he still needed an income. There was no precedent for him to follow in making his decision to go to Washington. In the first place industrial folklore was a brand-new field almost wholly of his own creation. In the second place the idea of a trade union becoming a patron of the arts and letters was also new. But John L. Lewis knew what he wanted, and he sought out Korson to do it. There was no guarantee that the scheme would work, but Korson had confidence in his ability, and he trusted Lewis. To cover himself in case the plan failed, Korson took a leave of absence from Bucknell rather than resigning. It was understood that he would do some writing and editing for the *United Mine Workers Journal* while devoting most of his time to preparing the book on bituminous folklore. Though the work on the *UMWJ* turned out to be more time-consuming than expected, it was helpful in an unforeseen way. He had many bylines in the publication, so that when he made his field trips, he was instantly recognized and welcomed.

It was difficult for Korson to leave Pennsylvania, but the opportunity to embark on another major book was irresistible. The move from Pennsylvania to Washington was at first disturbing. After he slowly adapted, Washington began to seem like home to him. With Washington as his base, he began the field work on bituminous folklore. By his own account he faced a nearly overwhelming task compared with the small scope of the anthracite industry. Instead of covering only a single corner of one state, now he had more than twenty states to cover. Instead of traveling a few miles from one mine patch to another, now there were hundreds of miles between coal camps.

Two factors simplified Korson's task. One was that he decided to focus his attention on the oldest and most populous bituminous regions, which covered nine states. His reduced list included his own Pennsylvania plus Ohio, Illinois, and Indiana in the Midwest, and Virginia, West Virginia, Kentucky, Tennessee, and Alabama in the South. The other factor was the cooperation of the United Mine Workers of America. With their sponsorship it was much easier to build and maintain rapport. Korson himself described how this connection facilitated his work:

> My field work was done chiefly in isolated places where suspicion of strangers was traditional. On many of my trips, I was accompanied by one or two local union representatives known to the miners and trusted by them. The hospitality and graciousness of these backwoods coal miners, once their confidence was won, lightened my work and shortened my journeys on overnight train rides, all-day drives over tortuous mountain roads, and hikes to inaccessible places.[2]

With the help of the union, Korson gathered a great deal of material, but even so it took much energy and patience to track down all the leads that came to Washington. By the time he was finished it had taken nearly three years of traveling, listening, recording, reading, writing, and editing to put the book into final shape.

While all of this was going on, Korson had the satisfaction of doing a minor juvenile book—*Black Land,* mentioned earlier—in which he could use his knowledge of the bituminous fields. He was approached by Walter Prescott Webb of the University of Texas to prepare a book on the way of life in the coal fields for supplementary reading in the social sciences in the public schools of the United States. It was to be a manuscript of 15,000 words, to be published as one of a series of short books under the general title "American Way of Life Series." The series covered a broad scope of professions, occupations, and industries. For example, one book dealt with "The Way of Life in the Cattle Country," one with "The Way of Life on a Southern Plantation," one with "The Way of Life in the Army," and so on. In each case an attempt was made to show people doing their work against the physical background of geography and against the social and economic background of history.[3]

Working on this short book fit well into Korson's plans because he was already doing field work on a large scale. The book was published in 1941 by Row, Peterson and Company of Evanston, Illinois, under the title *Black Land: The Way of Life in the Coal Fields*. It was a beautiful book of seventy-two pages with many arresting black and white photographs. As a juvenile book, it lacked such scholarly apparatus as table of contents, index, and formal documentation. Nonetheless it is his best juvenile work. Korson used the loose fictional device of assuming the persona of a newspaper reporter sent to write a feature article on "Bituma, West Virginia." With this thin fictional cover he discusses the eight-hour-day movement, the variety of ethnic groups, unemployment, and other subjects with his usual underlying human sympathy. Even as a juvenile book, it evokes the power of James Agee and Walker Evan's *Let Us Now Praise Famous Men*. Because of the thirty-seven stark black and white photographs the book resembles a work of journalistic sociology. Among the striking photographs was one of a mobile loading machine, which could load ten tons of coal onto small trip cars in a minute and a half. Another striking photo showed the workers' shacks, which were without paint or grass. It was the best illustrated of any of Korson's books.

The year 1941 was more noteworthy for the Japanese sneak attack on Pearl Harbor on December 7 than it was for the publication of *Black Land*. The United States formally declared war in 1941, but Korson's war effort was to be confined to his editorial work for the Red Cross. He had done his share of fighting in Palestine during World War I; now he was too old to march off to combat again. Instead, during these years of turbulence and chaos, Korson worked quietly at his desk on his major work on the folklore of the bituminous industry. By 1942 the first draft of the manuscript was ready to be sent to the publisher, but a long year of editing and revising was still ahead. He was well aware of the difficulties that such a bulky manuscript presented, as shown in his letter of transmittal:

Herewith is my manuscript, the fruit of the three hardest-working years of my career. It is a bulky document, but I know you understand why I went into this work so thoroughly. In an effort to keep down the size of this manuscript I have withheld some material I might have otherwise used and have also kept out many ballads. But if you advise further cutting I am perfectly willing to go along on any suggestions you may care to make.[4]

Finally, in 1943, the book was published by the University of Pennsylvania Press under the title *Coal Dust on the Fiddle: Songs and Stories of the Bituminous Industry*. Drawing on oral sources, broadsides, songsters, local newspapers, and the *United Mine Workers Journal*, Korson produced a massive volume of some 460 pages. As previously mentioned, the publication of *Coal Dust* was a landmark in his career because it was his first book to receive serious attention in the *Journal of American Folklore*. Predictably, the reviewer, John W. Spargo of Northwestern University, disapproved of Korson's effort. For reasons already suggested, the folklore establishment's attack on the book was predictable, for if Korson's definition of folklore were to be accepted, it would have a revolutionary impact on the field.

By now the validity of Korson's viewpoint seems proved by its having survived Spargo's misinterpretation. Significantly, Spargo's attack avoided the functional question. It was clear to any reasonable observer that these songs behaved like folksongs: they were transmitted orally and existed in different versions. Instead Spargo objected with a traditionalist's bias that the material was of poor quality—which is perfectly true by literary standards perhaps, but it missed the point of the book:

> When the protest is the main, indeed, as here, well-nigh the exclusive interest, a more robust voice is needed than the coal-miners' muse was able to provide. Most of these ballads were written to celebrate one sad occasion or another, by writers whose names are known. To some it will seem noteworthy that miners should write ballads at all; but after reading a few of these carelessly-written versicles, some readers will take an attitude like the one Dr. Johnson expressed about a dog's ability to walk on its hind legs. Here is a sample, which is fairly typical (193):
>
>> Old Jim had toiled in Dalton mine for
>> many a weary year,

> He had drawn his car on its narrow track, nor
> showed a sign of fear.

Gone is the starry empery of the days of the border minstrelsy. Good Sir Walter's heart would have flamed with indignation to match even Mr. Korson's, but he would not have been proud of such quasi-literacy as this. From the collector's remarks, I gather he chose only a few of his better pieces for reprinting here.[5]

Clearly Spargo had thrown down the gauntlet. The review was indeed hostile, but not mean-spirited. The issue was real and the stakes were high. From the point of view of the antiquarian in the library, the miner-balladeers were simply second-rate poets. For the folklorist to accept contemporary industrial material seemed to open the door to work of hopelessly poor quality. Ben Botkin of the Library of Congress Archive of American Folk Song accepted Spargo's challenge and issued a spirited rebuttal in the *JAF*:

> John W. Spargo's review . . . suggests the need of repeating the admonition of Joseph Jacobs . . . that "in our study of folklore we should pay attention not alone to the Lore, but also to the Folk," especially the "Folk of to-day." It is hard to believe that fifty years after this statement we find a reviewer in the pages of this *Journal* writing about the coal miners of the United States as if they were performing animals:
>
> To some it will seem noteworthy that miners should write ballads at all; but after reading a few of these carelessly-written versicles, some readers will take an attitude like the one Dr. Johnson expressed about a dog's ability to walk on its hind legs.
>
> Mr. Korson is one folklorist who has paid attention not only to the lore but also to the folk. Through long and arduous journeys from one mine patch or coal camp and one coal mine to another he has come as close to living with the folk as a folklorist can be expected to come. And through equally long and arduous research he has come closer to understanding the life and lore of one segment of the folk than most folklorists can hope to do. In thus collecting the songs and stories of a contemporary industrial group and in studying them in their historical, economic, and sociological context, he is contribut-ing to folklore studies not only new material but also a new approach.[6]

Looking back on this lively dispute some thirty years later we must conclude that Spargo's disapproving criticism was actually a blessing, since it opened up a formal debate on the place of industrial lore in the academic establishment. Given the revolutionary nature of Korson's material, resistance was inevitable and legitimate. The fact that the debate was carried out in the formal journal of the field showed that the academic system was not entirely closed. There was indeed resistance, but Botkin's rebuttal showed that folklorists could be persuaded to change their minds. Korson had borrowed much of the vocabulary and conceptual apparatus of the folklore establishment, but he did not employ these borrowed elements in quite the traditional way. The inevitable result was what we must call a misunderstanding between two schools of thought. In a sense Korson and Spargo were practicing their trades in different worlds. One maintained that folklore was found in libraries; the other said that it could be found in collieries. The two folklorists saw different things when they looked from the same point in the same direction. With the passage of time, the number and strength of persuasive arguments in favor of Korson's position increased. More folklorists were converted, and the exploration of industrial folklore continued.[7]

To understand and appreciate fully Korson's *Coal Dust on the Fiddle* it should be seen as a documentary piece of writing, very much a product of the era in which it was written. Documentary writing in the late thirties and early forties was closely akin to the documentary motion picture of the same period. Historian Warren Susman has said of this period:

> It was an age increasingly self-conscious of itself; it sought increasingly to define itself in a series of images, often even contradictory ones, by which it hoped to understand and realize and even identify itself as a culture . . . A careful study of these images, often widely known and reproduced, helps us to understand as well that search for a culture, its nature, its fundamental tensions, its commitments.[8]

The goal of documentaries—whether on paper or on film— was to show people in real-life situations. Some documentaries studied a family, a race, or a group of people, such as the Eskimos in Robert Flaherty's classic *Nanook of the North* (1922). This film made history largely because it attempted to interpret, rather than merely photograph, human activity on the screen. Other documentaries showed events of social or scientific importance. For example, Pare Lorentz's *The Plow That Broke The Plains* (1936) showed the high social and economic cost of overfarming the prairies. Similarly Lorentz's *The River* (1937) showed efforts to control the floods of the Mississippi River Basin. In the same spirit, appearing one year before Korson's book was Robert Flaherty's *The Land* (1942), a study of American agriculture during the decade of the Depression.[9] Korson was very much aware of the developments in the culture around him and of the growing importance of the documentary. In a letter to his publisher he referred to his manuscript as a *picture*: "I have tried to integrate my material so that songs, ballads, stories, legends, and historical matter blend into a single picture—the way of life of the bituminous miners of the United States and Canada."[10]

One early reviewer of *Coal Dust on the Fiddle,* V. S. Pritchett of the *New Statesman and Nation,* recognized at once Korson's debt to the documentary film. Pritchett argued that the purpose of such films was to give men and women an occupational dignity. These films, like Korson's book, put work into a larger social context:

> Ordinary life was given, as it were, a cutting edge. The real revolutionary idea behind all those films and reports of the lives of seamen, pilots, bus drivers, railwaymen, factory workers, and so on, lay in the attempt to make us aware of an environment which none of us wanted to accept. For since the industrial revolution men have detested the machine that fascinated them, have been bored by the conditions of living which it created, and have tried to live by injections of day-dreams. They have turned from their own particular drudgery to romance. One of the objects of documentary was to stop this tendency to fragmentation in modern life and to build for us and show us the unity and fascination of our working environment.[11]

Not only did Pritchett praise Korson for capturing the immediacy of a documentary; he also praised the UMWA for taking a pioneering role in sponsoring the book. He went on to argue that unions have a responsibility to our common culture and that they should patronize literature, painting, and other imaginative work. Unions, he said, owed it to their cause, to say nothing of owing it to the public imagination, to see that their story was told. Pritchett was quite correct in pointing out the uniqueness of union sponsorship for a folklorist. Unfortunately no other union to date has followed the leadership of the UMWA to sponsor parallel work in metal mining, steel mills, textiles, printing, or other trades.[12] One problem of such sponsorship for the artist or writer is the question of integrity. To what extent does the writer feel so indebted to the sponsor that he or she is tempted to praise virtue and ignore fault? Pritchett avoided this question altogether; it was not raised until more than twenty years later.

In the foreword for the 1965 second printing of *Coal Dust on the Fiddle* John Greenway wrote that he could find nothing worth mentioning that was wrong with the book. He went on to commend Korson "for his skillful handling of two difficult problems: accepting the aid of the United Mine Workers without repaying it with dishonest favoritism, and compressing the life and lore of hundreds of thousands of bituminous miners in 22 states into a truthful composite." Though I am not in complete agreement with Greenway's analysis, these two points are central to any criticism of the book. Certainly there is no question that Korson was successful in his compression of material, but the matter of favoritism deserves further attention. In retrospect, Greenway's statement on Korson's neutrality seems kind and well-intentioned, but quite naive. To think that Korson could have been a guest in labor's house for three years without wanting to repay the kindness assumes either superhuman restraint or monumental ingratitude. Korson consistently presented the UMWA in favorable ways. Aspects of bituminous labor history that were not advantageous to the UMWA cause were often simply omitted. For example, one will look in vain in *Coal Dust* for any mention of the rival Communist-led National Miners Union. Similarly, because of her strong ties to the NMU, the celebrated Aunt Molly Jackson was never mentioned. For Korson, a strong UMWA was an article of faith, a means of preserving the corporate-liberal state.

To the extent that Greenway perceived the book as balanced and even-handed with respect to the conflicts between the United Mine Workers and the coal operators, we can thank Korson's editors at the University of Pennsylvania Press. In the early drafts of the book Korson himself made no secret of his point of view. All of his experiences as a boy in Wilkes-Barre and as a young reporter in Pottsville would naturally give him a keen sympathy for the plight of the miner. More importantly, his intellectual stance as a mature adult was supportive of unions as a countervailing force to management for the long-run strength of capitalism. In response to Korson's first draft of the manuscript, Editor Ruth Keener of the

University of Pennsylvania Press, after consultation with three readers, urged him to strike a more impartial pose:

> The basic criticism in each report is that you have written a tract instead of a book of folklore . . . at a glance I too would agree that you have attempted too much and possibly lost your original intention of repeating *Minstrels of the Mine Patch* for the Bituminous miners in your zeal for the United Mine Workers cause. I would say it would be much better to forget the propaganda completely, just sketching the general conditions of the industry in your introduction, and then let the ballads and stories speak for themselves as one reader has suggested and as you did in the first book. Then more selection should be exercised in the use of your folklore material and the sources cited more explicitly whenever possible.[13]

Taking Keener's advice, Korson toned down some of the strident partisanship of the first draft. As an experienced newspaperman he was accustomed to dealing with editors and was prepared to mollify them. When it came to making revisions, he was not hypersensitive or thin-skinned. Despite the need to tone down the rhetoric, Korson's basic sympathetic and warm-hearted treatment of the miners showed through. Korson may have fixed his eye on the general nonfiction book trade, especially schools and libraries, but there was another important audience—the miners themselves. He knew that this book placed in the hands of his informants and their buddies would increase their self-esteem and self-respect. One suspects that John L. Lewis realized this all along in view of the extensive favorable coverage given the book in the *United Mine Workers Journal*. Reviewer Dorothy Rigdon of the *UMWJ* pinpointed the motives that miners would have for embracing *Coal Dust on the Fiddle:*

> Miners everywhere will enjoy reading this book. The older men will live over again in its pages the good and bad old days. The younger men will learn from it the background of their hazardous but noble occupation. *It will give them pride in their ancient craft, and, at the same time, will strengthen their loyalty to the Union because only through the Union could the miners have lifted themselves out of the wretchedness described in "Coal Dust on the Fiddle."*[14]

In terms of structure and organization, about 60 percent of the book was the author's text and the other 40 percent consisted of the words of some 140 original songs (along with the tunes of 13 of them transcribed by Ruth Crawford Seeger) in circulation among the miners. Within each chapter the appropriate songs and stories were commendably arranged chronologically, though some readers objected to the songs being placed at the end of each chapter rather than having them woven into the body of the text. The chapters of *Coal Dust on the Fiddle* were grouped in three general sections, an arrangement that is helpful in gaining an overall view of the material. Part One presents the way of life in the coal camps; Part Two presents the folklore of the coal mines, at the workplace; Part Three is a presentation of the union in song and story, which stresses accounts of the famous strikes and massacres.[15] This three-part division might at first suggest that the pro-union material was somehow separated out into a third distinct category, but in fact a strong pro-union slant underlies the presentation of the entire book.

For example, in Part One, Chapter 2, we find a description of the local union meeting: "The local union meeting is the coal-region version of the traditional New England town meeting. I have attended many of the meetings and have addressed some. The impression I have carried away is uniformly favorable, and the experience has strengthened my faith in the democratic processes of our nation."[16] This is not to argue that Korson was insincere or that he was consciously writing pro-union propaganda. No doubt Korson was indeed favorably impressed with union meetings. The point here is that in *Coal Dust* we are confronted with much more than a simple anthology of folklore. Instead we have a book with a definite and coherent sociopolitical point of view.

Looking at Part Two, we find much the same thing. Given Korson's commitment, it was virtually impossible to confine a pro-union attitude to the back of the book. For example, in Part Two, in a section ostensibly dealing with convict miners, we find:

> Aside from the rich profits accruing to them, the corporations fought to perpetuate the convict-lease system because it was a powerful weapon against unionism. So long as convict mines continued producing coal, no strike could be successful. It was this factor that doomed the big strikes of 1908 and 1920 and broke the back of unionism in the Alabama coal field for many years.[17]

The story of the bituminous industry is so inextricably bound up with the union movement that it would be unreasonable to expect Korson to have been able to disentangle the two. The problem is simply too complicated to permit rigid separation of the union material into a self-contained section.

In terms of method, Korson broke no new ground in writing *Coal Dust on the Fiddle*. He was simply extending the techniques and procedures that he had perfected in the anthracite fields of Pennsylvania. Now, for the most part, he applied the same method to the bituminous fields of the South. The parallels between *Coal Dust* and *Minstrels* are many and striking. Chapter 1 in *Minstrels* was "The Mine Patch"; chapter 2 in *Coal Dust* was "The Coal Camp." Similarly, what was chapter 6, "Injury and Death," appears, in effect, in the new book as chapter 13, "Mine Disasters." In the same way chapter 7, "The Strike" of *Minstrels,* is closely akin to chapter 19, "Strike Songs and Ballads," in *Coal Dust.*

This is not to suggest that Korson unimaginatively applied an old prosaic formula to a new problem. Quite the contrary. He was sensitive to the differences between the two industries. Where differences existed, he was keenly aware of the need to communicate the distinction to the reader. Nonetheless, as a writer he did have an artistic problem that he was unable to overcome completely, the problem of the sequel. By definition a sequel is something that follows; hence for any writer, either of fiction or nonfiction, there is an inevitable loss of freshness and originality. The problem is a classic built-in dilemma for the writer. If a work is successful, the public wants another like it. But if the sequel is too much like the original, there is disappointment.

Korson was not the first to face this problem. Writers of fiction had suffered with it for years. Critics agree that Robert Louis Stevenson's *David Balfour* is a somewhat disappointing sequel to his *Kidnapped.* Similar problems can be cited for Samuel Butler's *Erewhon Revisited* or for Aldous Huxley's *Brave New World Revisited.* Today we would probably identify Korson's approach as "oral history" or "history-from-below." His discussion of method in the Preface was very modest:

> In the field, while devoting most of my time to collecting songs and ballads, I tried not to neglect stories, legends, folk remedies, sayings, and unwritten history.
>
> I felt, too, that the significance of the material could be fully grasped only against the social background of the bituminous industry. This, however, is informal history, and documentation is incidental to a reconstruction of the life of the bituminous miners a generation or two ago.

My research was not limited to oral sources. Broadsides, pocket songsters, local newspapers, and the files of the *United Mine Workers Journal* yielded ballad texts which are identified in the headnotes. These printed sources give continuity by filling gaps in the bituminous mining history and tradition.

For inclusion in this volume, a ballad had to pass the test of literary interest and direct relationship to the bituminous coal industry (to the exclusion of anthracite ballads and non-mining labor songs), as well as to American folk tradition.[18]

In the long run, folklorists will probably agree that *Minstrels of the Mine Patch* was a hard act to follow. While *Coal Dust on the Fiddle* is competent and thorough, it lacks the unity and pioneer spirit of the anthracite book.

Coal Dust on the Fiddle was received as a valuable addition to our knowledge of the bituminous industry, but inevitably the publicity and the attention given to the book raised the issue of Korson's skill as a writer. In this matter most of the contemporary reviewers were cool and reserved. In all fairness to Korson, his purpose should be kept in mind. One way of classifying writing is as descriptive, narrative, and expository. Most of Korson's work was expository, meaning that his main purpose was usually to give information or to explain something. Most reviewers seemed to realize this distinction readily and applied reasonable standards. The consensus opinion is well summed up by Archie Green: "Korson made his living as a newspaperman and an editor. He sought no higher praise than that of any working journalist proud of his craft; he was pleased when a reader told him a story was warm or well written."[19]

In other reviews of the period we find echoes of the same assessment. David T. Bazelton said, "The writing is seldom more than competent reporting. This is true equally of the literary form and of the author's response to the poetic and political thunder of the material."[20] Similarly, Edward H. Robie described Korson as "a competent writer and reporter."[21] Even V.S. Pritchett, in the laudatory and supportive review discussed earlier, felt obliged to qualify his enthusiasm for Korson's writing: "He is a plain, clear writer of no very great distinction, but he is simple, sympathetic and diligent, and the result of his researches is a fascinating and moving social document."[22] In this single sentence we can see the conflict Pritchett must have felt. Though the writing was not distinguished, the story was indeed "moving." In light of the foregoing discussion of the largely cool reception given Korson's writing style; it is interesting to note that the reviewer for the *New York Times Book Review* was very responsive to Korson's style: "Mr. Korson writes the whole story with compassion, restraint, and the imagination necessary to recreate scene and feeling."[23] Even here, however, the word "restraint" suggests that Korson subordinated his views to getting the story across.

Though the bulk of *Coal Dust on the Fiddle* is composed of dutiful expository prose, there are some passages of very good descriptive writing. In these Korson appeals to the reader's imagination to create a clear and vivid picture in the mind. In the following passage, Korson uses descriptive skills to paint a vivid picture of the bituminous coal mine through an extended metaphor—comparing the mine to a city. The details in this passage are presented in a way that makes their location clear:

> The bituminous coal mine was a city buried deep in the earth, where work was carried on in a perpetual blackout. What to the confused visitor looked like an inextricable labyrinth was actually a systematically laid-out underground factory, cut out of rock and coal. From the drift mouth (or from the bottom of a slope or shaft, whichever the entrance happed to be) there ran an avenue called a "main entry" which was wide enough for a railroad track; this was the principal traveling way for the mine workers and for the transportation of coal. Driven off the main and at a right angle to it were headings or branch entries, like cross streets in a city. Off these branch entries were the "rooms," the daily workshops of the miners. It was a miner's task to win the coal by advancing on face of the seam until the room had been mined out, when he would move on to another room. The side walls, called "ribs" were also of coal, but they were left standing in columns to support the roof until all the rooms had been mined out. Then, one by one, they were retrieved by means of an extraordinarily hazardous operation variously called "ribbing," "robbing," "plugging the pillars," or "retreat." This was the "room-and-pillar" system of mining most commonly practised in this country.[24]

In addition to numerous effective descriptive passages like this, there were also some admirable narrative passages. Particularly impressive in this regard was chapter 16, "The Coal Creek Rebellion." Though ostensibly this seventeen-page chapter was written to provide a context for one twelve-line song, in fact the narrative there could easily stand alone. Basically this chapter tells the story of the struggle of the free miners in Tennessee in the

1890s to eliminate the convict lease system. Though the story was true rather than imaginary, it had much of the drama and power of fiction. Korson depicted the series of events that led to the miners' frustration and rage. The long-suffering mountaineer coal miners tried patiently to solve their problems through the regular legal channels. The prison inspectors, the General Assembly, and the State Supreme Court, each in sequence, turned them down. In the best Civil War bushwacking tradition, the miners formed a secret army to release the prisoners. The governor mobilized the entire state militia to quell the rebellion, but he enjoyed a Pyrrhic victory. The ensuing publicity inspired by the rebellion turned public opinion against the convict lease system, and in 1896 it was abolished.[25]

Korson's narrative consisted of events or incidents that were chosen from among the many historical facts available. Since he was concerned chiefly with events, he concentrated on action rather than character development or local color. Despite these limitations, the chapter does show him in command of the exacting craft of narrative writing. Korson himself felt that "The Coal Creek Rebellion" was the best piece of narrative writing in the book. In fact, he took so much pride in it that he once proposed to Sydney A. Sanders, his literary agent, that the story be made into a novel. Sanders' reply is fascinating because it touches all the points that make it difficult for the writer of nonfiction to shift gears into producing good fiction. In Korson's account the point of view was omniscient, but a good work of fiction would probably have to be seen through the eyes of a central character. Basically Sanders argued that a novel could not deal with oppression or labor-capital strife as such; instead it would have to deal with people:

> If you have visualized a novel dealing primarily with people; with a basic theme and plot that arises from people themselves and not from their labor troubles, that's something else. That will depend entirely upon what you put into it, and how you write it. With a novel of that kind, the labor background would be purely a background; not the motivation for the story. But as I said before, if you visualize labor-capital strife; focusing entirely upon the oppression of labor—then I just do not see it as a likely commercial undertaking.
>
> Anyway, George, I don't think there would be any chance of getting you a contract for such a novel no matter from which point of view you write it—until you have done, say, twenty-five thousand

words of it and have outlined the remainder reasonably fully. I don't
think you have yet written a novel and while I am sure you can do an
excellent story, this remains to be demonstrated. The novel
technique is far different from the non-fiction technique. Any publisher would need to see what your novel is going to be about, and
how you are going to write it.[26]

In addition to the literary problems of point of view and character
development, the practical problems of Korson's lack of experience
meant that he would be unable to get an advance to work on a
novel. For a man with the ongoing problem of making a living and
supporting a family, the practical difficulties posed an insurmount-
able obstacle. As a result, any ultimate verdict on Korson's ability
as a "writer" must remain purely speculative. Like Sydney Sanders, I think he could have done it, but the plain fact is that he never
got to it. Since historians and biographers must deal with what
happened rather than with what might have happened, we will
have to evaluate Korson as a folklorist rather than as a writer. As a
folklorist his contributions were substantial.

Inevitably a central concern of *Coal Dust on the Fiddle* was
the problem of ethnicity. As a Jewish writer confronting the
conflict between WASP coal operators and successive waves of
Irish, Italian, and Slav immigrants, one might expect Korson to be
highly sensitive to the nuances of differences among various ethnic
groups. Indeed, given his powers of observation and sensibility, we
might expect him to celebrate the ethnic diversity of different
instincts, habits, emotions, images, and traditions. Instead we find
that his commitment to the union led him to embrace the melting
pot concept of immigration and to play down ethnic differences:

> The miners were segregated into different parts of the camp accord-
> ing to race and nationality. English-speaking whites usually occupied
> the best row of houses; newly-arrived immigrants were assigned
> dilapidated shacks in another part of the camp called "hunktown" or
> "dago hill," and Negroes were assigned hovels beneath the dignity of
> chicken coops. Segregation fanned religious, racial, and political
> antagonisms, and thereby kept the workers disunited. The union,
> recognizing no such differences, worked to harmonize the diverse
> groups.[27]

Thus Korson portrayed the miners of all ethnic groups getting
along well together through the union in opposition to the common
enemy, the coal operator. His interpretation was indeed appropri-

ate for the 1940s, when the UMWA was still stressing unity above all else. We now know that over the ensuing thirty years this emphasis would be played down. But he could not have been expected to foresee the change in attitude toward ethnicity that would take place both in the culture at large and within the UMWA. By 1959 historian Carl Degler was suggesting that national traits of immigrant groups were not melting and fusing: "In view of such failure to melt and fuse, the metaphor of the melting pot is unfortunate and misleading. A more accurate analogy would be a salad bowl, for, though the salad is an entity, the lettuce can still be distinguished from the chicory, the tomatoes from the cabbage."[28]

Later, Michael Novak was suggesting in 1971 that it was time for America to understand and appreciate the diversity of her ethnic elements. Novak called for a new ethnic politics that would draw in resources other than Anglo-Saxon history and values.[29] One year later, in 1972, as if in confirmation of Novak's argument, the *United Mine Workers Journal* in an editorial explained why Democratic nominee Senator George McGovern of South Dakota did not appeal to "us hard hats and ethnics."[30] One can only imagine how surprised Korson might have been to see the *UMWJ* taking overt recognition of ethnicity as a political factor. Suffice it to say that in the 1940s Korson was aware of the differences among ethnic groups, but he chose to minimize them in order to stress union strength and solidarity.

Let us now turn from the question of ethnicity to the more central question of Korson's place in Anglo-American folksong scholarship. D. K. Wilgus has written that American folklorists have been guided by three traditions in collecting: "the academic, which, following Child, sought accurate transcriptions of text first and music later for scholarly study; the local-enthusiastic, which searched out and displayed the quaint, the unusual, the exciting, the enjoyable in undisciplined and mercurial fashion; and the musical-esthetic, which sought the distinguishable art form of the folk tune for appreciation and performance."[31] Korson would probably fit in the local-enthusiastic tradition; however, it is not an easy matter to make a rigid classification. Certainly Korson was interested in "accurate transcriptions," especially as shown in his collaboration with Melvin LeMon; and in *Coal Dust* he went to a great deal of trouble with the publisher to secure the services of

Ruth Crawford Seeger to make thirteen transcriptions, which add a great deal to the academic value of the book. Furthermore, though I am reluctant to place Korson in the category of musical-esthetic, in his folk festival experience he was always on the lookout for superior "performance." In short, all three of these traditions are at work in Korson's study of the bituminous industry.

Perhaps a more useful scheme of classification is Wilgus's division of books on the basis of intention and method into a number of types: "The academic collection presents texts (and sometimes tunes) in formal pattern imitative of Child's canon, with bibliographical and comparative notes. The running-comment collections surround the collectanea with essays, scholarly or colorful. An unordered, unannotated mass of texts characterizes the random-text collections. The singing books contain arranged folksongs for public or private performers."[32] This classification of folksong books on the basis of their aims and their editing principles seems both convenient and logical. Though Wilgus himself admits that there is no sharp line of demarcation between the strictly academic and the running-comment collections, it does seem as if the term "running-comment collection" were tailor-made for *Coal Dust on the Fiddle*. Certainly the book is not academic in the sense of dealing analytically with such formal elements as themes, stanza, and meter. Wilgus recognized that the term "running-comment collection" was a perfect fit for George Korson's work, since he used it as an example to explain the term:

> With few exceptions, these four qualities mark the running-comment collections: special purposes and types of material, proximity to sources, emphasis on the native or homemade song, and popular slant. George Korson's collection of miners' songs (*Songs and Ballads of the Anthracite Miner* [1927], *Minstrels of the Mine Patch* [1938], and *Coal Dust on the Fiddle* [1943]) illustrate all four qualities. Almost all the songs, in their present form, are peculiar to the mining industry and stem from the workers themselves. Collected from singers, from local broadsides, and from the files of the *United Mine Workers' Journal*, the crude songs are arranged by subject matter and form the nucleus of essays on the life of mine workers. Like the editors of *Minstrelsy of Maine*, Korson is able to trace items to their authors, even to record songs as sung by their composers. The earlier volumes, dealing with the smaller industry, presented a few variants, but the richer lore of the bituminous miners resulted in the printing of only one text of each song in *Coal*

Dust on the Fiddle. Both *Minstrels of the Mine Patch* and *Coal Dust* are collections of lore as well as songs, however, giving a wider coverage of the background.[33]

Although Wilgus's analysis of Korson's work is fair and reasonable, even sympathetic and supportive, it is interesting to note that he describes the songs as "crude." To the trained folklorist this unfinished quality may be seen as an asset, as testimony to the authenticity of the item. However, in 1943 not all of Korson's reviewers were trained folklorists. Predictably, several reviewers brought a strong belletrist bias to *Coal Dust on the Fiddle*. Applying the aesthetic standards of fine literature to folk materials, they naturally found the items substandard. For example, Edward H. Robie wrote: "As may be imagined, the songs are for the most part crude attempts at literary composition, and their themes are pretty much alike—the hard life of the miner and the oppression of the employer."[34] In a similar vein David T. Bazelton wrote:

> The bulk of the verse, presented without critical comment, is not very good. Since much of it was written to be sung to popular old tunes, the rhythms are conventional and unrelated, in any indigenous sense, to mining life. The expression is frequently sentimental or hifalutin, concerning itself with standard values and experiences in the standard way. One seldom finds here the originality of many Negro songs.[35]

This kind of criticism is manifestly unfair to both the collector and his material. It is unreasonable to expect "critical comment" on verse that is basically straightforward. And certainly one expects folklore to be formulaic rather than to be starkly original.

Fortunately at least one contemporary reviewer, John T. Frederick, writing in *Book Week*, compared Korson's work to that of other folklorists rather than to belletrist productions. Naturally, viewed in this light, Korson's book seemed much better. Applying the appropriate critical yardstick, Frederick wrote:

> The field of American ballad literature and folklore especially of regional and occupational groups, is richly interesting and rewarding to the reader and student.
>
> John A. Lomax did pioneer work in the field of cowboy songs, and he and his son, Alan Lomax, have edited a fine general collection of songs of the American people in "Our Singing Country." Carl Sandburg helped Americans to become interested in their folksongs, in his lectures and with his book "The American Songbag." Louise

Pound of the University of Nebraska has done very valuable work in the whole field of American folklore.

But no book I know gives so satisfyingly the whole body of experience of which ballads are an expression as does Korson in "Coal Dust on the Fiddle." It's a fine book for today.[36]

Coal Dust on the Fiddle sheds further light on Korson's views about labor and society. Korson believed that labor unions were socially desirable as a countervailing force against the excesses of capitalism. A comparison between *Minstrels* (1938) and *Coal Dust*, published five years later, shows the changes in his views. In the earlier book they are muted, but in the later they become more explicit. Korson had had five more years to confront the riddles of capitalism and the corporate-liberal state and such questions as, do the ends justify the means? Is capitalism inherently evil? Is revolution justified in the face of oppression? If coal is so vital to the nation's economy, why can't it bring profit to the operators and decent wages to the workers?

In turning from the anthracite industry to the bituminous industry, Korson had in effect left the North for the South, but the problems of labor-management strife went with him. Korson had changed his scene, but not his problems, and by 1943 he was at last ready to deal with them explicitly in the introduction to *Coal Dust*. Korson still strove to be fair and objective and to present both sides of the argument, but now he had a firm point of view on the topic. He granted that the operators themselves were victims of geologic and economic conditions beyond their control, but he insisted that the miners had the right to form a strong labor union:

> Occupying a strategic position in the nation's economy, the bituminous industry should have brought prosperity to the operators and a fair standard of living to workers. But the contrary has been the case. It has been a benighted industry, marked on the one hand by the miners' constant struggle for a decent living, and on the other by mine owners and investors seeking a return on their investments . . . America's industrial revolution was predicated on cheap coal which the operators were determined to produce, but they ran into a geologic-economic condition for which neither they nor the miners were responsible. Because of the position of the seams and the laborious and dangerous manner in which coal was produced, the labor cost was one of the highest in the country—nearly two-thirds of the cost of each ton. This labor cost, therefore, became the operators' principal point of attack. Wage cutting was a common

practice . . . With the bituminous industry under control of absentee powerful corporations the miners' only hope of advancing their economic interests lay in collective action. They felt they had a right to join a labor union of their own choosing, and the United Mine Workers of America, like its predecessors in the field, felt it had a lawful right to assist them in organizing themselves.[37]

In view of Korson's pro-union position, it is not surprising that his book was unfavorably received by management. As a liberal reformer he found himself under fire from the right. His treatment in *Coal Dust* was not as even-handed as it had been in *Minstrels,* so predictably he was attacked by the reviewer for *Mining and Metallurgy,* the magazine of the Institute of Mining and Metallurgical Engineers:

> Our chief criticism of the book is that the author gives the impression that every bituminous coal mine operator is a labor exploiter, slave driver, and capitalistic villain of the worst type, whereas the United Mine Workers is an organization of the highest and purest motives whose every action is above reproach.[38]

It would be misleading to suggest that Korson was working in a vacuum while the great events of the forties were swirling about him. Certainly a decade which brought to the world its greatest war in history, the horror of mass extermination camps, and the use of atomic weapons would touch anyone who professed an intellectual life—as a journalist, a writer, or simply as an articulate humanist. During this period Korson served as a writer, news editor, and foreign editor for American Red Cross publications while living in Washington, D.C. His chief contribution to the war effort was writing a morale-building book for the promotion of the Red Cross.

At His Side: The American Red Cross Overseas in World War II was published in New York by Coward-McCann in 1945. Basically the book told of the complex support role played by the Red Cross in dealing with the unprecedented, mechanized, and global conflict. With some 322 pages, an index, and maps, it was a substantial book; it was also Korson's most successful book commercially. This was no accident. The book deliberately included names of Red Cross volunteers overseas to encourage hometown sales. There was an expensive national promotion campaign including a full-page advertisement in *The New York Times.* The National Headquarters of the American Red Cross pushed the

Korson with wife and daughter, Washington, 1945.
Courtesy George Korson Folklore Archive

book vigorously in connection with its fund-raising drive. To gather material Korson interviewed returned overseas workers and used official narrative reports. Chapters in the book were arranged geographically. Written under the stress of wartime conditions, the book did have propaganda value at the time; but it is not a book of lasting interest and is not relevant to Korson's work as a folklorist.

Korson spent fifteen years with the American Red Cross from 1942 to 1957. Though the American Red Cross is a voluntary organization, it does require some full-time employees in its work of relieving human suffering. Since the organization has about 170 volunteers for each career staff member, there is no question about its voluntary nature. Korson's work as a professional writer and publicist required him to produce material that would further spur the volunteer spirit by appealing to the American tendency to take things into one's own hands. Much of the publicity effort of the Red Cross editorial offices went to working up free magazine and newspaper articles to pave the way toward voluntary action and to cheer volunteer efforts onward.

Like de Tocqueville a century before him, Korson recognized the strong appeal that voluntarism held for Americans. De Tocqueville wrote in *Democracy in America:* "I have often admired the extreme skill with which the inhabitants of the United States succeed in proposing a common object for the exertions of a great many men and inducing them voluntarily to pursue it."[39] Though Korson was not a misty-eyed do-gooder, he understood human motivations and the need for praise of voluntary efforts. His work at the American Red Cross was a means to an end—a way of putting bread on the table. We may wonder how he felt about his role as a professional cheerleader, but Korson seldom told people how he felt about things. He never said aloud that he hated the work, but he quit as soon as he was eligible for a modest pension.

Did Korson's commercial writing damage his scholarly ability? The answer is not altogether clear. Since his work in folklore was essentially scholarly rather than artistic, one can say that his prose was not damaged. Indeed his folklore books show the hand of a journalist in sentence structure, short paragraphs, and a high level of human interest. In this sense his work in folklore may have benefited from the discipline he brought to his craft as a journalist. But even granting this probability, it seems clear that many valuable years were lost producing articles that would be buried in back issues of the *Red Cross Newsletter.* Yet even with a full-time job Korson was able to write or edit ten books during his lifetime; one wonders what he might have done if he had had more time for his research.

In the postwar period Korson and his wife took up permanent residence in Washington, D.C. He was never again to return to Pennsylvania except for visits and field trips. In Washington the Korsons carved out a small, contented world for themselves. There were walks in the park and musical evenings at the Library of Congress. Rae's work, at the Library of Congress, complemented George's. She took an active interest in what he was doing, but she neither competed with him nor collaborated with him. The Korsons lived modestly and on a budget, but theater tickets were a happy exception to the rule of frugality.

The Korsons enjoyed the cultural life of the city. Another indulgence that Korson allowed himself was the acquisition of books. He found them irresistible and constantly added to his library, which at times seemed to threaten to crowd the family

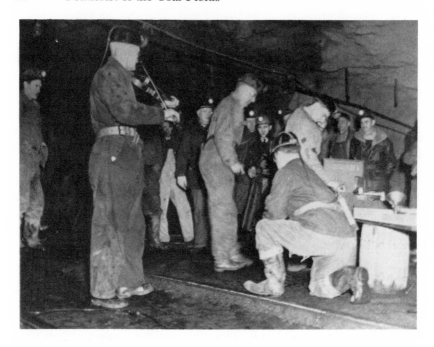

Korson adjusts the microphone while a miner waits to dance a jig. Scene
is Newkirk Tunnel Mine during 1946 Library of Congress field trip.
*Photo by Skippy Adelman (Black Star), courtesy George Korson Folklore
Archive*

right out of their apartment. The Korsons took pride in building
their modest social life around Washington's intelligentsia. The
Library of Congress often played host to visiting writers and poets,
many of whom were entertained by the Korsons. Though Korson
prized his private time with his typewriter, he was naturally
friendly and outgoing and so found himself drawn into Washington's
lively society.

Korson's first significant postwar folklore project involved a
Library of Congress field trip through the coal fields of Pennsylvania recording the songs of the anthracite miners during the
winter months of January and February 1946. The basic purpose of
the trip was to acquire recordings for the Archive of Folk Song in
the Library of Congress, to add to the repository of songs from all

over the world that had been collected since 1928. On this trip Korson was accompanied by Arthur Semmig, a Library of Congress engineer, which assured professional-quality recordings. Nonetheless, since the project was carried out in the field with portable equipment rather than under studio conditions, the results are disappointing to a person who is accustomed to smooth, polished, and slick commercial high-fidelity LP's. In 1947 Korson went over the field recordings and edited the Library of Congress record album *Songs and Ballads of the Anthracite Miners*. The following year the Archive of American Folk Song issued a 78 rpm set in five twelve-inch discs. In 1958 the set was remastered at 33 rpm as L 16.[40]

The jacket liner on the 1958 edition carried a cautionary note for the recording aficionado who was addicted to high-quality sound free of surface noise and was familiar with all the subtleties of RIAA crossover and the like. Such a listener was warned:

> These traditional songs, recorded with portable equipment in the field, are sung and played by people who learned them in the hand-me-down manner of folklore from their parents or neighbors. The singers are untrained musically, and their voices reflect the hills and plains of America rather than the broadcasting studio or the concert stage. This is not in any sense to minimize their worth, but, on the contrary, to point up the unique value of the recordings, for through them is preserved for the American people the pure tradition of folk song.[41]

The significance of the 1946 field trip is not at first apparent. We must remember that Korson by training and inclination was an old-line newspaperman. Previously his research tools had been a pencil and a notebook, and his productions rolled out of a typewriter. It is true, of course, that Korson and Melvin LeMon had used field recording equipment in the Pennsylvania anthracite region as early as 1935. It is also true that between 1938 and 1940, supported by a United Mine Workers' grant, Korson used portable equipment in the southern bituminous region.[42] However, in both of these earlier expeditions the recording equipment was used as an extension of note-taking.

In 1946, for the first time Korson used recording equipment with the deliberate aim of preparing a record album for release. This represented for him a shift from a world based on the supremacy of literacy to a world oriented to electric technology.[43]

What made him shift? The obvious answer would be the tremendous breakthroughs in quality that came after World War II, but in this case the real answer lies elsewhere. The fact is that Rae Korson, as head of the Archive of Folk Song in the Music Division of the Library of Congress, persuaded George to go ahead with the recording of anthracite songs and later with bituminous songs. It was due to Rae Korson's vision and foresight that we now have this important resource, which Archie Green has called "the two best recorded coal-song documents in the United States."[44] Actually it is not surprising that Rae Korson had to prod George to move in this direction. To Korson, a ballad was valuable chiefly as an artifact of social history, not as a piece of music. Rae Korson helped to fill in this blind spot. As she explained to Alice Lesoravage, an *Allentown Morning Call* reporter, some twenty-four years later: "My husband had little knowledge of music . . . That's where I came in. Because I studied music, I could help him with manuscripts and research."[45]

Rae Korson had helped many people in this way. Scholars in the world of folksong depended on her cataloging and organizing— not to mention her research. At the Library of Congress she helped to prepare many music education books, theses, manuscripts, and books on folk music. At one point Austin Fife, a former president of the American Folklore Society, said that every notable work in the field of folksong since 1944 has some acknowledgment of Rae Korson's help. In addition to folklorists, entertainment personalities also have enlisted her aid. These include Harry Belafonte, Odetta, Judy Collins, and Pete Seeger. Even Tiny Tim once made a visit to the Archive of Folk Song.[46]

Advance planning was essential for the 1946 field trip. Because the trip required the services of both a recording engineer and a professional photographer, the overhead costs were high and time in the field had to be held to a minimum. In addition, Korson could take only a little time off from his job with the American Red Cross. He wrote ahead to Edith Patterson at the Pottsville Free Public Library to help line up Bill Keating and other miner-balladeers for recording sessions.[47] He also arranged with Edward A. Lynch of the Philadelphia and Reading Coal and Iron Company to take his crew into one of the mines in order to record some ballads in a sort of induced natural context. Lynch and Korson settled on the Newkirk Tunnel Mine, a water level drift operation near Tamaqua, Pennsylvania.[48] In advance of the trip Korson

Edith Patterson and Korson, 1946.
Black Star Photo, courtesy George Korson Folklore Archive

---

planted several stories about the event in the local papers, which helped bring out some old-timers he had not recorded before. [49]

All of this careful advance planning paid off in a successful recording expedition. As a result the student of Korson's work now has access to aural as well as visual documents of the folk culture of Pennsylvania's anthracite miner. The extra dimension provided by this long-playing record has been described by Archie Green:

> Reading a blues or ballad imprisoned in print may in itself be a fulfilling or draining experience. However, hearing the same piece directly from a folksinger, or indirectly via a disc, imparts a sense of emotional immediacy and tension beyond the feeling evoked in letters. Sound recordings preserve the subtle inflection, unique accent, pulsating rhythm, or irregular tempo of a singer which is inherent in live performance but which is extremely difficult to convey in textual and musical transcription. [50]

Songs and Ballads of the Anthracite Miners (L 16) includes twelve songs and two fiddle tunes. While all of the songs deal with industrial lore, three of them are closely identified with the labor-union movement ("Me Johnny Mitchell Man," "On Johnny Mitchell's Train," and "Union Man"). The time span covered by this album runs from 1869 ("The Avondale Mine Disaster") to 1944

Korson, with cap in hand, and Jerry Byrne, behind Korson, are in the audience in the Newkirk Tunnel Mine, 1946, as James Muldowney plays his fiddle.
Black Star Photo, courtesy George Korson Folklore Archive

("Union Man"). The predominant musical style on the album is Celtic, as shown in the fact that none of the singers used instrumental accompaniment.[51] For the reader who is familiar with Korson's *Minstrels of the Mine Patch*, listening to this record is especially rewarding.

For example, the first song on Side A is everyone's favorite, Bill Keating's "Down, Down, Down." On first listening to it the ballad seems almost spoken rather than sung. It also becomes evident that Keating composed like most broadside balladeers, by fitting new words to a familiar old tune. The most amazing feature is the ballad's seemingly interminable length of thirty-eight stanzas—a tribute to Keating's prolific ability to create verse. One obvious objection to this ballad that could be raised by folklore purists is that it does not meet the criterion of anonymity, since clearly Korson knew that Keating had written it. Viewed this way it could be seen as simply doggerel set to music. Though this is a

Korson takes notes while Arthur Semmig records a solo by William E. Keating, the mine patch singer and ballad writer.
Black Star Photo, courtesy George Korson Folklore Archive

serious objection, it is not an overriding one, since clearly "Down, Down, Down" is a product of mining folk culture. A parallel case can be made for Woody Guthrie; he is a spokesman for the people, but he is not anonymous. If Woody Guthrie is a folk poet, then so is Bill Keating.

Another interesting aspect of this particular recorded version of "Down, Down, Down" is that for many years it was incorporated with a large working model of a coal mine and a breaker at the Wyoming Historical and Geological Society in Wilkes-Barre, Pennsylvania. It was a table-top display about six feet long and three feet deep, containing a great deal of detail work. The model was very popular with schoolchildren who came to visit the museum on class field trips. By dropping a nickel into a coin slot, a child could activate the descent of a miniature miner doll down the elevator shaft into the mine. Meanwhile a recording of "Down, Down, Down" began to play as the miner descended. As different aspects of the mine were described, small light bulbs would go on. Unfortunately the display was destroyed in the Hurricane Agnes flood of 1972.[52]

While "Down, Down, Down" is reckless and cheerful, written in a devil-may-care spirit, another song on the disc, "The Avondale Mine Disaster," written in 1869, is very somber. Musically similar in being sung without accompaniment, the two songs create an entirely different mood. Avondale was the anthracite industry's first major tragedy, in which 110 men and boys were lost. All the facts concerning the Avondale incident are set down by Korson in *Minstrels of the Mine Patch*.[53] There we are told that the men and boys had no chance of escape from the fire which broke out because there was only one outlet, a shaft built up into a rickety breaker, itself a fire hazard also. Like other broadside balladeers, the author (whoever he was) was anxious to set down the particular facts of this event. It resembles a standard Irish ballad in its narrative progression. For example, the climax comes one verse before the end, giving the singer a chance to moralize in the last stanza. But it is one thing to read the 1869 lyrics and Korson's 1938 commentary in *Minstrels* and quite another to listen to the mournful voice of John J. Quinn recorded in 1946 in Wilkes-Barre. It is a convincing demonstration that folk songs must be heard rather than read.

Also represented on the album was the work of the best known of all anthracite bards and minstrels, Con Carbon, who was celebrated throughout the anthracite region for his tenor voice, Irish wit, and keen sense of mimicry. It was impossible for Korson to record Con Carbon, who had died in 1907, but he is represented by Jerry Byrne's stirring version of "Me Johnny Mitchell Man," which expresses Slavic solidarity with the Welsh and Irish miners through John Mitchell and the union. In the liner notes Korson describes the song as sung in "Slavic-American dialect." Actually, of course, the song is an Irish miner's imitation of the way a Slav sounded to him. It is not really a Slavic song, but rather a good-natured parody as seen from this transcription of the chorus:

> Vell, I'm dunt 'fraid fer nottink,
> Dat's me nevair shcare,
> Comin' strike tomorra night?
> Dat's de business I dunt care.
> Right-a here I'm tella you,

Jerry Byrne, whose rendition of "Me Johnny Mitchell Man" is recorded in album L 16. He worked as a fire boss, inspecting for gas accumulations before the other miners reported for work, doing what Korson called "the loneliest job in the mines."
Courtesy George Korson Folklore Archive

Me not shcabby fella
I'm a good union citizen,
I'm Johnny Mitchell man.[54]

In listening to this song on the record it is clear that, though the words are imitative of a Slavic accent, the tune is not Eastern European. Rather it is a British song with such familiar patterns as 1, 4, 5 chord.[55]

The latest song among the *Songs and Ballads of the Anthracite Miners* LP is "Union Man," composed in 1944. This song, commenting on the wage-price spiral of the early 1940s, was of course too recent to have been included in *Minstrels* and serves to bring the album up to date. The song points up both the strengths and weaknesses of using the coal mine site for induced natural context. We do hear distracting voices and chuckling in the background, but this disadvantage is more than offset by the shouting, foot-stomping, beam-shaking atmosphere of levity. The song is a triumph of enthusiasm. However, the music is wholly unlike that of all the other songs on the disc, which are basically Anglo-Celtic songs of the latter half of the nineteenth century. Korson made no mention in the liner notes for the album that the music for "Union Man" is distinctly Eastern European and closely akin to a polka tune. The interesting point is that quite unlike "Me Johnny Mitchell Man" of 1902, by 1944 the Slavic influence had been so well absorbed in the anthracite region that it went unnoticed even by Korson.

The year 1947 brought a number of developments of interest to Korson. Like many other friends of organized labor, Korson was distressed to see the passage of the Taft-Hartley Law over the veto of President Truman in June 1947. It was widely denounced by unionists as "a slave-labor law."[56] Overseas there was some good news. In 1947 the British government asked the United Nations to solve the problem of Palestine. After much discussion, the United Nations decided to divide Palestine into two independent states, an Arab state and a Jewish state. A year later these developments would result in the proclamation of the new State of Israel.[57] In a sense Korson had lived to see the success of something he had fought for some forty years earlier.

Meanwhile, in the folklore world the year 1947 found Korson not only wrapping up the anthracite record album but also, as mentioned earlier, co-editing *The Child's Book of Folklore* with Marion Vallat Emrich. This modest book of 240 pages was published in New York by Dial Press in 1947. Since it was for children, illustrations were absolutely necessary; and John O'Hara Cosgrave II was given the commission. In a "Preface for Grown-Ups" the editors claimed that this was the first collection of "American folklore of, by, and for children." Most of the material was culled from printed sources. The editors intended it for use in kindergartens, elementary schools, playgrounds, summer camps, and the home. The book contains thirty-five folk songs and ballads, fifty-three categories of beliefs and customs, and thirty folk tales. In addition there are three categories of rhymes: teasing, memory book, and tongue twisters. Also there are four types of games: outdoor, counting-out, indoor, and singing. Originally the book was designed to be produced in an oversize format, but production costs were prohibitive. Later a tape of the book was made for blind children.

The story behind *The Child's Book of Folklore* involved an unusual four-way collaboration. In the postwar period both Rae Korson and Duncan Emrich were working with folklore in the Library of Congress. Since they were congenial co-workers, the idea of collaborating on a book of folklore came up from time to time. They took the idea up with Harry Hoffman, an editor with Dial Press, who suggested that a child's book would probably reach the widest market. Everything seemed fine. They had a good idea and a willing publisher, but then a problem came up. The Library of Congress, like many other research libraries, had rules restricting librarians from working on books, on the reasonable grounds that they might be too tempted to use time on the job for personal advantage rather than rendering service to the library patrons. Then Rae Korson came up with a solution to the problem: let their respective spouses write the book. So the book conceived by Rae Korson and Duncan Emrich was actually completed by George Korson and Marion Vallat Emrich. Conveniently enough, both families had teenage daughters who became interested in the project. Though their daughters had outgrown such things as jump rope rhymes, they were able to help collect them. Most of the material was collected by Rae Korson and Marion Emrich, but the introduction was written by George Korson. Ironically, this little book, which stayed in print for nearly thirty years, made more money in royalties for the Korson family than any other he wrote.

In the 1940s Korson produced two major publications. The first was *Coal Dust on the Fiddle* (1943), which we have examined in some detail. The second was *Pennsylvania Songs and Legends* (1949), an original collection of related essays on Pennsylvania folklore edited by Korson. As already discussed at the beginning of this chapter, the 1949 book grew out of Korson's work with the Pennsylvania Folk Festival movement of the 1930s, since it was through the role of festival director at Bucknell that Korson had made his reputation as a statewide folklore authority, and made the personal contacts necessary to assemble a list of distinguished contributors.

Pennsylvania Songs and Legends was originally published by the University of Pennsylvania Press in 1949. However, most readers of today are familiar with the reprint edition brought out by Johns Hopkins Press in Baltimore in 1960. Both editions carry illustrations by Charles P. Allen and transcriptions by Ruth Crawford Seeger. This is the only scholarly book that Korson edited rather than wrote himself. Even so it represents a great deal of work. It is a tribute to his prestige that he was able to get fourteen separate contributors to agree to write for him; it is a tribute to his tact and diplomacy that he got all of them to finish their assignments while remaining on amicable terms. The guiding idea behind the book was that folklore enriches history and fills in the gap of simple and everyday matters that the historian customarily neglects. For this book Korson himself contributed one chapter on coal miners.

As for the other contributions, Samuel Preston Bayard wrote "The British Folk Tradition," which advanced the thesis that Pennsylvania bridged the gap between the northeastern tradition and the southern tradition. William S. Troxell, who served as a dialect columnist of the *Allentown Morning Call,* collaborated with Thomas R. Brendle, Minister of the Egypt Reformed Church in Egypt, Lehigh County, Pennsylvania, to collect over 200 songs that might otherwise have been lost. Twenty-eight of their songs appeared in this book, published for the first time. Their chapter was called "Pennsylvania German Songs." J. William Frey contributed "Amish Hymns as Folk Music." He said that although the Amish were aloof from frolics and dances, they did draw on folk tunes for their hymns.

Merle H. Deardorff wrote "The Cornplanter Indians," the only chapter dealing with Indian material. He presented some of the Seneca myths and legends from Warren County. Henry W. Shoemaker wrote "Central Pennsylvania Legends," which is probably the weakest chapter in the book. His three legends, "The Phantom Panther," the "Story of Altar Rock," and "Conrad's Broom," are reported essentially directly as collected. No attempt at any generalizations or conclusions is made. Robert J. Wheeler wrote "Pike County Tall Tales." Wheeler, an Allentown businessman and politician, was already past seventy when this book was published. In 1936 he had won the statewide tall-story contest held at the Pennsylvania Folk Festival at Bucknell University.

Howard C. Frey wrote "Conestoga Wagoners," in which he advanced the thesis that the wagoners preferred anecdotes with a single narrative motif rather than long-winded stories. Lewis Edwin Theiss wrote "Canallers," which portrayed a life characterized by crime, rowdyism, feuds, and fighting. Freeman H. Hubbard wrote "Railroaders," with tales of the night express, wrecks, blockades, floods, blizzards, runaway trains, holdups, and heroic engineers. J. Herbert Walker wrote "Lumberjacks and Raftsmen," about an era at its peak in Pennsylvania between 1850 and 1870. He writes about Cherry Tree Joe McCreery, a legendary giant lumberjack and raftsman. Harry Botsford wrote "Oilmen," in which he describes Gib Morgan, the gypsy driller, a sort of wandering minstrel who preferred entertaining to oil drilling. Finally Jacob A. Evanson wrote "Folk Songs of an Industrial City," which included the Slovak, Finnish, and Greek songs found in Pittsburgh.

The basic idea behind *Pennsylvania Songs and Legends* was that by picking a dozen contributors of sound reputation, one could quickly produce a volume of folklore representative of the state. At first this commendable idea seems so simple that one wonders why it was not tried before and why Korson's example has not been imitated in other states. The plan behind the book was deceptively simple. The contributors were selected on the basis of covering folklore from the ethnic viewpoint, the regional viewpoint, and the occupational viewpoint. Each contributor was to write an essay of some thirty-five pages, and Korson would write a straightforward introduction. Though the plan for the book was clear, carrying it out was very difficult.

To say that Korson was the editor of *Pennsylvania Songs and Legends* is true, but somewhat misleading. The image behind the word "editor" suggests that he sat comfortably at his desk with a neat pile of manuscripts making a few changes here and there in wording and punctuation before shipping the package off to the printer. However, looking behind the scenes into the story of the making of the book reveals that there was more to it. Korson conceived the idea and then had to sell it to the University of Pennsylvania Press. Then, in turn, Korson had to recruit contributors (he called them "collaborators"). It was a delicate task, because he could offer each person only a modest advance, which immediately made it difficult to recruit professional writers. Nearly all of the contributors who were interested had full-time jobs as professors, teachers, publishers, businessmen, and so on.

As might be expected, at times the whole project seemed nearly unmanageable. The contributions were uneven in length and style and thoroughness, but even more serious was the problem of deadlines. Again and again the publication date had to be set back because contributors were late. Ultimately Korson could take pride in the book, but there must have been moments when the whole project seemed troublesome and unwieldy. According to his close friend Frank Hoffman,

> As I remember talking with George about it, that was one of the less happy publications he was involved in. He, I think, agreed to do this and then ran into a great deal of trouble with a number of people producing what he felt was the kind of thing that should be published (Henry Shoemaker would be a good example), and getting them to get the material in and then submitting them to editing. I don't think that he was altogether happy with it and I think, as they say, given his druthers he would have liked to have thrown out about one-third of what he finally did publish and get it from somewhere else or do without it entirely. But, I guess on the terms of the contract for the book he couldn't do that.[58]

Despite all these difficulties, Korson pushed the book through so that it would be ready for the fall trade of 1949. It was an impressive volume consisting of thirteen chapters plus an introduction by Korson. The book included music and words for 109 songs as well as the words of many additional songs and ballads. Significantly the book was not simply an anthology; instead it was a collection of original essays. Most reviewers recognized and respected the freshness of the book as compared with the usual scissors-and-paste anthology. Thus the book was generally well received. For example, Bertrand H. Bronson, writing in the *New York Times Book Review*, said, "The authors have a vital and dynamic conception of folklore. To them it is not primarily antiquarian but a process continuously operative, or ever-renewed adaptations to the forms and pressures of a changing environment."[59]

For Korson the publication of *Pennsylvania Songs and Legends* was the crowning achievement of the decade of the 1940s. Soon after publication of the book, Arthur Kaufmann, executive head of Gimbel's Department Store in Philadelphia, read the book and was so impressed that he decided to feature it in the store's annual Pennsylvania Week promotion of October 17 to 22, 1949. *Publishers Weekly* called it "one of the most elaborate promotions ever arranged for one book by one store."[60] Working with several publicity officers, Korson organized a folk festival of over 200 men, women, and children in costumes, who participated in 32 acts in the week-long festival. Taking up nearly all of Gimbel's bank of windows along Market Street were dioramas and displays—one window for each chapter of the book. It was evident that Gimbel's supported the book not so much as a commercial venture but rather as a demonstration of Pennsylvania loyalty. It was a splendid promotion for a splendid book. Even today the book stands as a model of its kind, which folklorists from other states could well emulate. [61]

4

Return to Pennsylvania
The 1950s

Old Pennsylvania. Her sons, like the soil,
a rough outside, but solid stuff within;
plenty of coal to warm her friends, plenty
of iron to cool her enemies.
                              —A toast by Nicholas Biddle[1]

The decade of the 1950s was a period in which George Korson faced a number of painful choices. On one hand he had more opportunities to collect folklore. He received many speaking invitations, and publishers were interested in his manuscripts. On the other hand declining health and heart trouble forced him to curtail his activities. Another problem involved the matter of residence. Though Korson had lived in Washington since the fall of 1938, working first with the UMWA and later the Red Cross, his roots were still in Pennsylvania. So Korson continued to make Washington his home base while making field trips and visits to Pennsylvania. On these trips, he continued to be somewhat limited by the fact that he never had an automobile nor had he learned to drive.

Despite Korson's heart condition and his homesickness for Pennsylvania, two significant accomplishments came out of the 1950s, one a matter of public service and the other a major publication. From 1957 to 1960 Korson served three terms as president of the Pennsylvania Folklore Society. In this position he led the Society through a difficult transition phase. He had to identify the problems of the Society, solve them, and proceed to set long-range goals. Also during this period Korson did the field work and prepared the manuscript of *Black Rock*, a study of the mining folklore of the Pennsylvania Dutch, in which "folklore helps us to understand these traditionally agricultural people as they became adjusted to an industrial environment."[2] The center of Korson's life in the 1950s was his role in two activities, the revival of the Pennsylvania Folklore Society and the publication of *Black Rock*. But these and other activities were increasingly affected by his poor health, which he took very seriously.

In 1950 Korson suffered a heart attack. Of all the events in his personal life this is the only one that he described in writing. In the George Korson Folklore Archive is an unpublished and undated manuscript titled "Never Underestimate an Author's Will to Live." Written entirely in the first person with vivid imagery and personal detail, it is entirely untypical of Korson's usual style. This nine-page fragmentary account is the sole item of a strictly autobiographical nature I have been able to locate. By his own account, Korson sat at his desk smoking an after-lunch cigar in the national headquarters of the American Red Cross in Washington on July 21, 1950, when suddenly he felt a piercing, crushing pain across his chest. In the belief that smoking had caused the acute pain, he threw away his cigar. Still the pain persisted. He broke out into a profuse sweat that had nothing to do with the temperature of that midsummer day. Since it was still several hours before quitting time, he continued sitting at his desk. By 4:30 the pain had become unbearable. Quietly he walked to the hall elevator, rode down to the street floor, summoned a passing taxicab and directed the driver to his apartment house. Upon his arrival, Korson paid the driver, and unassisted, he walked through a long hallway to his apartment.

Only when he arrived home did he ask his wife to call their family doctor. The doctor immediately recognized Korson's symptoms—paleness, severe chest pains, profuse perspiration, falling blood pressure, and fading pulse. It was a coronary thrombosis, or heart attack. Korson was rushed to the George Washington University Hospital in an ambulance owned by an undertaker. The hospital electrocardiograph confirmed his doctor's diagnosis. He was confined to bed for more than a month.

Korson had been a confirmed cigar smoker, enjoying as many as ten a day. With his approaching discharge from the hospital, he began anticipating the pleasure of smoking again. One day he confided this thought to his doctor, who told him it was impossible if he wanted to live. In Korson's own words, "As the will to live was stronger than the desire to smoke, there and then I gave up a habit that had held me captive for more than a quarter of a century."

After recuperation Korson resumed his editorial duties at Red Cross national headquarters. Since he had made a reputation for being a hard worker during World War II, he had no trouble convincing his associates that he was ready for more work despite his cardiac condition. His physician pointed out that a good mental attitude was essential to complete recovery from a heart attack. While trying to follow his advice, Korson was haunted by two anxieties. First, he questioned his ability to sustain a heavy work schedule without running the risk of another heart attack. The other anxiety concerned folklore, and was the source of much soul searching. Would he ever be able again to get out in the field and collect folklore and folksongs?

Recurring heart trouble made it seem increasingly doubtful that Korson would ever have the stamina again to undertake any extended folklore field research. In 1953, and again in 1956, he was readmitted to the George Washington University Hospital for treatment of coronary insufficiency. One evening in 1954 Korson and his wife were entertaining a young friend in their apartment to celebrate his approaching release from the Marine Corps. He described later what happened:

> In the midst of a delicious steak dinner I had a paroxysmal pain unlike anything I had experienced before. This pain seemed to have started in the region of the chest overlying the heart from where it radiated to the left shoulder and down the left arm along the ulnar nerve. I gripped my shirt and groaned, then, slowly, I made my way to my wife's bedroom. I dropped on the bed with an apprehension of impending death. My wife called our doctor who lives in suburban Chevy Chase, Maryland, about a half hour's drive away from us. This must have been the most torturous half hour of my life. It was filled with excruciating pain.

When the doctor arrived, he diagnosed the crushing pressure on Korson's chest as angina pectoris and gave him a small tablet of nitroglycerin to place under his tongue for speedy absorption. The severe constriction in the region of his heart was relieved almost instantly, but with the side effect of a throbbing pain in the head. From that point on, Korson was never without a supply of nitro-glycerin tablets.

It would be wrong to suggest that Korson spent the entire

decade of the 1950s grimly forgoing cigars, watching his diet, and taking medication. Actually it was a period full of many personal and family rewards and satisfactions. His daughter Betsy took a job on the *Arlington Daily Sun* in Arlington, Virginia. While she was working in Arlington, her father found her an even better job as woman's page editor of the Bethlehem, Pennsylvania, *Globe Times* (circulation then 25,000) with two assistants under her. She started work in October of 1951 there, but after a few weeks she met Dr. Harold Glazier, a Bethlehem dentist, and by April 1952 she had married and quit her job.

In time Betsy and Harold had three children: Nancy, born in 1953, Daniel, born in 1955, and Steven, born in 1959. By all accounts Korson was an attentive and devoted grandfather.

Nancy tells how her parents used to take the children to Washington for Thanksgiving with their grandparents every year. Korson would stand in the lobby of the apartment building in his coat and tie waiting for them to arrive, but trying to be casual about the whole thing:

> When we'd go to Washington to visit he used to get really excited and he used to go downstairs at least fifty times. He would tell my grandmother, "I'm going to get a paper and to check the mail." But really he was going to look for us. When we finally came, we'd say "Oh, Grandpa, I hope you weren't waiting for us long." And he would say, "Oh, no." My Grandmother would tell us on the side that he had only been sitting downstairs for hours waiting for us.[3]

In addition to the rewards of family life, Korson's growing reputation brought many visitors and correspondents—professors, scholars, and writers. They were all received with courtesy and some became close friends. Among this group was a young carpenter from San Francisco who collected books, pamphlets, and records on American trade union history. In a letter of March 30, 1956, Archie Green wrote to Korson introducing himself and explaining why Korson's books had exerted such a magnetic appeal:

> I feel keenly that current research in Industrial Relations and Labor Economics is too technical—health and welfare laws, wage studies, collective bargaining, and personnel management procedures. It is true that these studies reflect the status of the labor movement today. But since I work every day with my hands in exacting and demanding labor, I know that beneath the level of technical research

the labor movement is made up of vital, breathing human beings. Perhaps your own research meant so much to me because it made me live vicariously the life of a miner.[4]

Another faithful correspondent was a professor of business administration from Dartmouth College who was researching the Molly Maguires. In a letter of August 18, 1958, Wayne G. Broehl, Jr., wrote to Korson introducing himself and explaining his research. Broehl had received an Alfred P. Sloan Foundation Grant to study the Molly Maguires. Of course, Broehl went to Pottsville where he met Edith Patterson, who put him in touch with Korson. Six years later Broehl, with the help of Korson and others, wrote a new book on the controversial Molly Maguires. It has since won wide respect as a balanced piece of labor history.[5]

Fame also brought many speaking invitations. Though Korson had great flair and drive as a writer, he was never a successful platform speaker. He rarely sought speaking invitations, though he bravely accepted them if they seemed important. For example, he found it hard to resist an invitation from Richard M. Dorson to speak at the Folklore Institute in Bloomington, Indiana, during the summer of 1958, especially since Vance Randolph was also coming.[6] Korson was much more comfortable writing his ideas down, rather than delivering them before an audience. When he did speak, he tended to write out the entire address, jokes and all. This arrangement added to Korson's comfort, but deducted from his audience appeal.

When, years later, I asked Richard Dorson about Korson's talk on "Ballad Hunting in the Coal Fields" at the Folklore Institute, he said that he had not heard it himself but that the general impression was that Korson was not a strong speaker.[7] Nonetheless, it was a good opportunity for Korson. The main purpose of the institute was to bring active folklorists to Bloomington so that they could swap ideas and give the students a chance to get to know them. Korson did his share of socializing and exchanging shop talk, and was photographed with five colleagues at the Brown County Park. Originally taken as a casual snapshot by young folklorist Jan Harold Brunvand, the photograph later gained some fame in the profession, since it is the only known occasion that brought together Richard Dorson, George Korson, R. D. Jameson, Vance Randolph, Archer Taylor, and Stith Thompson.[8]

From travels and public appearances, Korson returned to

Noted folklorists at 1958 meeting of Folklore Institute of America (from left to right): Richard M. Dorson, George Korson, R. D. Jameson, Vance Randolph, Archer Taylor, and Stith Thompson.
Jan Harold Brunvand photo, courtesy George Korson Folklore Archive

work in Washington to his job as editor of the official national magazine of the American Red Cross. Both in public and in private he maintained that it was a privilege to work with General George C. Marshall, and that he found his co-workers congenial and the conditions pleasant. He enjoyed having a permanent job and the benefits that went with it, such as seniority, pension, vacation pay, and so on. At the same time, despite his basic contentment with the Washington scene, he still maintained many ties with Pennsylvania. In the early 1950s he was vice president of the Pennsylvania Folklore Society, a charter member of the Pennsylvania Historical Association, an associate member of the Pennsylvania German Society, and a member of the Pennsylvania Historical Junto of Washington, D.C. Of these activities, he was most active in the latter, which was a loosely organized group of Pennsylvania "expatriates" who resided in Washington.[9]

The story of Korson's involvement with the Pennsylvania Folklore Society helps to bring out a side of his accomplishments that would be missed if we examined only his writings. The Pennsylvania Folklore Society ran into trouble in the choice of its second president, a man named Henry Shoemaker. Shoemaker had a genuine love of his native Pennsylvania, and he was a gifted storyteller. Unfortunately, as a folklorist he was one of those amateur gentlemen who made no effort to separate the embroidered colorful romantic creation from the authentic oral narrative. Actually the story goes back to 1920, when the society was organized at Bishop's Court, the home of Bishop James Henry Darlington, D.D., LL.D., in Harrisburg. Darlington was not a particularly aggressive leader of the society, but he was committed to the pursuit of truthful accounts. Darlington served as president until his death in August of 1930.

Then the society slipped into a period of somnolence. In September a small group of members met at Restless Oaks, Henry Shoemaker's country residence near McElhattan, Pennsylvania, and Shoemaker was elected president of the society. There was only one problem. Because of his political connections, Shoemaker at the time was serving abroad as American minister to Bulgaria. Naturally, with an absentee president, nothing happened with the society. When Shoemaker returned in 1935, a full luncheon meeting was held at Bucknell University in Lewisburg, and, with 100 in attendance, Shoemaker was once again elected president of the society, a post that he retained until 1956.[10]

Coming from a long line of Pennsylvania ancestors, Shoemaker had a long and varied career as a businessman, diplomat, banker, newspaper publisher, soldier, and public servant. Despite this active and busy career, Shoemaker always found time to collect folklore. As a boy he heard his first Pennsylvania legends while vacationing at his grandmother's home near Pennsylvania's Bald Eagle Mountains. There, by his account, he listened by the hour to Isaac Steele, an old Seneca Indian, whose memory went back to the early 1800s. Beginning in 1903, Shoemaker started to write down the tales he had heard in his wanderings through the mountains of central Pennsylvania.[11] Unfortunately Shoemaker could never content himself with simply writing down what he had heard. Instead he would "improve" what he had collected, providing suitable embellishments as he went along.[12]

For the next thirty-five years Shoemaker turned out an enormous number of books and pamphlets on Pennsylvania folklore. The best known of these were the twelve-volume Pennsylvania Folklore Series, published between 1907 and 1924, and *Mountain Minstrelsy of Pennsylvania*, published in 1931. In addition to these works were collections of Scotch-Irish and English proverbs and sayings, old words, and place names in the Pennsylvania mountains.[13] Though his tales and anecdotes often have a thin thread of truth, serious scholars of Pennsylvania history and folklore have not relied on his work because it is difficult, if not impossible, to sort out the authentic oral narratives from material that is pure invention. Shoemaker's tales are often very entertaining, dealing as they do with such stock characters as the big Pennsylvania landholder, the staunch innkeeper, the mighty huntsman, and the beautiful sloe-eyed Indian maiden. Delightful as these tales are, they have no place in the scientific study of folklore.

Though Shoemaker was not really a folklorist, he did win a wide following of readers throughout the state. His enthusiasm and colorful imagination won him many friends. Frank Hoffman wrote a laudatory memorial article about him for the *Keystone Folklore Quarterly* shortly after his death:

> Henry Shoemaker did not formulate any theories concerning folklore. His interest lay in the material itself and in the people who possessed it as their natural heritage—lumberjacks, farmers, Indians, raftsmen, miners, itinerant workers, hunters, guides, innkeepers—anyone and everyone who had a story to tell or a song to sing. At a time when few people realized the wealth of lore that was there for the asking, he roamed the mountains and forests of his beloved Central Pennsylvania, listening and writing. Thousands of tales, legends, songs, and ballads were laboriously transcribed by hand in a day when portable recording equipment was unknown. In the course of these trips he also collected hundreds of friends, for to him a teller or singer was as important as the tale or song he possessed. And these friendships formed in lumber camps, crossroads stores, hunting lodges, and along mountain trails were as highly cherished as any formed in the capitol buildings of Harrisburg and Washington or at diplomatic functions in Lisbon, Berlin, or Sofia.[14]

It has been said that an institution is the lengthened shadow of a single man. Certainly this was an accurate way to describe Henry Shoemaker's relationship with the Pennsylvania Folklore Society as of 1956. Having served as president for more than twenty-five years, Shoemaker had grown accustomed to making nearly all the decisions about the society by himself. In favor of doing business this way, it can be argued that the society enjoyed stability and continuity of policy. On the other hand, it also made for a certain amount of stagnation and inertia. Some younger members felt discouraged from offering new suggestions.

In 1956 a crisis in leadership developed. For years Shoemaker had served as chairman of the State Historical Commission, State Archivist, and director of folklore for the State Historical and Museum Commission. Suddenly in 1956, for reasons that are not altogether clear, Shoemaker was dismissed from the Commission. He lost his post and his office in the Museum Building. Some feel that his dismissal may have been related to haughty treatment of subordinates. (He retained the habit of firm command from serving as a full colonel in the Pennsylvania National Guard, and he encouraged everyone to call him "the Colonel.") Whatever the cause, the dismissal left Shoemaker crushed and depressed. Matters came to a head in April 1956 when Adlyn M. Keffer, secretary of the society, attempted to plan the spring meeting. She arranged for the meeting to be held in the Museum Building, but when she told Shoemaker about the arrangements, he responded, "I will never set foot in the Museum again."[15]

Hoping to mollify Shoemaker, Mrs. Keffer arranged for a new meeting place at the Harrisburg Public Library. But the problems had not ended. Shoemaker, still depressed at the time of the meeting, did attend, but did not have the stamina to preside. The meeting was turned over to Vice President George Korson. Until that moment, the vice presidency of the society had been strictly honorific, but it soon became apparent to everyone that Korson would have to be elected president as soon as possible. Despite the difficulties of commuting from Washington, Korson served three terms as president of the Pennsylvania Folklore Society from 1957 to 1960. When Korson took over in 1957, the secretary had a list of some 300 names, but fewer than 100 had paid dues for 1955–1956. The treasury had about $20; there was much to be done to breathe new life into the society.[16]

At the meeting held in Harrisburg on April 27, 1957, at the

John Harris Mansion, it was finally made official; Shoemaker retired and Korson was elected president. If there is a single word to characterize Korson's contribution to the Pennsylvania Folklore Society, it was his provision of real *leadership*. It is not easy to be a good leader, but Korson had a firm sense of direction tempered with modesty and a sense of humor. He also had a concern for continuity and saw beyond his own tenure of office. Korson had three objectives for the society—an increase in membership, the adoption of a new charter and by-laws, and the expansion of the quarterly.[17]

How did Korson go about achieving the three goals he had set for the society? First, to increase the membership, a campaign was launched on October 1, 1958, with a target of signing up one thousand new members.[18] Korson's concern for increasing the size of the membership was quite legitimate. The society's prospect for making significant contributions depended on developing wide participation, through personal discussions as well as by formal procedure. The campaign plans included enrolling all professional and amateur folklorists, professional and amateur folksingers, as well as librarians, historians, and teachers. By direct mail each member was asked to sign up at least two members. Brochures and application cards were distributed to all members. In addition, publicity releases were sent to state publications and weekly and daily newspapers.

The letter to the membership stressed the relationship between the success of the campaign and the success of the quarterly:

> We need more paying members and additional revenue from memberships to expand our facilities and do a more productive job for the Commonwealth of Pennsylvania. Much of Pennsylvania folklore remains to be explored, collected and recorded. A stronger society could maintain an archive for collected folklore and publish our Keystone Folklore Quarterly more attractively in letterpress. The quarterly is distributed free to members in good standing, and will continue to be free.[19]

Perhaps the stated goal of a thousand members was unrealistic. In fact, there was only a modest increase in dues-paying members from 100 to 200; but Korson was able to report truthfully by the end of his third term that the number of dues-paying members had doubled.[20]

The second major goal Korson set for the society was the

adoption of a new charter and by-laws. Korson did not seek to direct the society along the rigid lines of a table of organization. He recognized that a voluntary society like the Pennsylvania Folklore Society could never become a wholly logical or tightly rational organization, but he wanted the society to grow on its own rather than take its entire shape and color from one man, as it had done under the Shoemaker administration. Korson believed strongly in the principle of rotating the presidency and helped write it into the new constitution. In a letter to a friend Korson wrote:

> I think you should also consider the fact whether my serving a third term might not violate the spirit of the rotation principle, which I believe in strongly, and which I helped put into the constitution. In a large state such as Pennsylvania it is wise to have the presidency rotate among the various regions as a matter of right and for the maintenance of interest, especially when good men are available for this office.[21]

Korson also pushed for the membership to vote authority for the application of a state charter. He directed a lawyer to draw up a petition to be presented to the courts. He believed that a state charter would strengthen the society, since it would become eligible to receive tax-deductible financial grants from individuals, corporations, and foundations.[22]

The third major goal Korson set for the society was the expansion of the *Keystone Folklore Quarterly*, which had been founded by Frank Hoffman, who was teaching in the Bucknell English department. At the first meeting of the society that he attended Hoffman got up and said brashly, "Why doesn't this society have a journal?" Later Shoemaker told him to go ahead with the project, so he put together a little eight-page issue which he himself typed on stencils and had run off on a mimeograph machine, calling it Volume One, Number One, of the *Keystone Folklore Quarterly*. Years later I asked Frank Hoffman about his role as editor of the *KFQ* in relation to Korson as president of the society. Hoffman explained that it was gratifying to him when Korson became president because then he received real assistance:

> Up to this point it had been with Henry Shoemaker whose attitude was we would really like this, my blessings upon you, now go out and do it. I was at that time very much a novice in the whole game not only of folklore but academia and publishing. The whole thing on every level was something new to me. But then George came in, of

course, with his valuable experience in publicity and dealing with these matters. I always felt I could talk to George about the direction in which to go in formulating policy and what to accept and what to reject and how to go about doing it. [23]

In retrospect, Korson's stewardship of the society was fortunate not only because of its vigor but also because of its timing. Korson's term of office spanned the period 1957 to 1960. It was during this period, in the year 1958, that Henry Shoemaker died. Frank Hoffman points out that had Korson not taken over, the society might simply have faded out of existence with Shoemaker's death. In this connection it should be pointed out that Korson, true to his principles, used his period of administration to recruit and train new leadership. When Korson left the office in 1960, Myra Elmers was elected president. In some ways she was even better equipped for the job than Korson. For one thing, Myra Elmers had an automobile to get around the state, and she had the time and money to devote to the job. [24] Dr. George Swetnam was appointed to succeed Frank Hoffman as editor of the *Keystone Folklore Quarterly*. Swetnam was a newspaperman with the *Pittsburgh Press*, a Presbyterian minister, and author of works dealing with the history and folklore of western Pennsylvania. [25]

Korson's service as president of the Pennsylvania Folklore Society was one of his two most significant accomplishments of the 1950s. The other was the writing of *Black Rock*, a study of the mining folklore of the Pennsylvania Dutch. In 1955 Korson was invited by the Pennsylvania German Society to give a one-hour lecture at its annual meeting on the campus of the Pennsylvania State University. Organized in 1891, the Pennsylvania German Society is the oldest cultural-historical group among the Pennsylvania Dutch. Its goal is to perpetuate the memory of the German pioneers and their descendants, and to collect and preserve all records of the part they played in molding American character and institutions.

Nearly every year since 1891 the society had published a volume of Pennsylvania history and the Pennsylvania German influence on it. By the year 1955 the series had grown to fifty-six volumes. Korson's Pennsylvania Dutch friends were aware of one significant omission—a book telling the story of the major role their ancestors had played in the development of the anthracite industry, especially during the last half of the nineteenth century when, in Korson's words, the United States was emerging as a world economic power with anthracite as its chief metallurgical fuel. Naturally Korson had become familiar with this area of history and folklore through many years of research.[26]

With all this in mind Korson planned his October 1955 speech before the society on "The Pennsylvania German Influence on the Anthracite Mining Industry." Korson's wife and his doctor both questioned the wisdom of going ahead with the address, since one hour of speaking on his feet might involve too great a strain. But after much deliberation, Korson decided to risk it. Armed with two small bottles of nitroglycerin tablets he set out for Penn State. The lecture was well received; after the talk, members of the society gathered around Korson and urged him to expand the lecture material into a book.[27] After his return to Washington he received similar pleas by mail.[28] The challenge appealed to Korson, but the idea of risking another heart attack while writing a book caused him to hesitate. After a great deal of thought, he finally decided to apply for a Guggenheim Fellowship to conduct the research he needed to round out his account. He waited until October 15, 1956, the deadline, before mailing his application.[29]

An entire fall and winter of suspense passed by. Finally, in April 1957, Korson received a special delivery letter from the Guggenheim Foundation telling him that he had been awarded a fellowship.[30] He rejoiced. At long last he was receiving official recognition for his work. With this independent grant, he felt he could retire from the American Red Cross. His wife and his family were aghast. They felt that it would be wiser to take a leave of absence from the Red Cross, so that he could return to a stable and secure position when the Guggenheim ran out. But Korson felt that his life itself was in danger of running out. He wanted to do all the serious collecting and writing he possibly could. This Guggenheim Fellowship at last gave him the mechanism to make a clean break with the workaday world of journalism. He would stake everything on the study of folklore. Thus on June 21, 1957, Korson formally retired from the Red Cross and was given a luncheon by his associates and a gracious farewell from General Alfred M. Gruenther, president of the American Red Cross.

Receiving a Guggenheim was a big step for Korson. He had never received a major independent grant before. To be sure, his

Korson interviews William Breiner, who gave the real story behind the legend of Philip Ginder's coal discovery.
AP Wirephoto of 1960, courtesy George Korson Folklore Archive

previous work had been given some support from the UMWA, but this new kind of prestigious recognition with no ties to any special interest group reflected an increased national interest in his work.

With a sense of urgency, Korson lost little time in getting to Pottsville to make arrangements for his field work. He arranged to stay with an old friend, Dr. Harry Hoffman. There he spent the first few weeks lining up names of prospective informants and working out the mechanics of transportation. Through Harry Hoffman and Edith Patterson, Korson had little difficulty in assembling a long list of informants. Getting to the informants with a tape recorder, however, presented some difficulties. With his heart condition, Korson could not carry the tape recorder because it was too heavy. Another problem was that he had no driver's license. Public transportation was impractical because many of his prospective informants lived in remote places.[31]

Fortunately Korson found Carl F. Maurer, a sixty-three-year-old retired miner, who was able to help. Having worked in the coal mines of the Philadelphia and Reading Coal and Iron

Korson records humorous folk tales related by "Uncle Charles" Brenner, 80.
1957 photo by Bernard Dohn of the Allentown Call Chronicle, *courtesy George Korson Folklore Archive*

Company for many years, Maurer recognized immediately the value of what Korson was trying to do. Maurer expressed enthusiasm for the project at their first meeting, and he was even able to suggest prospective informants himself. Korson and Maurer entered into an agreement whereby Maurer would drive Korson about and help with the tape recorder for $10 per day. Out of this amount Maurer bought gasoline and oil, kept up his car insurance, and bore all other costs of operating the automobile.[32]

With his physical arrangements well in hand, Korson plunged into a strenuous schedule of interviews. Each day Korson and Maurer set out with the bulky Wilcox-Gay tape recorder. Most of the recording was done at the 3¾ speed, which Korson found suitable for his type of recording, consisting of long interviews in which pure folklore would emerge only at intervals. At the slower speed of 3¾ Korson could get a whole hour of recording without

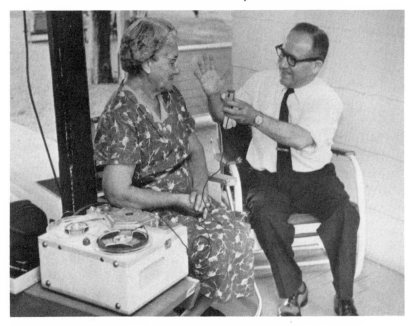

Korson gathers material for *Black Rock* from Mrs. Clinton Otto of Schuylkill County.
Courtesy George Korson Folklore Archive

moving. Even though the machine was bulky, Korson was pleased that the reel of tape unwound so quietly that the informants were scarcely aware of the machine.[33] To expedite work on the book, Korson arranged with the Thomas Secretarial Service in Washington, D.C., to make transcriptions of his recordings. Throughout the summer Korson mailed tapes back to Washington, so very little time was lost. Though ideally the collector should do his own transcribing, this arrangement was very efficient. Korson also took the precaution of providing his transcriptionists with adequate maps and glossaries.[34]

Although the work was strenuous, Korson survived it in good condition under the care of a heart specialist and with the help of his nitroglycerin tablets. He had a sense of exhilaration from meeting interesting people and discovering fresh material. Korson came away from Pottsville in the fall with a large collection of many reels of magnetic tape. In a mood of obvious excitement, he wrote his younger brother Meyer: "While still tired, I've begun to dig into the pile of stuff accumulated during the summer and fall. I've enough to keep a stenographer, a librarian, and perhaps a maid busy for a couple of months to help go through the mass of material. But no such luck. I shall have to do it all myself."[35] So Korson began to pull out the history and folklore of the West End from his transcripts, photographs, photostats, books, pamphlets, manuscripts, and notebooks filled with precious notes.

Korson plunged into a disciplined schedule of uninterrupted writing that fall, but by December a crisis developed. It became increasingly obvious that Korson would not be able to finish the book within the one-year period of the Guggenheim Fellowship. To have more time for writing the book, Korson had cut his field trip short and had over fifty hour-long tapes transcribed by his secretarial agency in Washington. By his estimate this step saved three to four months. Yet even with all this time-saving, Korson found it impossible to stick to the original schedule.

Faced with this problem, Korson applied for a one-year renewal of his grant. He kept writing, and by March he had finished the first chapter and a general introduction, running over fifty typescript pages. Things were going well. Then in April of 1958 came bad news from the Guggenheim Foundation: Korson's request for a second fellowship was not granted. The news came as a shock to Korson, but he quickly pulled himself together. He felt that as a person who had suffered a heart attack, he could not afford the luxury of brooding over this disappointment.[36] Determined not to return to commercial journalism, he needed to find some way around the loss of his foundation funds. In the face of this dilemma, he turned to his literary agent, Allan C. Collins of Curtis Brown, Ltd., who initiated some hard bargaining with The Johns Hopkins Press, which was interested in publishing the book. Collins argued that Korson would need a cash advance for financing in order to finish the book. By May of 1958 Harold E. Ingle, director of The Johns Hopkins Press, substantially agreed to Korson's terms.[37] Korson began to feel tension the moment his signature was on the contract. Now he was committed to deliver the manuscript in a little over a year. But when he looked at the mass of material in his apartment, he felt sure that it would take more time. He knew that he was breaking new ground and that the manuscript would have to be written with great care. Also the documentation slowed up production; this was his first book with extensive footnotes.

Two years of tough writing passed, and Korson produced a substantial manuscript. Still the end was not in sight. Then pressure from his publisher started to build up. The final push to wrap up the book subjected Korson to grueling, tension-ridden work. Those last few weeks are best described in Korson's own words:

> Early in 1960 I received a call from the Editor of the Johns Hopkins Press to meet him in the cocktail lounge of a plush Washington hotel. The editor is a kind and gentle man, and it took two stiff drinks for him to come out with some bad news: a final deadline for the manuscript to meet fall publication. I required two equally potent drinks, which went on the editor's expense account, and two tablets of nitroglycerin under the tongue, to accept the new deadline without protest. Anginal pains warned me that it would mean working under high pressure, against which I had been cautioned frequently by my doctor, but I really had no choice.
>
> My doctor's card, showing his home and office telephone numbers for emergency use, lay conspicuously on my dresser. Tension heightened as my writing schedule lengthened. During daylight hours I was at my typewriter "from c'n to cain't," with rest periods and coffee breaks in between. A sleeping pill closed my eyes at bedtime, but severe chest constrictions opened them again, and again, in the deepening night. I had learned the trick of placing a nitroglycerin tablet under my tongue in the dark without getting up, but in the period of my intensive writing I was driven out of bed often by excruciating anginal pain. I seldom switched on my bedroom light as I regarded it unseemly for a grown man to show tears even to a dresser mirror. To avoid waking my wife in the adjoining bedroom, I suffered in silence, but more often than not she heard my movements anyway.
>
> What she and I both feared, though we seldom talked about it, was another attack of coronary thrombosis which might prove fatal. There were nights when acute pain drove me to the telephone to call the doctor, but I exercised self-control. The telephone remained untouched.[38]

By September of 1960 Korson had finished the last details of indexing the book. Finally, to the great relief of his relatives and friends, the book was published on November 11, 1960, with the title *Black Rock: Mining Folklore of the Pennsylvania Dutch*. It was a big book, running more than 450 pages, and it retailed at $7.50, which was very expensive at the time. Simultaneously, The Johns Hopkins Press reprinted his *Pennsylvania Songs and Legends*, which also retailed at $7.50. The books were boxed together for the Christmas trade at $12.00 in the hope of wide sales.[39] Korson had the satisfaction of knowing that the publisher decided to push his book as its number one publication in the fall catalogue, and to feature it in many advertisements. In addition, a beautiful brochure about the book was printed and sent to ten thousand prospective buyers.[40]

An interesting sidelight connected with the publication of *Black Rock* was its special relationship with the Pennsylvania German Society. As mentioned earlier in this chapter, the book actually grew out of a lecture given before the society in October 1955. Between that time and 1960 Korson was in constant touch with William J. Rupp, publications officer of the society, who encouraged him every step of the way. The society was eager to add the volume to their series, but Korson was understandably interested in having The Johns Hopkins Press publish the book because of its excellent editorial and production staff, not to mention its facilities to distribute the book to a national audience. In the face of this apparent conflict, Korson came up with a clever proposal—that the first six hundred copies of the book be published for the Pennsylvania German Society and that the title page of this first edition carry the joint imprint of The Johns Hopkins Press and the Pennsylvania German Society. The idea won acceptance from all parties. From the standpoint of the society it gained an important volume without going to the expense and financial risk of a large enterprise. From the standpoint of the press it gained a substantial guaranteed bloc of sales for a very minimal production concession.[41]

Another link with the Pennsylvania German Society was the book's dedication to William S. Troxell, the *Allentown Morning Call*'s beloved columnist for more than thirty years. Troxell had been a leader in the Pennsylvania German cultural revival and had served as president of the Pennsylvania German Society from 1952 until his death in August 1957, the same summer during which Korson began field work on *Black Rock*. As a newspaperman and former columnist himself, Korson appreciated Troxell's gift in turning out daily essays that were bright and chatty, and included charming Pennsylvania German dialect anecdotes. His columns not only helped keep the Pennsylvania Dutch dialect alive, but also chronicled many of the day-by-day experiences of the farmers and villagers whom he visited on his daily rounds of the small towns of Lehigh and Northampton counties.[42] In addition, Troxell, in collaboration with the Reverend Thomas R. Brendle, had made their large collection of Pennsylvania German folk songs and ballads available to Korson in his *Pennsylvania Songs and Legends* of 1949. Not only did Korson admire Troxell's professional accomplishments, but there was another dimension to their relationship, which Korson explained in a letter to Troxell's widow:

> There also was a personal reason. Bill and I had been good friends for nearly a quarter of a century. He, Rev. Brendle and I had worked together on folklore projects for many years, as you know, and often their participation made the difference between success and failure as far as my own efforts were concerned. Now that Bill is no longer with us I felt that I should show my gratitude by dedicating this book of Pennsylvania German history and folklore to his memory.[43]

We have examined the creative origins of *Black Rock* in Korson's mind, the problems involved in field work, the challenge of the writing itself, the details of its publication, and the nature of its special relationship with the Pennsylvania German Society. Let us now look at the finished product and its critical reception.

Any discussion of *Black Rock* must begin with an examination of its organization and structure. This massive book is arranged in twenty chapters, but it is virtually two books in one. The first nine chapters constitute a sociological history of the anthracite industry among the Pennsylvania Dutch. With chapter 10, Korson takes up the study of their folklore including folk speech, courtship and marriage customs, folk medicine, the lore of the breaker boys, folk songs, and ballads.[44] In the preface to the book, Korson gives the rationale for this dual structure. He justified the lengthy historical section of chapters 1 through 9: "This book is about a hitherto obscure chapter in American history—the period in the latter half of the nineteenth century when the United States emerged as a leading industrial power by using anthracite as its principal metallurgical fuel." In the same paragraph Korson mentions his second purpose, which dominates chapters 10 to 17: "This is a study of the Pennsylvania Dutch in an unfamiliar setting, in which folklore helps us understand these traditionally agricultural people as they became adjusted to an industrial environment."[45] Korson's effort to use folklore as a means of understanding the history of the Pennsylvania Dutch is significant, since the historical record for this group had been amply documented. With no shortage of published sources, clearly the folkloristic findings were likely to be supplementary.[46]

Unfortunately there was a real loss of unity and coherence in attempting the admittedly difficult strategy of linking folklore and history. All too often the reader was left to make the interconnections between the folklore of the second half and the history of the first half. This failure to achieve an organic and systematic whole lies at the heart of the book's difficulty for readers. One of his most perceptive reviewers, Preston A. Barba of Muhlenberg College, noting the defensive tone of the preface, voiced the objection this way:

> As a scholar of integrity he distinguishes between fact and fancy, engaged not so much in disentangling the threads of history and of lore, as in interweaving them into a whole fabric. And yet the further one follows his fascinating narrative the more one is inclined to believe that the subtitle of this book is a misnomer, and that Korson the historian has outdone Korson the folklorist.[47]

While acknowledging Korson's failure to make the book into a unified whole, we must not lose sight of the two great strengths of the work. The first is the demonstration of Korson's great warmth and charm, so much in evidence when he was out in the field collecting. The second chief merit of the book lies in the fact that it gave Korson the opportunity to wrap up many bits of history and folklore of the anthracite region, in which he had specialized.[48]

A brief look at Korson as a collector will demonstrate his warmth and charm. From the anecdotes in the book we realize Korson's eagerness to accept the informants on their own terms. Though Korson participated in the life of the community, he never forgot to observe or inquire. Part of the charm of *Black Rock* lies in Korson's willingness to share the thrill of discovery with the reader. In addition Korson, with admirable modesty, was willing to tell an occasional story on himself. For example, in chapter 10 he tells of the collecting situation in the home of William A. Stutzman. After a long interview session, Korson and his driver, Carl F. Maurer, were invited to dinner. Though Korson neither smoked

Miner with Pick

Long before machine mining came into widespread use, the Pennsylvania Dutch miner had to master a set of tools with which he worked in his daily task "at the face." First of all, there was the pick, symbol of his craft, for undercutting the seam to prepare it for blasting.

—*Black Rock*, p. 178

Courtesy Wyoming Historical and Geological Society

nor drank on this occasion, he did break his doctor's orders in overeating rich foods. In fact, away from the watchful eye of his wife, Korson managed to break both medical taboos (wittingly) and religious taboos (unwittingly) as he joined the Stutzmans for dinner:

> Typically Pennsylvania Dutch, the round dining table, set in the middle of the large kitchen, groaned from its heavy burden of steaming food, the sight of which caused my gustatory nerve to

Miner Securing Powder

The black powder in use then was dangerous. The miner bought it at the company store by the keg and stored it at home. In a powder can called a "cadger" he carried one day's supply.

—*Black Rock*, p. 179

Erskine Solomon photo, courtesy Wyoming Historical and Geological Society

---

tingle—a large platter of meat, a mound of mashed potatoes with butter melting in the middle, dishes of corn, beans, pickled beets, and homemade bread and coffee. I must not overlook the two big pies—one lemon, the other apple—only a minute or two out of the oven, which were cooling tantalizingly at the far end of the table— that is, far from me. I looked in vain for the seven sweets and seven sours, the mythical favorites of feature writers who deal with the Pennsylvania Dutch.

Everything tasted so good that I readily accepted Mrs. Stutzman's offer of seconds—with one exception. Pie. Having had more than I should of the roast meat, I had no room for a second helping of apple pie. The roast meat had been especially good, and

Miner with Old Hand Drill

In regular anthracite mines, blasting was hazardous and required skill and experience. A miner had to know how to drill a hole in the seam and how to handle explosive cartridges. Today this work is performed by specialists, professional shot-firers.

—*Black Rock*, p. 324

Erskine Solomon photo, courtesy Wyoming Historical and Geological Society

---

so, impulsively, but with all the sincerity in the world, I complimented the cook on her roast beef.

"Oh, it ain't roast beef," she chuckled.

"No?"

"No, it's roast pork."

Roast pork is usually not in my diet, but it certainly tasted good that day.[49]

If Korson had been strictly observant of kosher dietary laws, this would have been a serious transgression; but it is obvious from the tone of the anecdote that he was simply enjoying telling a story on himself by making himself the butt of the joke.

Fire Boss Testing for Gas

By inventing a safety lamp in 1815, Sir Humphrey Davy convinced British miners that mine gas is a natural phenomenon; a fine wire gauze inclosing the flame to keep it from igniting mine gas was the Davy lamp's safety feature. Fire bosses in the Swarta mines used it on their daily examinations of the mines. A fire boss started his rounds at 4 A.M., or three hours before the miners reported for work.

—*Black Rock*, p. 181

Erskine Solomon photo, courtesy Wyoming Historical and Geological Society

Besides demonstrating Korson's consummate ability as a collector, *Black Rock* also provided Korson with a medium for enlarging his body of writing on the history and folklore of the anthracite region. Ignoring for a moment the central question of whether the book actually showed how the Pennsylvania Dutch adjusted to an industrial environment, the fact remains that Korson used this vehicle as a wrapping-up operation. Some of the most effective passages in the book present fascinating details of the folk culture of the Pennsylvania anthracite miner. We find, for exam-

Colliery Bath House

Before the installation of showers at collieries, anthracite miners were obliged to go home in their working clothes, which were dripping wet from perspiration and sulphurous mine water, while their necks, backs, and faces were black with coal dust.

—*Black Rock*, p. 212

Erskine Solomon photo, courtesy Wyoming Historical and Geological Society

ple, vivid descriptions of the miner's principal tool, the pick; the hazards of blasting and of gas explosion; the difficulties of keeping clean; the treatment of mules; the provisions for injured miners; the pastimes of mine patch children; and even some irreverent graffiti describing mining machinery. For faithful Korson readers who are already familiar with *Minstrels of the Mine Patch*, this book can be read as a captivating sequel, even though much of the mining material is peculiar to neither the Pennsylvania Dutch nor the West End of Schuylkill County.

In my discussions with folklorists throughout the country in

Veterinarian Treating Mule

Because they knew how to handle animals, many Pennsylvania Dutch farmers became mule drivers and mule bosses in the mines. They carried folk remedies from the farm to the mine mule stable. Some of the mining companies' graduate veterinarians were Pennsylvania Dutch.

—*Black Rock*, p. 268

Erskine Solomon photo, courtesy Wyoming Historical and Geological Society

---

gathering material to evaluate Korson's contribution to American intellectual life over the past few years, I was consistently struck by a disturbing paradox concerning *Black Rock*. Nearly everyone I talked with knew that Korson himself considered this, his eighth book, to be the very best he had written. But even his most loyal and trusted friends, including Archie Green and Wayland Hand, do not share this opinion.[50] How can this discrepancy exist?

One pitfall of the book was that Korson brought to the project highly refined skills and resources of specialized knowledge. But a large part of his earlier success was due to his ability to see things whole. The earlier books succeeded better in communicating to those outside his field. Korson did not entirely avoid pressure

Colliery Ambulance

The number of injured and killed anthracite mineworkers increased as the industry dug deeper into the earth for hard coal seams. One of the principal factors contributing to the high accident rate was insufficient information among miners and colliery officials alike as to the cause and methods of preventing accidents.

—*Black Rock*, p. 260

Erskine Solomon photo, courtesy Wyoming Historical and Geological Society

---

toward myopic specialization. In essence, then, *Black Rock* was too narrow in scope. But in addition to this overriding shortcoming, four specific areas caused problems: (1) the Philip Ginder material, which opened the book, involved close technical arguments that lost the general reader; (2) by Korson's own account he was unable to find a single Pennsylvania Dutch folksong that made a reference to coal mining, and this had been a central goal of the investigation; (3) in an attempt to be comprehensive, Korson produced a book that many considered to be overly long for the general reader; and (4) in an attempt at scholarly precision, Korson became preoc-

Mine Telephone Station

An important reform in providing care for injured miners was the installation of underground telephone stations. This development was described by Korson: "They installed a telephone to call the ambulance driver in an emergency, thus eliminating the whining colliery siren that used to sound over a wide area whenever men were hurt inside the mine. No longer need anxious wives and weeping children take up a vigil in front of the mine portal waiting to see who was brought up severely injured or killed."

—*Black Rock*, p. 263

Erskine Solomon photo, courtesy Wyoming Historical and Geological Society

cupied with his "source notes" and lost his earlier broad appeal. In a sense all of these objections reflect the fact that Korson had built up a strong following of readers who had certain fixed expectations of a Korson book, including lively human interest and readability. For the most part, this audience, composed of both folklorists and general readers, was unhappy with the "new" (more scholarly) Korson.

The first problem concerns the Philip Ginder chapter, a well-documented and painstakingly crafted thirty-one-page essay. Basically Korson took the legendary account of Ginder as dis-

Culm Bank

Now at the lower end of town we used to have culm banks anywhere from seventy to a hundred feet high. We, as young boys in this town, used to go to the colliery and get long pieces of sheet iron. We would curl up the end like a toboggan, put a wire on the back end of it, pull the sheet iron up to the top of the culm bank and then ride down on it.

—William W. Lewis, in *Black Rock*, p. 330

Erskine Solomon photo, courtesy Wyoming Historical and Geological Society

coverer of anthracite and attempted to find the factual basis behind the story of 1791. The old story told of a poor hunter who went up on Summit Hill mountain to bring down game for his family. When he failed to kill a single bird or animal with his gun, he turned homeward, only to stumble over a piece of black rock, which turned out to be coal. But Korson's research showed that Ginder was a miller, not a hunter. The reason he went up on the mountain was not to hunt but rather to look for suitable millstones for a gristmill.[51]

Korson had to write the Ginder chapter with great care

Quintuplex Pump

One day when the devil was walking about,
He wanted a man who was heavy and stout
To look after the pumps and engines in Hell,
And take charge of the imps and young devils as well.

—Graffiti from the gangway of Beaver Brook Mine,
reported in *Black Rock*, p. 348

Erskine Solomon photo, courtesy Wyoming Historical and Geological Society

because the historical details are mired in controversy. For example, Pottsville residents continue to insist that their own folk hero, Necho Allen, had discovered anthracite the year before in Schuylkill County. To an outsider, however, the whole thing seems to be a tempest in a teapot. Actually, of course, the Indians knew about coal (though they did not put it to effective widespread use), and the first white men to "discover" anthracite were Moravian missionaries, years before either Ginder or Allen.[52]

Unfortunately Korson's argument was just tedious enough to

Monument to honor the legendary discovery of coal in Pennsylvania in 1791.
Allentown Call-Chronicle *photo, courtesy George Korson Folklore Archive*

---

discourage readers from outside the anthracite region. Wayland Hand, for example, said to me:

> I knew that George thought that his *Black Rock* book was the best, but I didn't. The first book was the most exciting book in terms of what he had to say about the mine patch. The third book had more stuff on the legends and the beliefs of miners which is my own field so I naturally responded warmly to that. *Black Rock* I thought was just out of context somehow. I never finished it; I bogged down in the Ginder stuff.

This comment highlights a problem inherent in Pennsylvania German scholarship. The Ginder problem, which a prominent outside folklorist yawned through, touched off a raging controversy among the specialists. One might speculate that part of Korson's bad press for *Black Rock* stemmed from a feeling that he was poaching on well-patrolled preserves, especially with regard to the Ginder episode.

Preston A. Barba of Muhlenberg College, for example, finds Korson's versions unconvincing because the chronology does not line up well with certain established facts of millstone manufacture. Barba writes of Ginder:

> He was not the first to discover anthracite coal; but in 1791 he came

upon anthracite coal, not while hunting game, as the legend goes, but while looking for conglomerate rock from which to cut his millstones. If the tax lists of "over-the-mountain" settlers include the name of "philip kinder" as early as 1754, one can only wonder how he took up milling in 1791; and further, where those early settlers procured stones for their gristmills in the intervening years. It could hardly have been unknown to them that millstones of high quality were being quarried in Lancaster County as early as the 1770's.[53]

Barba's criticism was strong, and although Korson never dealt with his objections, others soon did. As we shall see shortly, George Swetnam later advanced a plausible hypothesis to explain the dating problems. Barba also found another problem with Korson's Ginder scholarship, which was less crucial. This second objection dealt with the spelling of Ginder's name:

> In considering the various spellings of the hero's name, the author finds "Ginter" most frequently in print, but for himself accepts "Ginder," apparently without realizing that both forms are only a Palatine dialect coloration of "Guenther" (also without *h*), common both as a German given name and family name, from the Old High German components *gund* (battle) and *heri* (host or army).[54]

Another Pennsylvanian who was unconvinced by Korson's account was George Swetnam, who seriously questioned William Breiner's accuracy. An interesting point in Swetnam's criticism is that he came up with an explanation for the chronological problem pointed out by Barba:

> Only in one place along this course do we feel that Mr. Korson has seriously erred, and that in the very first chapter in his discussion of the historical facts about Philip Ginder, the folk hero who is credited with discovering that anthracite coal would burn. It is a little puzzling to find him challenging the statement of Dr. Thomas C. James, who had known and talked to Ginder, because his statement was made 18 years after the conversation it reported; it is even more surprising to find him impugning it on no better evidence than the opinion of a failing, 90-year-old man who *was not born until more than 60 years after* the death of the man about whose affairs he speaks so glibly. But any folklorist who has worked in the field has at some time felt the almost hypnotic spell of an aged man who is completely wrapped up in the facts he reports. It is almost impossible not to believe him, whether he is right or not.
>
> On the basis of the evidence presented, we feel, most historians

would suspect there had been two Philip Ginders: the father, who had owned property in another county prior to 1791, and the son, newly arrived and on his own in the wilderness, who was ekeing out his living as a hunter when he burned the first chunk of anthracite in his fire. The dates involved almost force some such opinion upon the student.[55]

Swetnam's criticism seems balanced and fair concerning the relative reliability of James and Breiner. In addition, Swetnam's hypothesis of two Philip Ginders is persuasive and compelling. In short, then, Korson's chapter on Ginder failed to hold the interest of the general reader and left the authorities room to argue with him.

The second problem, Korson's inability to find a single Pennsylvania Dutch folksong that made a reference to coal mining, was a keen disappointment to him. Given his success in uncovering the folksong tradition of the anthracite region in his 1927 *Songs and Ballads of the Anthracite Miner*, it was only natural that he would just assume that he could re-create his earlier success in a slightly different locale. It takes only a little imagination to see how dejected Korson must have felt when the time for his field work ran out and he had to leave Pottsville for Washington without the trophies he had sought. In chapter 20, "Songs and Ballads," Korson was forced to report:

> Now to the question asked earlier in this chapter: What did the Pennsylvania Dutch miners contribute to the folk song tradition? Under my 1957 Guggenheim grant, I had sought to record a comprehensive collection of folklore reflecting Pennsylvania Dutch folkways in a coal mining environment. The results have been gratifying in all types of folklore except one—folk songs. I had hoped to unearth enough evidence to show a parallel Pennsylvania Dutch folk song tradition based on the anthracite industry. While I recorded some songs in the Dutch dialect (they form part of this chapter), not one makes any reference to coal mining.[56]

Theoretically, in the social sciences, negative findings should be as significant as positive findings. In this case perhaps we learn something about the Pennsylvania Dutch coal miners by knowing that they did not have any dialect coal songs. But the social sciences are unlike the physical sciences in this respect. There are too many variables. One is always left with the suspicion that given sufficient time and energy, someone someday might just find the missing evidence. Though *Black Rock* remains an admirable book, this shortcoming did dampen Korson's spirits, since it weakened his strongest chapter.

The third problem that plagued *Black Rock* was the feeling of many readers that it was too long. It should be pointed out in this connection, however, that it was the general reader rather than the academic reader who most often voiced this complaint. There is no evidence that the book is padded with irrelevant material; the real problem is that people did not expect this kind of substantial work from Korson. The great thing about *Minstrels of the Mine Patch*, after all, was that it gave the folklore back to the folk. *Minstrels* was a readable book, which was often a prized possession in mining families, while *Black Rock* never achieved this status. Instead it was written for the cognoscenti. Academic reviewers recognized this at once and described the book as "definitive." For example, Willard Rhodes, writing in *Western Folklore*, said: "*Black Rock* will undoubtedly be recognized as the definitive work on the folklore of this area, for the violent technological, sociological, and cultural changes of the past two decades make it unlikely, even impossible, that future scholars will add anything significant to Korson's important work."[57] Meanwhile Paul Trescott of the *Philadelphia Sunday Bulletin*, writing outside the gentlemanly walls of academe, said more frankly: "The author has devoted to his task the months and years of work which are necessary if the product is not to be superficial. To anyone familiar with that part of the country and the people, his latest is a fascinating book, though in part perhaps overly long."[58] Of course, ultimately there is no right answer to the question of length. Actually some things are missing from the book that would have been helpful. It has been pointed out that there is no bibliography nor a discussion of sources or method of collection. Especially suitable for this book would have been photographs or illustrations beyond the simple line drawings by Stanley Mossman and used as chapter heads. Granting that these would have added to the cost, there should have been the maps that a book of this nature requires.

A large part of the length problem stems from the dual nature of the book in trying to cover both history and folklore. Charles O. Houston, Jr., voiced the objection this way:

> This book is arranged in twenty chapters, of which the first nine are
> devoted to a rather uneven chronological background of the anthra-

cite industry among the Pennsylvania Dutch. With Chapter 10, the author takes up in considerable detail the various aspects of life in the region, principally the customs, behavior, and folklore. The chronology is never completed and there is a considerable "paste and scissors" character to the last eleven chapters.[59]

I find Houston's charge of a "paste and scissors" character not quite fair, since it tends to suggest that Korson was getting his material from old printed sources rather than from fresh field work. Nonetheless the second half of the book does have an uneven and choppy aspect. In practice, the question of length is often ignored, since bringing it up at all seems to smack of anti-intellectualism, but for folklorists it must be squarely confronted. How much collectanea can we justify setting in type? One reviewer dealt forthrightly with this matter and even suggested a practical remedy:

> In his earlier work Korson was probably gravely hampered by spatial limitations, but his new book gave him an opportunity to record formally his rich collectanea. His source material is so extensive, however, that even here he complains of lack of space for "use of more of my field of recordings." (It might be worthwhile to note that the University of Kentucky Press has found a workable solution in the Microcard for handling field notes and sources too bulky to be set and printed letterpress.)[60]

The fourth and final problem about the book is the question of documentation. In an attempt at scholarly precision, Korson became preoccupied with his "source notes" (footnotes) and as a result lost some of his earlier broad appeal. Korson felt that he had set for himself a very high performance standard, which would produce a "magnum opus." In a letter to his junior colleague Archie Green, Korson explained his approach:

> The index, which was quite a chore, is off to the printer at last. It's an analytical index, and so detailed and long, and it should be helpful to researchers. BLACK ROCK probably will be considered the most scholarly of my books, if only for the source notes. These notes take up more than thirty pages of fine print at the back of the book. To have source notes was my voluntary decision. I was working in a virgin field—the Pennsylvania Dutch as anthracite miners—and felt the notes would strengthen the book, give it an added dimension. But they added at least six months to my work-time on the manuscript.[61]

Understandably Korson was proud of what he had done. Since the book had been written on a Guggenheim Fellowship, he felt that it had to be a crowning achievement; but the search for sources tended to become obsessive. In his bid for methodological precision, Korson took more interest in research than in interpretation. In the last analysis, *Black Rock* was a good book but not, as Korson believed, his most monumental.

Despite the shortcomings of the book, one final factor must be added to the account. In previous chapters I have pointed out that a strong union was for Korson an article of belief, a means of preserving the corporate-liberal state. *Black Rock* gave Korson still another opportunity to reiterate this belief. As in his earlier books, Korson assumed the role of reformer, not of revolutionary. Still there can be no doubt about his sympathies. In his last chapter Korson discussed the well-documented anthracite strike of 1902. By the time of his 1957 field trip, the printed record of that strike could be considered complete. Yet Korson was proud of the fact that fresh material of that historic event could be found through folklore. Korson uncovered a fascinating story about how a Pennsylvania Dutch farmer played a key role in the strike. Korson was not content to show the Pennsylvania Dutch as a colorful ethnic group on the fringes of coal mining. Instead he wanted to show that the Pennsylvania Dutch farmer and the coal miner were inextricably tied together by the economic system.

The story that underscores this point was given the title "How the Lowly Potato Saved the Union in 1902." John Mitchell had been president of the UMWA since 1899 and had spent three years quietly trying to organize the miners into a disciplined body. Strikes had been avoided in 1900 and 1901 largely because Mark Hanna, the Republican party boss, had urged J. P. Morgan, head financier behind the industry, to order the operators to settle with the workers in order to avoid raising questions of social injustice, especially important during the McKinley-Bryan presidential campaign. But by 1902 both sides felt that a showdown could not be avoided any longer. A strike was called in May of 1902.

At first the miners took to the strike cheerfully, but as the strike dragged on through spring and summer, the miners began to suffer. Families were living on bread and water, supplemented only by relief packages from the cities. At this point real starvation was a threat to many of the striking 140,000 miners.[62] Korson wrote: "Realizing that the lowly potato was a staple item of the miners' diet, President Mitchell hoped and prayed for a bumper crop that fall. With potatoes plentiful and cheap, he knew that the striking miners could hold out indefinitely until he got the operators around the collective bargaining table."[63]

Thus John Mitchell understandably felt that his prayers had been answered when he learned that the potato crop raised by the Pennsylvania Dutch farmers of Schuylkill County was unusually abundant. Korson wrote of Mitchell:

> At the same time he learned that the top man there was John Schrope, who had a yield of 500 bushels to the acre, exceptional, indeed, for those days. An agricultural expert has calculated that Schrope's 500 bushels were the equivalent of about 30,000 pounds, enough, he said, to sustain 150 large families for a month.[64]

Korson went on to point out that Mitchell made a special trip to see the mound of potatoes in John Schrope's barn, and he had a photograph taken of him standing at the top of it. This is not to suggest that Mitchell urged the farmers to give their crops away to the desperate miners. The point is simply that the abundance of this inexpensive staple was one more important factor in the miners' ability to hold out longer in this bitter and protracted strike. The Pennsylvania Dutch farmers understandably felt that they had made a real contribution to the miners' cause. Certainly the episode helped to create good mutual feelings between the miners and the farmers.

In the end, of course, it was not the potato that saved the union in 1902. It was Theodore Roosevelt. As the strike dragged on into the fall, everyone could see the horrors and suffering of a winter without coal. Korson had described the outcome of the strike years earlier in *Minstrels:*

> Public opinion, in and outside the region, raised a clamor for an end to the strike. Mitchell as usual was ready to arbitrate, but the operators remained obdurate until Theodore Roosevelt, then President, threatened to take over their properties if they still refused. A White House conference was followed by the appointment of a Board of Arbitration, and the strike was at an end on October 23, 1902.[65]

Korson never lost an opportunity to address himself to the struggles between capital and labor. Since *Black Rock* was financed by the Guggenheim Foundation, not the UMWA, Korson was in no way obligated to the union as a special interest group. Unfettered with any obligation, he still gave this favorable episode a prominent position at the conclusion of his book.

5

Years of Fulfillment
The 1960s

George Korson's personal touch was the key to the secret of the
riches he was able to delve up from the hearts and memories of at
least two generations of coal miners, young and old.
—Gerhard Heilfurth[1]

The period of the 1960s was for Korson a bittersweet time. To be
sure, he enjoyed the public recognition that came to him. His
name was chosen for inclusion in the *Dictionary of International
Biography.* He was elected as Life Fellow of the International
Institute of Arts and Letters. His two major books, *Minstrels* and
Coal Dust, were reprinted in affordable editions and gave him a
new generation of readers. He was celebrated in reviews and
lionized on his visits to Wilkes-Barre, where he arranged to donate
his papers to King's College. He had time to complete projects that
he had set aside for years. For example, in 1965 he finally brought
out an album of bituminous miners' songs, which both his wife and
Archie Green had been urging him to do for years. He also was
able to publish an expanded case study of an old song he had first
collected in the 1920s, "My Sweetheart's The Mule in The Mines."
The 1960s also gave Korson the opportunity to develop further his
ideas on the value of the union movement to American society. His
long years of advocacy of the United Mine Workers of America
gave him instant recognition and ready access to union material.
There were also the private pleasures of quiet moments spent in
his study transcribing his field recordings.

At the same time the 1960s held for Korson some painful
experiences. He was hospitalized for angina pectoris twice, once in
1963 and again in 1966. And Korson saw his old miner friends

Daniel Walsh, described in *Minstrels of the Mine Patch* as "a veteran miner himself, gifted with a rich though uncultivated tenor voice, he puts so much heart into his singing that even the most callous cannot resist being moved." *Photo courtesy George Korson Folklore Archive*

---

gradually dying, one by one. Tall, lanky Daniel Walsh of Centralia died in 1962. Then the gifted poet William Keating of Pottsville died in 1964. Walsh left behind the memory of singing "The Old Miner's Refrain" for Korson at Centralia, Pennsylvania, in 1946:

> Where are the boys that worked with me in the breaker long ago?
> There are many of them now have gone to rest;
> Their cares of life are over and they've left this world of woe;
> And their spirits now are roaming with the blest.[2]

One of the most meaningful gestures of recognition for Korson was his election as a Fellow of the American Folklore Society. In the late 1950s a small group of prominent folklorists including Francis L. Utley, Wayland D. Hand, and Herbert Halpert decided that they ought to create some way of honoring the senior folklore researchers who had done outstanding work. Later they were formally named as a committee by the American Folklore Society. Among the earliest nominees, ardently backed by Herbert Halpert, was George Korson. It was a natural choice. Years later I asked Professor Hand about the committee's decision. He told me, "There was never any question about his entrance on the basis of his field work . . . it was a sort of foreordained spot that came to him without any question."[3] Finally on December 21, 1960, it was made official: MacEdward Leach as secretary-treasurer announced that Korson had been elected as a Fellow of the American Folklore Society.[4]

On the heels of this honor came another: the University of Chicago Folklore Prize for Korson's book *Black Rock*. The announcement was made by George J. Metcalf, chairman of the Department of Germanic Languages and Literature, on June 22, 1961.[5] Probably this recognition was extended because of the proved worth of all of Korson's work, rather than for the particular merits of *Black Rock*. Indeed established practice in prize politics clearly invites such an interpretation in this case. In no way does this question the integrity of the committee. Instead it is a reflection on the slow process of formal recognition characteristic of academe in general and folklore in particular.

Over the years Korson had built up a tremendous admiration for John L. Lewis. There were two reasons for this admiration, one practical and the other ideological. Practically, Korson felt that Lewis had been wise in not standing in the way of mechanization, which gave the coal industry a chance to compete with oil and natural gas. Intellectually, Korson believed that vigorous unionism resulted in a fair division of the spoils of capitalism and helped to avoid Marxism in America.[6] The respect between the two men was mutual. Lewis, himself an avid reader, was one of Korson's earliest admirers and supporters.

In view of this long relationship it is not surprising that Korson's brother-in-law, M. Hughes Miller, president of the Bobbs-Merrill Publishing Company, approached him to do a book on John L. Lewis. It was to be included in the series "Childhood of Famous Americans."[7] The series numbered over 100 titles, but John L. Lewis was the first labor leader to be chosen. It was natural that Bobbs-Merrill approach Korson, not only because of his family ties with the firm and his first-hand knowledge of Lewis, but also because of Korson's commitment to education. This was to be his third juvenile book, following in the path of *Black Land* (1941) and *The Child's Book of Folklore* (1947). One problem in writing the Lewis book was that the rules and regulations for the format of the series were strict.[8] But as a professional writer Korson regarded this as a challenge rather than as an annoyance.

An immediate problem that Korson faced in carrying out this assignment was Lewis's consistent refusal to reminisce about his career. After his retirement in 1960 from the presidency of the United Mine Workers of America, Lewis, then eighty years old, received many appeals from large universities to deposit his papers with them. He refused them all. No living American up until that time was offered more money for his memoirs by book and magazine publishers than John L. Lewis; one publisher is even said to have offered $250,000.[9] Unfortunately for Korson, there was hardly anything in print about Lewis's childhood. In a letter to M. Hughes Miller, Korson explained just how desperate the situation was: "Throughout the years, a high official of the organization, who is close to Lewis and a good friend of mine, has kept a file of Lewis's references to his childhood memories, but it is pretty thin. I have just obtained a verifax copy of every paper in it."[10]

Aware of Lewis's great reluctance to talk about himself, Korson realized that he could not go to him directly and risk a flat refusal to cooperate. Therefore he adopted an indirect approach by contacting Lewis's brother Denny. Denny approached his famous brother, who responded in a letter to Korson: "Bobbs-Merrill can, of course, publish any book it wishes. I would, however, prefer to have them do it on their own responsibility. I dislike greatly to talk about myself and do not think I could fittingly contribute anything in relation to my boyhood days." In spite of this rebuff the letter then went on graciously to congratulate Korson for the contribution he had made to the "historical romance of the coal industry."[11] Although on the surface the letter was not encouraging, Korson's friends within the UMWA assured him that this was indeed a friendly letter and that he could write a Lewis volume without interference, though the entire work would have to be unofficial. On the basis of this advice Korson decided to go ahead with the project.

Given Korson's close knowledge of Lewis and a dash of creative imagination, he probably could have written this juvenile work with dispatch. Instead he did a good deal of solid research for it. Korson scoured old newspapers in Lewis's hometown of Lucas, Iowa. He interviewed members of Lewis's family, including his brother Denny Lewis of Washington, D.C., president of the union's District 50. Korson also interviewed another brother, Howard Lewis, who was mayor of Benton, Illinois, as well as two sisters, Sarah Lewis Collins in Kansas City, Missouri, and Hattie Lewis in Springfield, Illinois. The trip to the Midwest involved a calculated risk to Korson's health, but he knew from experience that letters with questions would not elicit information as effectively as personal interviews. As a result of this research, the manuscript was based largely on original and fresh material, not a rehash of old stories already in print. [12]

Korson was proud of his finished manuscript. Like other books in the series, the subject's early life was given expanded treatment, and his adult accomplishments were telescoped into a few pages at the end. John's Welsh coal-mining family was presented in detail, along with an account of his struggle to get an education.

Korson had fully expected the little book to join the "Childhood of Famous Americans" series in 1962 or 1963. Then in April of 1963 a problem developed. The company, it seemed, had a policy of restricting books in the series to "persons no longer living." [13] Korson was shocked. He had known of the policy, but he had been led to believe that the company had waived its policy, because it gave him a contract knowing that Lewis was still living. The company offered to publish the book as an independent trade juvenile biography rather than as a title in the series. Korson countered with the suggestion that the company hold the completed manuscript until after Lewis's death. It is an irony of history that Korson was in his sixties and Lewis was in his eighties; nonetheless, Lewis outlived Korson. The book, *John L. Lewis, Young Militant Labor Leader*, was not published until 1970. Sadly, Korson never saw it in published form.

When Korson left the Red Cross he vowed not to drain off his energies in journalism but instead to focus all his efforts on folklore. But in the early 1960s, after making a vigorous effort to complete *Black Rock* and the Lewis biography, Korson never again mustered up the stamina to take on a major book project. Because of his health problems Korson needed to pursue a low-key life-style. In 1961 he began freelancing as a newspaperman and magazine writer. In this capacity he acted as a Washington correspondent for a small string of national trade papers. [14] Undoubtedly this kind of journalistic work interfered with his real interests, such as the Lewis book and the album of bituminous miners' songs, but economic necessity continued to push Korson into a certain amount of "meat and potatoes" writing. The folklore projects simply had to await his free time.

In 1962 Korson took a temporary job as a consultant with the Bureau of Mines in the Department of the Interior.[15] Then as now, the bureau put out many publications, but except for news releases, they were all of a technical nature. Korson was called in to prepare "a booklet or a pamphlet that would tell about the work, philosophy and accomplishments of the Bureau since it came into existence more than half a century ago, and also project its future program."[16] Naturally the bureau expected such a pamphlet to be simply written and readable so as to reach a wide audience. As it turned out, it was a job that sounded easy at first but presented special challenges. Since Korson had to digest a great deal of technical information and then present it in an understandable way, he found it a difficult assignment.

Meanwhile the obituaries from Pottsville piled up on Korson's desk. In August of 1962 Korson learned of the death of Daniel Walsh, who had once sung the popular stage song "Down in a Coal Mine" for Korson and Melvin LeMon back in the 1930s.[17] It seemed to be a time of troubles. In 1963 Korson was hospitalized for angina pectoris. He had to take about a half dozen medications a day, and go to a laboratory every other week for blood tests.[18] While Korson was in the hospital recovering and trying to rest, he was stunned by the news of President John F. Kennedy's assassination in Dallas. Overwhelmed with emotion, Korson wrote to his brother Selig, a physician in Iowa: "Washington was deep in sorrow following the murder of President Kennedy. You must have watched the events on your TV. Not in many years were we as depressed as during those weeks of mourning."[19]

Never one to brood, Korson in 1964 seemed to snap back. In October of that year he was a featured speaker at the annual meeting of the Pennsylvania Historical Association in Wilkes-Barre. Professor Edwin B. Bronner of Haverford College was in charge of the program, and he came up with a double bill most appropriate for Wilkes-Barre because it featured two native sons. The first speaker was Professor Harold E. Dickson of Penn State, who gave an illustrated lecture on Pennsylvania painters, emphasizing George Catlin. The second speaker was George Korson, who presented five recorded songs from his album *Songs and Ballads of the Anthracite Miners.*

Speaking at the old familiar Hotel Sterling that crisp October evening, Korson opened his remarks with an acknowledgment of the symbolism involved in his return to Wilkes-Barre:

> It is my good fortune to be in Wilkes-Barre, city of my boyhood dreams, the city of many memories.
>
> More important, it is a richly historic city, with its roots going back to the American Revolution and even earlier in history.
>
> This year marks the 40th anniversary of my first contact with anthracite miners' folklore. Although I began my field researches in Schuylkill County, I have, by no means, overlooked Luzerne County.
>
> I made my first ballad-hunting trip in the Wyoming Valley in the spring of 1925. Throughout the years I returned many times to interview informants, to collect folklore, and to check historical facts in the Wyoming Historical and Geological Society and the Osterhout Public Library.[20]

Being featured as a keynote speaker before the Pennsylvania Historical Association was undeniably a form of recognition of Korson's accomplishment. But the year 1964 brought an even more significant recognition—the reprinting of *Minstrels of the Mine Patch.* This reprinting brought Korson a new generation of readers. The project was the idea of Dr. Kenneth S. Goldstein, founder of Folklore Associates, which had been created to reprint and distribute distinguished books of folklore that had been out of print for many years and for which there was still a demand. Goldstein was primarily interested in books that had stood the test of time. As a rare-book dealer since the 1940s, Goldstein knew what prices people were willing to pay. He had noted that there was a constant demand for books like *Minstrels of the Mine Patch,* even at a rate several times the original list price. For a variety of reasons, including a political interest in organized labor as well as a personal friendship with Korson through membership in the Pennsylvania Folklore Society, Goldstein decided to approach Korson.[21]

At first Korson's literary agent was cool to the idea of Folklore Associates taking on the project. However, Korson wrote a letter to his agent endorsing the Goldstein proposal:

> For your information, Dr. Goldstein is a rare combination of scholar

and businessman in the folklore field. He performs a useful service. For many years he has run a mail order folklore book business, and he has recorded, edited, and issued many commercial albums of folk songs . . . He has already brought out many important books in this field, including a five-volume set of the Child ballads, a folklore classic. Apparently he has good sales and is filling a need.[22]

When the book came out in 1964, it appeared with a dedication to Edith Patterson and a new fourteen-page foreword by Archie Green. Korson proudly referred to it as the "third edition" of *Minstrels,* since it had been published in 1938 and had undergone a second printing (without revision) in 1943.[23] The foreword by Green was especially important, since it represented both the first attempt at presenting a retrospective biographical sketch of Korson's life and the first serious extended essay presenting Korson's contributions to American intellectual life. Green identified all of the central questions—the dichotomy between rural and industrial lore, the prior neglect of industrial lore, and most important, union support of Korson's work.[24]

One melancholy event marred the bright triumphs of 1964. In May of that year Korson visited Bill Keating at the Veterans Administration Hospital in Wilkes-Barre. Korson found him in good spirits, but he later wrote Edith Patterson that "he was a shell of the old Bill Keating."[25] Nonetheless, Keating not only remembered Korson but was enthusiastic at the sight of him. Keating told Korson to get out his pencil and paper, since he had a dozen songs in his head that he wanted to sing. Keating was anxious to go home, but his doctor would not discharge him, believing that his days were numbered. Indeed by December of 1964 Keating was dead. In sorrow Korson wrote to Edith Patterson: "Everytime one of these old miners of mine passes on I am saddened. They were part of my life, as you are . . . Keating was a natural folk minstrel and with the proper education he might have gone far as a song writer. I believe that his song, 'Down, Down, Down' will live long."[26]

In 1965 Korson had the satisfaction of seeing *Coal Dust on the Fiddle* reissued by Folklore Associates. This time Kenneth Goldstein asked John Greenway to write the foreword. At the time Greenway was serving as associate professor of anthropology at the University of Colorado and as editor of the *Journal of American Folklore.* Greenway was a logical choice, since he also had studied the songs of the coal industry. In his fourteen-page foreword,

Greenway brought the story of bituminous mining up to date. It was a sad account of mechanization and severe decrease in the number of employed miners. Because Archie Green had presented biographical material and a discussion of Korson's contributions to folkloristics just the year before, Greenway took an entirely different approach. As a cultural determinist, Greenway tried to show the history of coal mining in the context of the evolution of American civilization. Greenway's point of view was interesting, but not entirely successful because the space available for the foreword did not permit him to develop his ideas fully.

Ever since the 1947 release of Korson's Library of Congress record album *Songs and Ballads of the Anthracite Miners,* all of his supporters had been waiting for the obvious next step, a disc for the bituminous miners. Korson kept putting his friends off, saying that he was busy working on a book. Of course, one book always led to another, and the record album continued to be delayed. With the 1960 publication of *Black Rock,* Korson began to run out of believable excuses. In a letter of 1960 Archie Green gave Korson a gentle nudge: "Now don't forget, George, as soon as the book is out of the way you *must* issue a 12″ record of Bituminous Miners' Songs. Do not delay!"[27]

Still Korson stalled. Basically he believed that books were more important than records, but Archie Green had a long memory. Again in 1961 Green prodded Korson: "Now, George, I close with a reminder to you. You said, long ago, that when you finished the book you'd start on an LC album of Bituminous Songs as a companion to the early album. We all want you to get one out!"[28]

Under this constant pressure from both Archie Green and his wife Rae, Korson gave in and produced *Songs and Ballads of the Bituminous Miners* in 1965. The most striking thing about this album in comparison with the earlier album of anthracite songs is the introduction of authentic instrumental accompaniment. In the earlier album not a single singer used any instrumentation. Several singers on the bituminous songs album used the guitar to second the voice. Though the songs were still simple and narrative, the plucking and twanging of the guitar helped to fill them out, to add an extra dimension to the distinctive, high-pitched, wailing, untrained Appalachian style.[29] To some this album with its hillbilly and blues character must have seemed a quaint anachronism, coming out in 1965 when rock music was the popular style. There

The Korsons review a manuscript around 1960.
Photo courtesy George Korson Folklore Archive

---

was a vivid contrast between the bituminous miners, rooted in places like Harlan County and committed to the United Mine Workers, and the nihilistic and alienated young singers in rock bands in the big cities.

Still the sound of the bituminous miners seems somehow more familiar than the sound of the anthracite miners on their album, perhaps because hillbilly music is akin to the Nashville sound of country music, whereas the Celtic sound of the anthracite album bears little relation to anything on radio or disc of today. Though the bituminous album seems more contemporary than the anthracite one, it is still an archival album rather than a polished, commercial record. In this respect it is like other Library of Congress albums. Dr. Harold Spivacke, chief of the Music Division, once said of the archive's releases: "I really think our kind of recordings are not commercially feasible. Our function is to be the pioneer."[30] This sentiment was echoed by Rae Korson, head of the archive, who said: "This is social history. We don't try to compete with the hi-fi and stereo recordings, however."[31]

The 1965 album included seventeen songs and one duet, "Payday at the Mine," played on fiddle, with guitar, by Charles Underwood at Price Hill, West Virginia, in 1940. The time span for the bituminous songs album runs from "Two Cent Coal" of 1876 to

"Harlan County Blues" of 1937. This sixty-one-year period was marked by bitter labor-management disputes in the bituminous coal fields. While all material on the album was industrial, six pieces have overt connections with the union movement: "The Coal Loading Machine," "Sprinkle Coal Dust on My Grave," "That Little Lump of Coal," "Harlan County Blues," "This What the Union Done," and "We Done Quit."[32] This heavy emphasis on union material is not surprising in view of the intense loyalty that miners felt for their union and in view of Korson's commitment to unionism as a means of preserving the corporate-liberal state. For the reader who is familiar with Korson's *Coal Dust on the Fiddle*, listening to the bituminous miners album is especially rewarding because it brings some of the fine old songs to life.

Events in the history of bituminous coal mining are usually marked in prose and picture, not often in sound. Yet American bituminous coal miners do have a rich heritage of songs reflecting both their hopes and sorrows.[33] Thus it must have been gratifying for Korson when his album received a number of sympathetic reviews. For example, Dave Wilson, writing in *The Broadside*, said of Korson's album: "Not only is this a valuable musical and social document, but it is an aesthetically pleasing addition to the record collection of anyone who appreciates traditional American music."[34] About a month later Robert Shelton writing in *The New York Times* said: "This fascinating collection tells in melody and lyrics much about the mining life and much about a major battleground where the war on poverty is being waged."[35]

All of this praise was certainly well-deserved. Most reviewers were content to applaud Korson's success as a collector, to cite a few of their favorite examples, and to commend the Library of Congress for a worthwhile project. One review, however, stands out because of its thoughtful criticism. Archie Green, writing in *Ethnomusicology*, raised two key points. The first objection deals with the omission of references to commercial records:

> Like most Library of Congress album brochure writers, Korson does not employ any discographical references to commercial records, and hence scholars are denied needed tools. Not only did race and hillbilly Artist and Repertoire men (record company scouts) parallel Korson in the field, but in recent years Merle Travis, Mike Seeger, Pete Seeger, A. L. Lloyd, Ewan McColl, Ian Campbell, and other singers have recorded important mining pieces complementary to

Korson's work. Only two comparative items need to be cited to underscore a shortcoming in the brochures: L 16, "A Celebrated Workingman," cf. "The Celebrated Working Man" by A. L. Lloyd on *The Iron Muse* (Topic 12 T 86); L 60, "The Dying Mine Brakeman," cf. "The Reckless Motorman" by Sarah and Maybelle Carter on *More Favorites by the Carter Family* (Decca DL 4557).[36]

The second, and potentially more serious, objection deals with the fact that the headnotes seem to deal with the songs as *texts* without reference to musical qualities:

Korson's notes for L 16 are restricted to texts and headnotes condensed from *Minstrels of the Mine Patch*. The L 60 brochure is similarly restricted to *Coal Dust on the Fiddle*. However, a prefatory statement does sketch the rise of song in pre-automated bituminous folk culture. Beyond a straightforward assertion that L 60's "songs have historical as well as intrinsic cultural value" Korson nowhere states that the album itself has any special significance apart from its implied supplementary role to his books.[37]

Green's second objection deserves amplification. Indeed the brochure that accompanies the bituminous album is astounding for some of the things left unsaid. It is almost as if Korson never listened to the tapes in preparing the notes, but instead confined his efforts to a reading of the transcripts. To be sure, many matters of text-tune fit are highly complex and challenge even the abilities of the specialist. Nonetheless, a casual playing of the album should yield some noteworthy observations on its musical properties.

On the first side we find "The Dying Mine Brakeman" (A5) sung with guitar by Orville J. Jenks at Welch, West Virginia, in 1940. Green has pointed out that no mention is made in the headnotes of a parallel song, "The Reckless Motorman," which was available on a Carter Family commercial record. Also not discussed in the headnotes is the simplicity of the tune, based totally on two chords, or the overall sound of the song resembling a cowboy song from the country-western tradition, rather than the gospel tradition that characterizes many of the other songs on the album.

A second example is "The Coal Loading Machine" (A6), sung by the Evening Breezes Sextet of Vivian, West Virginia, at Welch, West Virginia, in 1940. Though the sound of this song is totally different from all others on the album, no discussion is offered in the brief headnote. It might have been pointed out, for instance, that since this group was a polished sextet, the resulting sound is highly rehearsed, almost resembling a studio performance. The tune here is reminiscent of "She'll be Coming 'round the Mountain."

A third example is "Sprinkle Coal Dust On My Grave" (A7), sung with guitar by Orville J. Jenks at Welch, West Virginia, in 1940. It was the story of an old miner unjustly fired who asks his friends to sprinkle coal dust, rather than flowers, over his grave. Surprisingly, the brochure headnotes make no mention of the fact that the tune is that of "The Little Log Cabin in the Lane," a very common one.

A fourth example is "Coal Diggin' Blues" (B2), sung with guitar by Jerrel Stanley at Braeholm, West Virginia, in 1940. No discussion was offered in the brochure concerning the yodel, the switch from ordinary voice to falsetto and back again (which was probably picked up from the Jimmy Rodgers records popular in the early 1930s). Again no discussion was offered here about the potential interplay between folksong and commercial discs, though the evidence for such interaction was unmistakable. Likewise no mention was made of the fact that it was a straight black twelve-bar blues song in a white version.

A last example is "Payday at the Mine" (B6). The brochure simply gives the facts concerning collection in a seventeen-word description: "Played on fiddle, with guitar, by Charles Underwood, at Pinehill, West Virginia, 1940. Recorded by George Korson." Not discussed was the use of the fiddle to imitate other sounds, specifically a railroad train. This playful upbeat use of the fiddle gives the song a sort of clownish ending.[38]

I suspect that Korson as an old newspaperman was committed to print as the prime medium of communication. Though he certainly loved the miners and was dedicated to the UMWA, it seems evident that he really had little taste for their *music.* Basically it was the narrative aspect of the song that caught his interest, not the tune. Korson viewed the music as simply a vehicle to get the message of the song across. He was interested in putting the songs and stories that he collected into the total context of the folk culture of the bituminous miner. He was not interested in folk music per se, but in telling the miners' story to the world.

Generally, the bituminous album is more musical than the anthracite album. The very first song on the bituminous album is sung a cappella by G. C. Gartin at Braeholm, West Virginia, in

1940. Even without instrumentation it sounds more musical than the anthracite songs, perhaps because it is in the southern gospel-country tradition:

> The miner is gone
> We'll see him no more,
> God be with the miner
> Wherever he goes.
> And may he be ready
> Thy call to obey,
> And looking to Jesus
> The only true way.

In its overt reference to Jesus the song is very hymnlike. In fact the whole song resembles a prayer, as seen clearly in the third stanza: "God be with the miners,/Protect them from harm/And shield him from danger/With thy dear strong arm."

One possible explanation for the bituminous album sounding "more musical" than the anthracite album lies in the fact that Korson had more to choose from in assembling the bituminous one. All of the anthracite album was recorded in northeastern Pennsylvania. By way of contrast, the bituminous album represents Alabama, Kentucky, Ohio, and West Virginia, as well as Pennsylvania. By simply having a larger sample of songs to choose from, Korson could favor those with more musical properties. It may simply be a matter of more miles, more states, more contacts, more informants, more money, and more support. All of this combined to give Korson a broader base, which then enabled him to be more selective on the album.

Tempting as this hypothesis is, I think it misses a key distinction, the cultural differences between the folk culture of the anthracite miner and the folk culture of the bituminous miner. To describe how these cultural differences are reflected in the tone quality of the music is difficult. One of the difficulties is that the vocabulary for the description of tone qualities tends to consist of pejorative terms. With this qualification in mind, the anthracite music may be placed in an Anglo-Celtic tradition—tight, flat, strained, rasping, squeaking, and pinched; the bituminous music is in a southern mountains tradition, richly influenced by black blues and white gospel. The music of the bituminous miners may not necessarily be more musical in an absolute sense, but we tend to perceive it as more euphonious because the folk music that is popular today comes out of a southern tradition. Of course, it is important to remember that these two groups of singers were aiming at *different* tone qualities: the anthracite miners are singing in a tradition where the verbal meaning is more important than the musical meaning; they are singing in the old traditional manner of British ballad singers. It is easier for most of us to understand the even-toned quality of the bituminous album, and one part of the explanation may be that southern white gospel music has a strong black influence. This was noticed early by one of Korson's reviewers:

> Then listen to George Davis of Glomawr, Kentucky, sing his own composition "Harlan County Blues." I'm left wondering how a white mineworker could sound so much like a lot of Leadbelly I have heard before. George Korson, who recorded most of the songs on the album, traces the development of much of the music found among the mineworkers and shows how Negro miners created songs which were not only borrowed by White miners, but which also influenced musical styles among the miners.[39]

After wrapping up the bituminous album, Korson had hoped that he might be able to slow down in 1965. It did not work out that way. He was approached by Justin McCarthy of the *United Mine Workers Journal* with a proposal for a new project. The year 1965 represented the seventy-fifth anniversary of the founding of the UMWA and a suitable occasion for writing a history of the organization. McCarthy proposed that Korson publish the history serially in the *United Mine Workers Journal* with the eventual idea of making the series into a book.[40] To help with the project Korson enlisted the aid of Judith Mikeal Gross. Born and raised in West Virginia, she was the daughter of a coal miner. Her qualifications included a master's degree with a thesis on the nineteenth-century labor organizer Mother Jones.[41]

The important thing about this venture was not that Korson wrote a history of the United Mine Workers but that the union asked him to do it. The senior editors of the *UMWJ*, Justin McCarthy and Rex Lauck, knew quite well that a history of the union would not simply be a "chronicle" or set of all the singular facts related to the union. Instead it would have to be a "narrative" or "interpretation," which would include the chronicle of events within a causal framework. For these union officials to trust Korson with such a delicate and sensitive assignment meant nothing less than that they trusted him completely. Their jobs could be at stake if, for example, the history were offensive to John L. Lewis. Their trust was based on Korson's proven pro-union position developed in his writings of over forty years.

Though Korson's history did win the endorsement of the union, it suffered from some of the same faults that plagued the first nine chapters of *Black Rock*. The history was essentially a library project, a research project. This had never been Korson's forte. Away from the stimulus of field work, the history lacks the colorful imagery and the human interest that Korson handled so well in his earlier years. The project failed to excite him, and unfortunately this shortcoming showed up in his writing.

Korson died before he was able to finish the history and prepare the manuscript for publication as a book. But even if he had lived there would have been serious problems with the project. One problem, which could have been easily worked out, was that the pieces were written for installment publication; that fact would have to be disguised with some editing and smoother transitions. But there was a more serious problem. The bulk of what Korson wrote was a history of the union under John L. Lewis. However, in a book-length treatment Korson would have been obliged to go back to the beginnings of the union and trace its early history. After establishing this framework, Korson could then have shown the many years of Lewis's administration in proper perspective.[42] The main problem was that Korson was trapped by his own success in dealing with the UMWA. His history was too much an "official" history, as one prospective publisher politely explained in a letter of rejection:

> I have just finished reading the few chapters of your *History of the United Mine Workers* which you were good enough to send me a bit over two weeks ago. The book, I suspect, will be a tough one to sell to the general public, and, for this reason, I have a strong hunch that it won't be right for us. The approach, so far, seems to be appropriate to the membership of the union but not likely to be fitting to the uninformed reader. What you have is primarily a "company" history. If my judgment is correct, it's not a book for us. I wish it were such that we could do it for I would really love to work with you on it.[43]

In 1965 some of Korson's frustration in not readily finding a publisher for his union history was offset by the satisfaction of presenting his complete collection of tapes, manuscripts, books, photographs, and letters to King's College in Wilkes-Barre. The beginning of the story of that donation goes back a few years earlier. One day, the story goes, George Korson walked in off the street to the library of King's College, which had been established after World War II by the Holy Cross Fathers in response to the postwar demand for college education among veterans. As a native son of Wilkes-Barre, Korson was naturally curious to see what the new college was like. And as an author, Korson was curious to see what the new college library stocked. Without introducing himself, Korson inquired of Mary Barrett, the librarian, what they had in the way of folklore books. Miss Barrett replied apologetically, "Well, to tell the truth, we don't have many folklore books, but we do have everything ever written by George Korson. He's my favorite folklorist!"[44] Naturally, this kind of enthusiasm was a factor when it came time for Korson to decide where to leave his personal papers, letters, and manuscripts.

In the 1960s several libraries had expressed interest in the Korson papers, but three stood out as the strongest prospects: the Library of Congress, Penn State, and King's College. Rae Korson advised against the Library of Congress. She doubted that the staff would go to the trouble of sorting, arranging, and cataloging the collection. Meanwhile two professors at Penn State, Alfred Buffington and Maurice Mook, urged the university librarian there, Ralph W. McComb, to negotiate with Korson. McComb had a special interest in manuscripts and rare books, and he did pursue the matter. However, Korson finally decided to give the papers to King's College.

The decision was facilitated by the efforts of Charles McCarthy, a prominent local historian and a mutual friend of both Mary Barrett and George Korson. In 1964 McCarthy, knowing of Korson's engagement to speak before the Wyoming Historical and Geological Society in Wilkes-Barre, was active in setting up a luncheon invitation for George Korson to meet with King's College officials.[45] Mary Barrett handled the luncheon arrangements. The affair was held at the Hotel Sterling in downtown Wilkes-Barre. Barrett invited Korson's old newspaper colleagues, Korson family members still living in town, and Con Carbon's niece, Sherin

Morrison. For entertainment, a group from the King's College Glee Club dressed in miner's outfits with lunch buckets sang some of the songs Korson had collected years earlier.

All of this attention must have helped swing the decision to give the papers to King's College. Still it took a full year before Korson made his final decision. During that period, he was in weekly telephone contact with Mary Barrett, talking over old times and conducting low-key negotiations about the papers.[46] Korson felt that, since his material had come out of the anthracite region originally, it was appropriate to return his things to the region. In making the decision Korson said, "I feel strongly that this collection belongs in the Wyoming Valley because I believe scholars who will use the collection will better understand the music and legends in the area where they were created."[47] The decision was made easier by his knowledge of the library's enthusiasm for his work and the college's promise to take the best care of it in the future.[48]

By September of 1965 all of the negotiations with King's College had been completed, and plans went ahead to make a formal announcement of the gift. Basically the college agreed that on the top floor of the new library, then in the planning stage, a separate room would be set aside and identified as "The George Korson Folklore Archive." There might be other rooms with the papers of other notable persons, but Korson's collection was to be separate. Korson agreed to give the college all his papers. In accepting the gift, the Reverend Lane D. Kilburn, C.S.C., said:

> King's College is honored to be the recipient of this outstanding collection which will attract historians, folklorists, and sociologists from the entire nation. In addition it will serve in itself an enrichment of local history resources. Korson could not have chosen a better time for making his presentation since the college is in the planning stages of a new library and will be able to include in its plans quarters for The George Korson Folklore Collection. The college is grateful to Miss Mary I. Barrett, librarian, for her devoted efforts to enrich the community through the library holdings. It was largely a result of her sensitivity and appreciation in the area of local history and development that this acquisition was made possible. King's College will always be deeply indebted to Mr. Korson and grateful to him. The permanence of the collection will serve as a timeless memorial of his scholarly work.[49]

Once the decision was made to give his research materials to

Korson presents his records of a life's work—books, periodicals, discs, tapes, and papers—to King's College in 1965. Receiving the gift are Rev. Lane D. Kilburn, CSC, college president, and Mary Barrett, the college librarian who conceived the idea of The George Korson Folklore Archive. *King's College photo, courtesy George Korson Folklore Archive*

the library of King's College, Korson spent considerable time happily engaged in sorting out books and papers. He looked forward to continuing his research and writing, while directing the management and arrangement of his material to make it available for subsequent scholars. The library meanwhile agreed to set aside a private study for him to carry out his work. Sadly, Korson himself never finished the job of putting all these papers in good order. After his death in 1967, Rae Korson continued the sifting and sorting; and later the project was wrapped up by Judith Tierney, Special Collections Librarian, who spent over a year patiently assembling everything.

In retrospect, it seems to have been a wise decision for Korson to have left his papers to King's College. Larger and more prestigious institutions, such as the Library of Congress, might have accepted Korson's papers, but it is doubtful that they would have gone to the same trouble in sorting, arranging, and cataloging the collection. Thus the collection is currently in a very accessible and useful state.

Korson's final contribution to folklore was an article entitled "My Sweetheart's the Mule in the Mines," which appeared in *Two*

Penny Ballads and Four Dollar Whiskey, a hard-bound annual put
out by the Pennsylvania Folklore Society. The annual was edited
by Kenneth S. Goldstein and Robert H. Byington and published
by Folklore Associates in 1966. Appropriately, Korson's article took
a retrospective look at his early collecting days. Planning for the
annual went back to 1963, when members of the Pennsylvania
Folklore Society first contemplated an annual patterned along the
model set by the Texas Folklore Society. Planning moved along
when Kenneth Goldstein, on behalf of Folklore Associates, offered
to underwrite the project.

Though the title "My Sweetheart's the Mule in the Mines"
would suggest that the article was a case study of a single folk song,
the subtitle for the article, "Memoirs of Tom and Maggie Hill,"
comes closer to an accurate description. The article developed
Korson's role as a collector of folklore, with special attention to a
single informant, Tom Hill of the Schuylkill Valley, who lived at
Tucker Hill, a mine patch that was part of the nearby Silver Creek
Colliery. Korson first met Tom Hill in 1924, and over the years he
found Hill to be an excellent informant on two topics, the Molly
Maguires and mine mules.

The rhetorical device of building the article around a single
informant and his family was a clever response to the assignment
Korson had been given. The editors wanted a piece that would be
personal and anecdotal. In his original letter of instructions Robert
Byington wrote to Korson:

> What we would like is an article of personal reminiscence about your
> many and varied experiences as a collector of Pennsylvania lore, the
> more anecdotal and even sentimental, the better. You have covered
> a lot of Commonwealth ground over the years, George, and it stands
> to reason that the ground was studded with interesting people and
> interesting experiences. We are hoping it will not be too much
> trouble for you to recollect some of them for us.[50]

It is fortunate for us that Byington framed his request in these
terms. Korson was basically a modest man and had said little about
his early collecting experiences. In fact, Korson left behind very
little material of an autobiographical nature. There are no
memoirs, diaries, or even field journals. But in this case Byington
had specifically asked for a "personal reminiscence." Since Korson
was a professional writer with a lifetime of experience in giving
editors what they asked for, he complied. The article is especially

helpful in setting out Korson's account of his early newspaper experience in the Schuylkill Valley:

> Between September of 1923 and the fall of 1925 I was on the staff of the Pottsville *Republican* with a unique assignment. My job was to circulate among the mining families of the Schuylkill Valley to stimulate their interest in becoming steady readers of my newspaper. Up to then, in their isolation, they had managed to get along without reading any papers. I won them over by running their names in news stories and treating them with respect. My wakeful hours were spent in the valley garnering news. I observed the mining folk under a variety of circumstances—at wakes and weddings, at dances and union meetings, at baseball games and pigeon shoots—and by visiting miners' homes. I covered the deputy coroner's inquests. His duty was to fix responsibility for deaths of workers in Schuylkill Valley mine accidents. The deputy coroner held his inquests evenings in the back of his speak-easy (this was still Prohibition). I learned much about the mining craft from listening to the testimony. Many of the witnesses were elderly. After inquests I would linger to listen to their reminiscences and anecdotes.[51]

This passage underscores Korson's *participation* in the daily activities of the community. Working as a newspaperman allayed suspicion, established rapport, and provided him a natural role in the life of the community.[52]

Turning from this general description of his early collecting experience, Korson took up the case of informant Tom Hill. The most interesting theoretical point to emerge in the essay is that the folklorist benefits from maintaining rapport with an informant over a long period of time. In 1924, when Korson first interviewed Tom Hill, he obtained a single version of "My Sweetheart's the Mule in the Mines":

> My sweetheart's the mule in the mines.
> I drive her without any lines,
> On the bumper I stand,
> With my whip in my hand,
> My sweetheart's the mule in the mines.[53]

Though Korson might have suspected that what he had collected was a bowdlerized version, it was all he got that day. About nine years later Korson visited the Hill family again. He asked Tom if he could recall any additional verses of the song since their last meeting. Before Hill had a chance to respond, his grandson volunteered a new stanza:

> My sweetheart's the mule in the mines,
> I drive her without reins or lines,
> On the bumper I sit,
> I chew and I spit
> All over my sweetheart's behind. [54]

It is a classic case of the value of a follow-up interview. Of course, such a repeat visit is possible only if the collector has succeeded in establishing reliability and genuine interest in the traditions of the people. Korson's success in dealing with the Hill family over an extended period of time is almost a textbook case to illustrate a point made by Kenneth Goldstein in *A Guide to Field Workers in Folklore:* "Participation opens new avenues to understanding his informants and the community and should lead to the collection of more and better data to be used in problem solution. [55]

Korson was always loyal to Pennsylvania. At considerable risk to his own health he made the effort to attend Pennsylvania Folklore meetings in Harrisburg in the spring of 1966 and again in the spring of 1967. At one of these meetings Henry Glassie, then serving as State Folklorist of Pennsylvania, tried to express some of the debt that the folklorists of Pennsylvania owed to Korson. At the time many people felt that the folklife movement, building strength in the late 1960s, was wholly a European import grafted onto the American scene. Glassie said that this was not the case at all, that there were American antecedents for the folklife movement and that Korson's work was a prime example of this, since as early as the 1920s he had argued that folklore must be studied in the total context of the way of life of the people. Korson received this accolade with great delight and felt that it was an appropriate summing up of his contribution to folklore. [56]

In the late 1960s Korson's health grew steadily worse. His good friend Warren E. Roberts, himself a onetime heart attack victim, told me that Korson never made a good recovery. Korson was by now visibly a sick man. For example, one day Roberts and Korson were going up a flight of stairs. Roberts said by then he could have bounded up the stairs, but Korson had to go slowly, one step at a time, and to stop frequently to catch his breath. [57] Then in the fall of 1966 X-rays revealed that Korson needed a prostatectomy. Korson was mindful of the dangers involved. In December of 1966 he wrote to his sister Ann Lane: "The urologist postponed surgery because of my heart condition. However I shall have to undergo surgery some time next spring. As you know, it's not a serious operation, but the state of my heart condition adds an element of danger to it."[58]

In May of 1967 Korson had the operation and came through it without complications. Shortly after the operation he came home from the hospital to his apartment. There he began to recuperate, spending much time on the sunporch, which had been made into a room for his books. His daughter Betsy brought him a new padded chair for the sunporch. After he had been home for a few weeks, early on the morning of May 23 he felt an attack of massive pain. He was rushed to the hospital in a semiconscious state and placed at once in intensive care. This was his seventh heart attack; time had run out for George Korson at age sixty-seven. Later that morning he died.

Laudatory obituaries appeared in *The Washington Post, The Wilkes-Barre Times-Leader,* and *The New York Times.*[59] The funeral was scheduled for Friday, May 26, at Beth Israel Memorial Park in Cedar Knolls, New Jersey.

Korson's was a small funeral. On that rainy Friday afternoon at the graveside only his family and a few close friends were able to come. Rabbi Max Wasser of Bethlehem, Pennsylvania, gave a prepared eulogy. Then a truly moving thing happened. Ben Botkin stepped forward and said, "Would you mind if I say something?" No one knew that Botkin had planned to speak; he had written something on his own. In a halting voice Botkin read above the sound of the falling rain:

> George Korson, whom I've known for the past twenty-five years or more, was a great folklorist because he believed in the folk and their common humanity as well as in the lore and its fantasy and faith. He was a great collector because he collected people as well as songs and tales. George himself became something of a folk figure and a legend among the miners who were his people. And he has become something of a legend among folklorists as one who restored humanity to folklore and folklore to humanity. For this as much as for his work he will be remembered by his colleagues and his readers, who are the richer and the sweeter for the richness of his labors and the sweetness of his spirit. Now his voice is stilled, but his words will live on as part of our folk heritage.[60]

Epilogue

Coal-mines and all that is down there, the lamps in the darkness, echoes, songs, what meditations, what vast native thoughts looking through smutch'd faces . . . In them the development good—in them all themes, hints, possibilities.

—Walt Whitman[1]

Inescapably the coal industry has served as a magnet, drawing the attention of poets and painters, ecologists and regional planners, radicals and revolutionaries. Walt Whitman saw the coal miner as a fine example of the common man, the working man. Writing in the nineteenth century, Whitman celebrated the coal miner, as he did other workers, as a noble individual. Whitman encouraged independence and self-reliance. By contrast, Korson knew that as an individual a coal miner was unknown. Only collectively could he make his presence felt. Korson wrote:

> The miner understands his position well, and so is strong for organization. Bitter experience has taught him that if he has rights to preserve, or wrongs to adjust, or economic security to win, or happiness to attain, he can achieve them only as a collective unit. Hence he worships his union as a religion. A union button restores his self-respect, revives his self-confidence and gives him the feeling that he really belongs in the society of civilized human beings—a society that doubtless would shun him but for the respect it holds for his collective strength.[2]

The miner has had so many troubles—from child labor abuse to silicosis—that he has become virtually a symbol.[3] Many radical and left-wing groups have taken the miner's cause as their own. Conflicts between the UMWA and the coal operators have become so predictable and so ritualized that they seem to represent a central built-in problem of the corporate-liberal state, the conflict between labor and management. Thus the work of George Korson is inevitably seen in the spotlight of this arena. The folklore of coal miners reflects the conflicts of American industrial society. Folklorist Wayland D. Hand once put it this way: "The preeminence of the study of mining lore from the folkloristic point of view, and from purely human and social factors, is clearly established if one takes into account, as one must, considerations of capital and labor, political rights, and the rights of labor and of unionization."[4]

It seems clear that as a pioneer industrial folklorist, George Korson had to face the conflict between reform and revolution in the American corporate-liberal state. For Korson this was not an idle armchair decision. For example, in the early thirties there were bitter labor struggles in Harlan County, Kentucky. The picture was complicated by the dual-union rivalry between the UMWA and the Communist-led National Miners Union. By 1931 wages and employment had been cut so drastically that the miners were desperate. A brief strike led by the United Mine Workers fell apart. There were charges that the UMWA had "sold out" its local membership. The National Miners Union came in to fill the gap. A leading figure to emerge in this struggle was Aunt Molly Jackson, described by Richard Reuss as "midwife, ballad singer, coal miner's daughter, sister, and wife, and militant unionist."[5] She wrote and sang a number of songs describing the wretched conditions of the coal miners. One of the most moving was "Kentucky Miners Ragged Hungry Blues":

> I'm sad and weary, I got those hungry ragged blues
> I'm sad and weary, I got those hungry ragged blues
> Not a penny in my pocket to buy one thing I need to use.
>
> I woke up this morning with the worst blues I ever had in my life;
> I woke up this morning with the worst blues I ever had in my life;
> Not a bite to cook for breakfast; poor coal miner's wife . . .
>
> This mining town I live in is a dead and lonely place;
> This mining town I live in is a dead and lonely place;
> Where pity and starvation are pictured on every face.[6]

Aunt Molly Jackson's songs attracted widespread attention among left-wing intellectuals and workers all over the country. Why did Korson choose to ignore this material obviously steeped in the folkways of the southern mountains? Korson knew that folksongs were weapons, but there were limits beyond which he would not go. Folksongs in the service of the UMWA were acceptable, but "agitation-propaganda" songs in behalf of Communism he deliberately omitted. Korson knew directly the struggles and conflicts that the miners' organization went through in the 1920s and 1930s. He saw Communists as "union wreckers, aliens, and subversives."[7] Yet, like Samuel Gompers, Korson could not simply accept capitalism as the status quo. As Thorstein Veblen sought to use economics in the service of social change, so George Korson sought to use folklore in much the same way. Politically Korson was neither a radical nor a revolutionary. Instead he was a liberal-centrist reformer. Basically he believed that strong labor unions were socially desirable to balance the excesses of capitalism.

As a lifelong friend of the miners, certainly Korson was sensitive to the abuses of industrialism; but as a conventional liberal democrat, he believed that trade unions and the New Deal held the answer to the problems confronted by the miners. Among intellectuals and historians of the left today, it has become popular to judge the New Deal as a failure, to argue that the New Deal partially succeeded in coping with the Depression, but that it preserved the basic problems of the system. However, to judge Korson's political response to the problems of the 1930s by the standards of the present is manifestly unfair.

It is true that politically Korson was more of a liberal than a revolutionary. However, folkloristically Korson—despite his liberal manner and outlook—was in fact a revolutionary, although a quiet one. Folklore theory before Korson's time had a distinct rural and Anglo-American bias. Without formal education in folklore, Korson simply ignored these biases. His two great books, *Minstrels* and *Coal Dust,* dealt with both industrial lore and immigrant lore. These books represented a real shift in vision and definition. The folklore establishment was slow to accept Korson's paradigm. However, once his work was accepted, the study of American folklore would never again be the same.

The real lesson to be learned by an examination of George Korson's intellectual perception of American coal miners is that in assessing the work of any folklorist we must take into account his world view of his life and his times. We can appreciate the power of ideas and ideologies that govern the folklorist's selection of materials and his analysis of them.

A final word about George Korson the man. In trying to sum

up his personality in a single word, Henry Glassie once suggested that the best word would be "sweet."[8] Korson himself might have resisted the label, since he could be tough when he had to be. One need only recall his early days as a combat soldier or hardboiled newspaperman, but underneath all that Korson was indeed a sweet man, a man without malice. With a chubby, boyish face and elfin eyes, he was kind to everyone, with a remarkable disposition that allowed him to speak ill of no one.

Korson's ever-present smile was beguiling, since it represented a genuine love of people. The naturally gregarious Korson was never a schemer or a manipulator. People enjoyed his conversation and his company because he was both kind and honest. Though Korson never wrote an autobiography, perhaps someday a selection of his letters may be published. They span nearly his entire life and show him to be a warm and faithful friend and an earnest scholar in the pursuit of truth.

Notes

Much of the background information in this book comes from interviews with Rae Korson, George Korson's wife (Washington, D.C., February 17, 1973), Betsy Korson Glazier, their daughter (Bethlehem, Pennsylvania, August 30, 1974), and Fran Wruble, George Korson's sister (Wilkes-Barre, Pennsylvania, August 28, 1974).

Complete publishing information for all sources can be found in the Bibliography.

Preface
1. Quoted in Golden, p. 19.
2. Green, *Only a Miner*, pp. 3–31.
3. Ibid., p. 13.
4. Richard D. Altick, *Lives and Letters: A History of Literary Biography in England and America* (New York: Knopf, 1965), pp. 351–400.
5. Green, "Foreword," *Minstrels of the Mine Patch*, pp. iii–v.
6. Green, *Only a Miner*, p. 13.
7. There is one item dealing with the folklore of steel, Jacob A. Evanson, "Folk Songs of an Industrial City," in Korson, *Pennsylvania Songs and Legends*, pp. 423–66.
8. Green, *Only a Miner*, p. 23.
9. See Redfield and Yoder, "The Folklife Studies Movement."
10. New York: Praeger, 1970.
11. In this respect Korson is similar to John Dos Passos. See George J. Becker, *John Dos Passos* (New York: Frederick Ungar, 1974), p. 3.
12. Altick, p. 382.
13. Barrett to Gillespie, January 17, 1977.
14. Wyoming National Bank, p. 8.
15. Browne, pp. 7–8.
16. *Zora Neale Hurston: A Literary Biography* (Urbana: University of Illinois Press, 1977).
17. *Stith Thompson: His Life and His Role in Folklore Scholarship* (Bloomington, Ind.: Folklore Publications Group, 1978).
18. Murray G. Murphey, *Our Knowledge of the Historical Past* (New York: Bobbs-Merrill, 1973), p. 144.
19. Brom Weber, ed., *The Complete Poems and Selected Letters and Prose of Hart Crane*, Anchor Books (Garden City, N.Y.: Doubleday, 1966), p. 6.

Introduction

1. This introduction was originally presented in a somewhat shorter form at the American Folklore Society Meeting in Portland, Ore., October 31, 1974.

2. Dexter Perkins, *The American Way* (Ithaca, N.Y.: Cornell University Press, 1957), pp. 1–28.

3. Ibid., p. 137.

4. The question "Is snobbery the Achilles heel of liberalism?" was discussed at a workshop held at the 5th Annual State Convention of the New Democratic Coalition at Pittsburgh, Pa., January 20–21, 1973.

5. Howard Mumford Jones and Richard M. Ludwig, *Guide to American Literature and Its Backgrounds since 1890*, 3d ed. (Cambridge: Harvard University Press, 1964), p. 121.

6. Leach, "The Men Who Make Folklore," p. 15.

7. Ibid., pp. 22–23.

8. Green, "The Workers in the Dawn," p. 257.

9. The yeoman farmer as image and symbol is discussed in Tate, pp. 54–55.

10. Karl Lehmann, *Thomas Jefferson: American Humanist* (New York: Macmillan, 1947), p. 181.

11. Dorson, *American Folklore*, p. 75.

12. Pp. viii–ix.

13. Denisoff, p. 37.

14. P. 20.

15. Ibid., pp. 164, 166.

16. Ibid., p. 13.

17. Interview with Archie Green in Washington, D.C., November 17, 1978.

18. P. 6.

19. Reuss, pp. 161, 164.

20. Hille, p. 7 (emphasis added).

21. Reuss, p. 170.

22. Louis Hartz, *The Liberal Tradition in America* (New York: Harcourt, Brace & World, 1955), pp. 259–83.

23. "Reflections: The American Condition," *The New Yorker*, February 4, 1975, p. 59.

24. Brooks, *Toil and Trouble*, p. 101.

25. Quoted in Brooks, *Toil and Trouble*, p. 114.

26. James MacGregor Burns, *Roosevelt: The Lion and the Fox* (New York: Harcourt, Brace & World, 1956), p. 218.

27. Green, "Foreword," p. iv.

Chapter 1

1. Philip Coyle, "Good-Bye Number Three," in Korson, *Minstrels*, p. 20.

2. Some of the material in this chapter was presented in a shorter form at a lecture before the Wyoming Historical and Geological Society, Wilkes-Barre, Pa., October 17, 1974.

3. Tierney, *A Description of the Archive*, p. 3.

4. "George Korson is Third to Hold Title."

5. Charles A. McCarthy, "National Boys' Club Week Recalls Mrs. Palmer's Work," *Wilkes-Barre Record*, March 29, 1966; and Korson, *Minstrels*, pp. 94–95.

6. Korson, "History of Wyoming Valley."

7. Korson, *Black Rock.*

8. Baumann, p. 75.

9. Eckardt and Eckardt, pp. 46–57.

10. Columbia University in the City of New York, *Transcript of Record,* "George Gershon Korson," December 19, 1941.

11. Korson, *Minstrels,* p. 1.

12. This distinction has been dealt with at some length by Kenneth S. Goldstein in *A Guide for Field Workers,* p. 3. If professional folklorists are defined as "those who have been academically trained in folklore studies," then clearly Korson was not a professional. However, there is no stigma necessarily attached here to the label "amateur," especially if we accept M. A. Murray's definition of an amateur as "the self-trained" folklorist, rather than an untrained enthusiast. See Murray, p. 8. It may help clarify the matter if we consider Korson a professional writer rather than an amateur folklorist.

13. Goldstein, *A Guide for Field Workers,* pp. 4–7.

14. Korson, "Indiana Speech."

15. Goldstein, *A Guide for Field Workers,* pp. 160–73.

16. Korson, "Indiana Speech."

17. *Morristown Jerseyman,* December 17, 1926.

18. Denisoff, pp. 64–66.

19. Malcolm Cowley, *Exile's Return: A Literary Odyssey of the 1920's* (New York: Viking, 1956), pp. 48–80.

20. Robert Fulton Richards, ed., *Concise Dictionary of American Literature* (New York: Philosophical Library, 1955), entry on Sandburg, pp. 197–98.

21. *Chicago Daily News,* August 11, 1928.

22. Searle, "Announcement," *United Mine Workers Journal,* Number 1, 1926, cited in Green, "Foreword," pp. x–xi.

23. Green, "Foreword," p. ix.

24. Korson, "Indiana Speech."

25. The distinction between subsidy publishers and the vanity press is discussed at some length in Edward Uhlan, *The Rogue of Publishers' Row* (New York: Exposition Press, 1956), pp. 231–38.

26. Advertising mat for Wilkes-Barre Newspapers, September 1927, George Korson Folklore Archive.

27. *Wilkes-Barre Record,* October 10, 1927.

28. *Wilkes-Barre Times Leader,* October 6, 1930.

29. August 20, 1927.

30. Ibid.

31. December 3, 1927.

32. February 1, 1928.

33. March 7, 1928.

34. August 1928.

35. December 30, 1927.

36. Compare Korson's position with the general description of "Liberalism in America" in Dexter Perkins, *The American Way* (Ithaca, N.Y.: Cornell University Press, 1957), pp. 29–56.

37. For an extended discussion of the shock of alienation experienced by immigrant families see Handlin, pp. 259–85.

Chapter 2

1. Korson, *Minstrels*, p. 13.
2. *Allentown Chronicle and News*, April 27, October 13, and August 29, 1931.
3. Pells, p. 200.
4. Udall and Wilson, p. A5.
5. Zelda Popkin, "Folk Festivals Lure: Annual Trips Begin in May to Centres of American Arts and Music," unidentified newspaper column, Spring 1935, enclosed in a letter from Henry W. Shoemaker to George Korson, April 20, 1935.
6. John M. Pickering, son of M. J. Pickering, interview at University Park, Pa., September 22, 1978. John M. Pickering helped Sarah Gertrude Knott assemble the records of the NFFA, 1934 to 1971 (the year she retired; M. J. Pickering had died in 1954), for deposit in the Folklore & Folklife Archives, Western Kentucky University, with copies to the Folk Music Division, Library of Congress.
7. Howe and Coser, p. 263.
8. *Allentown Morning Call*, May 5, 1935.
9. Knott to Korson, April 15, 1935.
10. Shoemaker to Korson, April 20, 1935.
11. May 5, 1935.
12. "Folklore is Preserved in a Festival," *Literary Digest*, August 1, 1936, pp. 21–22.
13. Rainey to Korson, May 29, 1935.
14. Pickering to Rainey, July 10, 1935.
15. Korson to Rae Korson, September 20, 1935.
16. Korson to Rae Korson, September 30, 1935.
17. At the George Korson Folklore Archive there are thirty-nine containers with correspondence. It is interesting to note that Container 5 has correspondence from 1918 to 1934, a span of sixteen years, while Container 6 has correspondence from January to June 1935, a span of six months. The point is simply that it was apparently not until 1935 that Korson became fully aware of the historical importance of his own work.
18. "Biography of A. C. Marts," *Bucknell Alumnus*, December 1944.
19. Korson, memorandum to Marts.
20. Arnaud C. Marts to J. Warren Davis, July 7, 1936.
21. Korson, "Folk Festival News."
22. Yoder, "Twenty-Five Years."
23. Marshall McLuhan, *Understanding Media: The Extensions of Man* (New York: McGraw-Hill, 1965), pp. 7–32.
24. Pennsylvania Folk Festival, *Program*.
25. Ibid.
26. Korson, "Financial Statement."
27. The term "fakelore" was coined by Dorson in 1950. See Dorson, *American Folklore*, p. 4.
28. Korson, "Plans for the 1937 Pennsylvania Folk Festival."
29. Korson, "Folk Festival News."
30. Korson to E. C. Nagle, August 4, 1937.
31. Pennsylvania Folk Festival, *Program*.
32. Hightower to Marts, August 2, 1937.
33. Sipley to Marts, February 14, 1938.
34. Pennsylvania Folk Festival, Advertising Flyer.
35. See, for example, Sipley to Korson, March 19, 1938; and Korson to Sipley, March 21, 1938.

36. Marts to Sipley, July 5, 1938; Walter Greenway to Korson, July 25, 1938; and Phelps Soule to Korson, October 4, 1938.

37. Melvin LeMon to Eugene H. Fischer, May 8, 1936.

38. Detail on the distribution of this songbook came from an undated, unsigned, untitled memorandum apparently written by George Korson in 1938 as part of a proposal to expand folklore research at Bucknell.

39. Soule to Korson, August 11, 1937.

40. Keating to Korson, November 25, 1938.

41. Among early reviews that made favorable mention of the physical appearance of the book were those of Lewis E. Theiss, "Minstrels"; and "New Book of Miners' Songs," *Pottsville Republican*.

42. Korson, *Minstrels*, pp. 2–4.

43. Green, *Only a Miner*, p. 23.

44. Redfield, p. 4.

45. Korson, *Minstrels*, pp. 14–15.

46. Ibid., p. 11.

47. Hand, interview at Portland, Oregon, November 1, 1974.

48. Green, *Only a Miner*, p. 24.

49. Green, "Foreword," p. xii.

50. *The Nation*, December 10, 1938, p. 630.

51. Green, "Foreword," p. xii.

52. Spargo, p. 91.

53. Thomas S. Kuhn, *The Structure of Scientific Revolutions*, Phoenix Edition (Chicago: University of Chicago Press, 1962).

54. Goldstein, *A Guide for Field Workers*, p. 48.

55. Green, *Only a Miner*, p. 24.

56. Korson, *Minstrels*, p. 11.

57. Ibid., p. 299.

58. Ibid., pp. 48–53.

59. Ibid., p. 39.

60. Ibid., p. 218.

61. Brooks, *Toil and Trouble*, p. 98.

62. Green, *Only a Miner*, pp. 17–18.

63. *Minstrels*, p. 242.

64. Kennedy to Korson, September 24, 1932.

65. November 14, 1938.

66. February 7, 1939.

67. Korson, *Minstrels*, p. 242.

Chapter 3

1. Korson, *Coal Dust*, p. 77.

2. Korson, *Coal Dust*, p. xv.

3. Webb to Korson, November 16, 1938; Eric Bender to Korson, April 13, 1939.

4. Korson to Phelps Soule, January 6, 1942.

5. Spargo, p. 91.

6. "Dust on the Folklorists."

7. Korson's fight for acceptance of his view of folklore is similar to that which scientists who advance a new paradigm must face. See chapter 12, "The Resolu-

tion of Revolutions," in Thomas S. Kuhn, *The Structure of Scientific Revolutions*, Phoenix Edition (Chicago: University of Chicago Press, 1962), pp. 143–58.

8. Susman, p. 329.

9. Donald Richie, ed., *The Museum of Modern Art Department of Film Circulating Program* (New York: Museum of Modern Art, 1973), pp. 26–30.

10. Korson to Phelps Soule, January 6, 1942.

11. May 13, 1944.

12. Green, *Only a Miner*, p. 13.

13. Keener to Korson, April 16, 1942.

14. June 15, 1943, p. 18.

15. Early reviews that addressed themselves to questions of the book's structure and organization include those of Elias and Robie.

16. Korson, *Coal Dust*, p. 44.

17. Ibid., p. 171.

18. Ibid., pp. xvi–xvii.

19. Green, *Only a Miner*, p. 11.

20. *The New Republic* 109 (November 22, 1943), p. 725.

21. Robie, "Book Review."

22. Pritchett, "Books in General."

23. Horace Reynolds, *New York Times Book Review*, July 25, 1943.

24. Korson, *Coal Dust*, pp. 121–22.

25. Ibid., pp. 353–70.

26. Sanders to Korson, November 2, 1945.

27. Korson, *Coal Dust*, p. 32.

28. Carl N. Degler, *Out of Our Past: The Forces That Shaped Modern America*, rev. ed., Harper Colophon Books (New York: Harper & Row, 1959), p. 296.

29. *The Rise of the Unmeltable Ethnics: Politics and Culture in the Seventies* (New York: Macmillan, 1971), pp. 237–91.

30. Justin McCarthy, November 15, 1972, p. 13.

31. Wilgus, p. xv.

32. Ibid., pp. xv–xvi.

33. Ibid., pp. 204–5.

34. Robie, "Book Review."

35. Bazelton, "Book Review."

36. July 18, 1943.

37. Korson, *Coal Dust*, pp. 14–15.

38. Robie, "Book Review."

39. Cited in David R. Maxey, "The Volunteers," *Look* 34 (June 16, 1970).

40. Green, *Only a Miner*, p. 416.

41. Music Division, Library of Congress.

42. Green, *Only a Miner*, p. 416.

43. Marshall McLuhan, *Understanding Media: The Extensions of Man* (New York: McGraw-Hill, 1965), p. 17.

44. Green, *Only a Miner*, p. 415.

45. *Allentown Morning Call*, October 3, 1970.

46. Ibid.

47. Korson to Patterson, December 28, 1945.

48. Lynch to Korson, January 21, 1946.

49. Korson to Lynch, February 6, 1946.

50. Green, *Only a Miner*, p. 33.

51. Ibid., p. 417.

52. Catherine H. Bryan, Assistant to the Director, Wyoming Historical and Geological Society, interview at Wilkes-Barre, Pa., August 1, 1974.

53. Pp. 180–82.

54. Con Carbon, "Me Johnny Mitchell Man." Transcription from liner notes of L 16.

55. My remarks on L 16 were written after a helpful discussion of the album with two of my folklore students, Neal Mowry and Hedy Goller. The discussion was taped at Douglass College on May 19, 1975.

56. Brooks, *Toil and Trouble*, p. 224.

57. Eckardt and Eckardt, pp. 181–85.

58. Hoffman, interview at Portland, Ore., November 2, 1974.

59. July 24, 1949.

60. November 26, 1949, pp. 2218–19.

61. The best short account of the Gimbel's Store promotion is given in *Publishers Weekly* above, but for details of the arrangements the correspondence is helpful. For example, see letters from Korson to Dick Taplinger of the Publishers Publicity Bureau on July 21, 23, and 27 of 1949.

Chapter 4

1. Biddle (1786–1844), was a Philadelphia financier; the toast is cited by Korson in *Black Rock*, p. 102.

2. Ibid., p. viii.

3. Nancy Joan Glazier, interview at Bethlehem, Pa., August 30, 1974.

4. Green to Korson, March 30, 1956.

5. Broehl to Korson, August 18, 1958; Broehl, *The Molly Maguires*.

6. Dorson to Korson, January 9, 1958.

7. Dorson, interview at Portland, Ore., November 2, 1974.

8. Dorson to Korson, February 27, 1958.

9. Korson to Arthur C. Kaufman, March 13, 1950.

10. Shoemaker to Korson, November 14, 1956.

11. My account of the life of Shoemaker is based closely on a draft copy of an article "Henry W. Shoemaker, 1882–1958" by Frank A. Hoffman, sent in a letter from Hoffman to Korson, January 28, 1959.

12. Samuel P. Bayard, telephone interview, January 10, 1979.

13. According to Hoffman, the most extensive bibliography of Shoemaker's publications is that compiled by Miriam E. Dickey in "Henry W. Shoemaker: Pennsylvania Folklorist" (master's thesis, Western Reserve University, 1955). It lists nearly two hundred items but still is incomplete.

14. Hoffman, p. 3.

15. Keffer to Korson, June 26, 1956.

16. Ibid.

17. Korson to Keffer, May 3, 1957.

18. Korson to J. Herbert Walker, August 20, 1958.

19. Korson, J. Herbert Walker, and Grace West Staley to the members of the Pennsylvania Folklore Society, October 1, 1958.

20. Korson to Keffer, March 12, 1960.

21. Korson to George Swetnam, April 8, 1959.

22. Korson to Ralph W. McComb, June 11, 1959.

23. Hoffman, interview at Portland, Ore., November 2, 1974.

24. Korson to Hoffman, June 16, 1960.
25. Korson to Jan Harold Brunvand, March 14, 1960.
26. My account of the origins of *Black Rock* in Korson's thinking is based closely on the manuscript "Never Underestimate an Author's Will to Live."
27. Korson to Philip M. Ginder, November 1, 1955.
28. Reverend William J. Rupp to Korson, November 14, 1955.
29. Korson to Henry Allen Moe, October 15, 1956.
30. James F. Mathias to Korson, April 11, 1957.
31. Korson to Rae Korson, c. July, 1957.
32. Korson to J. J. France, October 11, 1957.
33. Korson to Rae Korson, July 24, 1957.
34. Ruth Thomas to Korson, September 8, 1957.
35. Korson to Meyer and Ruth Korson, October 25, 1957.
36. Korson to James F. Mathias, December 18, 1957; Korson to John H. Kyle, March 6, 1958; Henry Allen Moe to Korson, April 2, 1958; Korson to Moe, April 7, 1958.
37. Details of the contract negotiations come from the following correspondence: Ingle to Collins, April 11, 1958; Korson to Collins, April 15, 1958; Collins to Ingle, April 18, 1958; Ingle to Collins, May 15, 1958.
38. Korson, "Never Underestimate."
39. Korson to Moritz Jagendorf, September 24, 1960.
40. Korson to Philip M. Ginder, September 28, 1960.
41. Details of the double imprint negotiations come from the following correspondence: Korson to Rupp, February 1, 1958; Rupp to Korson, February 27, 1958; Korson to Rupp, June 14, 1958.
42. *Allentown Sunday Call Chronicle*, August 11, 1957.
43. Korson to Florence Peters Troxell, October 28, 1960.
44. Among reviewers who commented upon the organization and structure of the book are Houston and Swetnam.
45. Korson, *Black Rock*, pp. viii-ix.
46. See Dorson, *American Folklore and the Historian*, pp. 142-44.
47. Barba, p. 314.
48. Trescott, "Book Review."
49. Korson, *Black Rock*, p. 192.
50. Green, interview at Washington, D.C., February 28, 1973; Wayland Hand, interview at Portland, Ore., November 1, 1974.
51. Korson, *Black Rock*, pp. 1-31.
52. Wiegand, "Book Review."
53. Barba, p. 315.
54. Ibid.
55. Swetnam, pp. 20-21.
56. Korson, *Black Rock*, p. 356.
57. Rhodes, pp. 288-89.
58. Trescott, "Book Review."
59. Houston, "Book Review."
60. Lawrence S. Thompson, p. 148.
61. Korson to Green, September 28, 1960.
62. Korson, *Minstrels*, pp. 214–18.
63. Korson, *Black Rock*, p. 396.
64. Ibid.
65. Korson, *Minstrels*, p. 218.

Chapter 5

1. Heilfurth, "George Korson," p. 69.

2. Korson, *Minstrels*, p. 273.

3. Hand, interview at Portland, Ore., November 1, 1974.

4. Leach to Korson, December 21, 1960.

5. Metcalf to Korson, June 22, 1961.

6. Korson to John Greenway, December 11, 1965.

7. Miller to Korson, January 31, 1961.

8. Phyllis Kirk to Korson, April 13, 1961.

9. Vance Trimble, "John L. Has Spurned Fortune for Memoirs," *Washington Daily News*, April 17, 1961, p. 9.

10. Korson to Miller, May 2, 1961.

11. Lewis to Korson, April 25, 1961.

12. Extensive reports on Korson's field trips and his contacts with informants may be found in the correspondence. See, for example, his letters to M. Hughes Miller of May 24, 1961; August 11, 1961; September 26, 1961; February 13, 1962; April 4, 1962. See also his two letters to Gloria R. Mosesson, a juvenile editor for Bobbs-Merrill, dated March 7, 1962, and May 26, 1962.

13. Korson to C. B. Ulery, managing editor, April 22, 1963.

14. Korson to George Swetnam, March 25, 1961.

15. Korson to Selig Korson, May 30, 1962.

16. Korson to Ed Pinkowski, July 14, 1962.

17. Korson to Jerry Byrne, August 11, 1962.

18. Korson to Selig Korson, December 14, 1963.

19. Ibid.

20. *Wilkes-Barre Times-Leader Evening News*, October 12, 1964.

21. Goldstein, telephone interview, Philadelphia, Pa., October 7, 1975.

22. Korson to Alan C. Collins, May 24, 1963.

23. Korson to Green, April 16, 1964.

24. Green, "Foreword," pp. i–xiv.

25. Korson to Patterson, June 10, 1964.

26. Korson to Patterson, December 22, 1964.

27. Green to Korson, August 25, 1960.

28. Green to Korson, July 2, 1961.

29. Hemphill, p. 77.

30. Robert Shelton, "The Fort Knox of Folk Song," *New York Times*, November 12, 1961.

31. Ibid.

32. Green, *Only a Miner*, p. 417.

33. A parallel argument is made for the history of the textile industry by Archie Green in "Born on Picketlines."

34. *The Broadside*, Cambridge, Mass., March 2, 1966.

35. April 24, 1966 (section 10), p. 22.

36. Green, "Record Review," pp. 362-63.

37. Ibid., p. 363.

38. My remarks on L 60 were written after a helpful discussion of the album with two of my folklore students, Neal Mowry and Hedy Goller. The discussion was taped at Douglass College, May 19, 1975.

39. Wilson, "Record Review."

40. Korson to Edith Patterson, February 5, 1965.

41. Korson to Justin McCarthy, September 27, 1966; Gross to Korson, September 27, 1966.

42. Allan C. Collins to Korson, August 4, 1966.
43. Arthur W. Wang to Korson, June 9, 1965.
44. Barrett, interview at Wilkes-Barre, Pa., August 10, 1972.
45. Charles A. McCarthy to Korson, July 27, 1964; Korson to McCarthy, August 6, 1964.
46. Barrett to Gillespie, January 17, 1977.
47. *Wilkes-Barre Record*, September 15, 1965.
48. Korson to Selig Korson, August 27, 1965.
49. *Wilkes-Barre Record*, September 15, 1965.
50. Robert H. Byington to Korson, June 17, 1963.
51. Korson, "My Sweetheart's the Mule," p. 2.
52. Goldstein, *A Guide for Field Workers*, p. 76.
53. Korson, "My Sweetheart's the Mule", p. 8.
54. Ibid., p. 10.
55. p. 76.
56. Glassie, interview at Cape May, N.J., October 4, 1975.
57. Roberts, interview at Cape May, N.J., October 4, 1975.
58. Korson to Lane, December 22, 1966.
59. *The Washington Post*, May 25, 1967, p. B7; *The Wilkes-Barre Times-Leader*, May 24, 1967; *The New York Times*, May 25, 1967.
60. Botkin, remarks at the funeral of George Korson.

Epilogue

1. Whitman, "A Song for Occupations" in Sculley Bradley, ed. *Walt Whitman: Leaves of Grass and Selected Prose* (New York: Holt, Rinehart and Winston, 1962), pp. 182–84.
2. Korson, *Minstrels*, p. 204.
3. The metaphor of coal as a magnet is advanced by Archie Green in *Only a Miner*, pp. 431–32.
4. Hand, "George Korson and the Study of American Mining Lore," address.
5. Reuss, p. 115.
6. Ibid., p. 116.
7. Green, *Only a Miner*, p. 18.
8. Glassie, interview at Cape May, N.J., October 4, 1975.

Bibliography

Abrahams, Roger D. *Anglo-American Folksong Style*. Englewood Cliffs, N.J.: Prentice-Hall, 1968.

————. *Deep Down in the Jungle . . . Negro Narrative Folklore from the Streets of Philadelphia*. Hatboro, Pa.: Folklore Associates, 1964.

Adams, James Taylor. *Death in the Dark*. Big Laurel, Va.: Adams-Mullins, 1941.

Alinsky, Saul. *John L. Lewis: An Unauthorized Biography*. New York: Putnam's, 1949.

Allen, Frederick Lewis. *Only Yesterday: An Informal History of the Nineteen-Twenties*. New York: Harper and Row, 1964.

Anderson, Jay, ed. "George Korson Memorial Issue." *Keystone Folklore Quarterly* 16 (Summer 1971): 50–113.

Arble, Meade. *The Long Tunnel: A Coal Miner's Journal*. New York: Atheneum, 1976.

Aurand, Harold W. *From the Molly Maguires to the United Mine Workers: The Social Ecology of an Industrial Union 1869–1897*. Philadelphia: Temple University Press, 1971.

Baratz, Morton S. *The Union and the Coal Industry*. Port Washington, N.Y.: Kennikat Press, 1955.

Barba, Preston A. "Book Review: *Black Rock*." *Pennsylvania History* 28 (July 1961): 314.

Baumann, Roland M. "Dissertations on Pennsylvania History, 1866–1971: A Bibliography." *Pennsylvania History* 39 (January 1972): 75.

Bayard, Samuel Preston. "The British Folk Tradition." In *Pennsylvania Songs and Legends*, edited by George Korson. Philadelphia: University of Pennsylvania Press, 1949.

Bazelton, David T. "Book Review: *Coal Dust on the Fiddle*." *The New Republic* 109 (November 22, 1943): 725.

Bethke, Robert D. "Drink, Song, and Social Relations." Paper given at the Annual Meeting of the American Folklore Society, Portland, Oregon, November 3, 1974.

Bimba, Anthony. *The Molly Maguires*. New York: International Publishers, 1932.

Bining, Arthur Cecil. *Writings on Pennsylvania History: A Bibliography*. Harrisburg: Pennsylvania Historical and Museum Commission, 1946.

"Book Review: *Minstrels of the Mine Patch*, by George Korson." *Time* (November 14, 1938).

"Book Review: *Songs and Ballads of the Anthracite Miner*, by George Korson." *Coal Age* (August 1928).

Botkin, Ben. "Dust on the Folklorists," *Journal of American Folklore*. 57 (1944): 139.

————. "George Korson (1899–1967)," *New York Folklore Quarterly*. 23 (1967): 237.

————. *The Illustrated Book of American Folklore.* New York: Grosset and Dunlap, 1958.

————. *New York City Folklore.* New York: Random House, 1956.

————. *Sidewalks of America.* Indianapolis: Bobbs-Merrill, 1954.

Botsford, Harry. "Oilmen." In *Pennsylvania Songs and Legends,* edited by George Korson. Philadelphia: University of Pennsylvania Press, 1949.

Brendle, Thomas R. *Pennsylvania German Folk Tales, Legends, Once-Upon-A-Time Stories.* Norristown, Pa.: Pennsylvania German Society, 1944.

Brendle, Thomas R. and William S. Troxell. "Pennsylvania German Songs." In *Pennsylvania Songs and Legends,* edited by George Korson. Philadelphia: University of Pennsylvania Press, 1949.

Broehl, Wayne G., Jr. *The Molly Maguires.* New York: Vintage/Chelsea House, 1964.

Bronson, Bertrand H. "Cultural Keystone," Review of *Pennsylvania Songs and Legends,* edited by George Korson. *New York Times Book Review,* July 24, 1949.

Brooks, Philip C. *Research in Archives: The Use of Unpublished Primary Sources.* Chicago: University of Chicago Press, 1969.

Brooks, Thomas R. *Toil and Trouble: A History of American Labor,* 2d ed. New York: Dell Publishing Company, 1971.

Browne, Ray B. "Introduction: The Proper Study for American Studies." in Ray B. Browne, Donald M. Winkelman, and Allen Hayman, eds. *New Voices in American Studies.* Lafayette, Ind.: Purdue University Studies, 1966.

Byington, Robert H. "Introduction: George Korson Memorial Issue." *Keystone Folklore Quarterly,* 16 (1971): 51.

————. "Working Americans: Contemporary Approaches to Occupational Folklife." *Western Folklore* 37 (July 1978): 142–245.

Carmer, Carl. *The Susquehanna.* New York: Rinehart and Co., 1955.

Child, Francis James. *The English and Scottish Popular Ballads.* 5 vols. New York: Dover Books, 1966.

Coffin, Tristram P. *The British Traditional Ballad in North America.* Philadelphia: American Folklore Society, 1960.

Columbia University in the City of New York, *Transcript of Record,* "George Gershon Korson," December 19, 1941.

Deardorff, Merle H. "The Cornplanter Indians." In *Pennsylvania Songs and Legends,* edited by George Korson. Philadelphia: University of Pennsylvania Press, 1949.

Denisoff, R. Serge. *Great Day Coming: Folk Music and the American Left.* Baltimore: Penguin Books, 1973.

Dennis, Norman, et al. *Coal Is Our Life: An Analysis of a Yorkshire Mining Community.* London: Eyre & Spottiswoode, 1956.

DeSantis, Vincent P. *The Democratic Experience.* Glenview, Ill.: Scott, Foresman, 1963.

Dix, Keith. *Work Relations in the Coal Industry: The Hand-Loading Era, 1880–1930.* Morgantown: Institute for Labor Studies, West Virginia University, 1977.

Dorson, Richard M. *America in Legend: Folklore from the Colonial Period to the Present.* New York: Pantheon Books, 1973.

————. *American Folklore.* Chicago: University of Chicago Press, 1959.

————. *American Folklore and the Historian.* Chicago: University of Chicago Press, 1971.

————. *Folklore and Folklife: An Introduction.* Chicago: University of Chicago Press, 1972.

Dreiser, Theodore. *Harlan Miners Speak.* New York: Harcourt, Brace, 1932; reprinted New York: da Capo Press, 1970.

Eckardt, Alice, and Roy Eckardt. *Encounter with Israel.* New York: Association Press, 1970.

Elias, Robert H. "Book Review: *Coal Dust on the Fiddle.*" *Pennsylvania History,* 10 (October 1943).

Erikson, Kai T. *Everything in Its Path: Destruction of Community in the Buffalo Creek Flood.* New York: Simon and Schuster, 1976.

Evans, Chris. *History of the United Mine Workers of America from the Year 1860 to 1890.* Indianapolis, 1918.

Evanson, Jacob A. "Folk Songs of an Industrial City." In *Pennsylvania Songs and Legends,* edited by George Korson. Philadelphia: University of Pennsylvania Press, 1949.

Fay, Albert H. *A Glossary of the Mining and Mineral Industry.* Washington, D.C.: Government Printing Office, 1920.

"First Pennsylvania Folk Festival Proves Great and Glorious Success." *Allentown Morning Call,* May 5, 1935.

"Folklore Is Preserved in a Festival." *Literary Digest,* August 1, 1936, p. 21.

Fowke, Edith, and Joe Glazer. *Songs of Work and Freedom.* Chicago: Roosevelt University, Labor Education Division, 1960.

Frederick, John T. "Book Review: *Coal Dust on the Fiddle.*" *Book Week,* July 18, 1943, p. 4.

Frey, Howard C. "Conestoga Wagoners." In *Pennsylvania Songs and Legends,* edited by George Korson. Philadelphia: University of Pennsylvania Press, 1949.

Frey, J. William. "Amish Hymns as Folk Music." In *Pennsylvania Songs and Legends,* edited by George Korson. Philadelphia: University of Pennsylvania Press, 1949.

Funk and Wagnalls Standard Dictionary of Folklore, Mythology and Legend. New York: Funk and Wagnalls Co., 1949.

Fuson, Harvey H. *Ballads of the Kentucky Highlands.* London: Mitre Press, 1931.

"George Korson." *Morris County's Daily Record,* May 25, 1967.

"George Korson Is Third to Hold Title of 'Man from Wilkes-Barre.' " *Wilkes-Barre Sunday Independent,* September 28, 1958.

"Gimbel Brothers Book Promotion." *Publishers Weekly,* November 26, 1949, p. 2218.

Glazer, Joe. Liner notes to *Down in a Coal Mine,* Collector Records 1923. Album dedicated to George Korson.

———. Liner notes to *Songs of Coal,* Sound Studios 12–1137.

Gluck, Elsie. Review of *Songs and Ballads of the Anthracite Miner,* by George Korson. *Justice,* December 30, 1927.

Golden, Harry. *Carl Sandburg.* New York: World Publishing Company, 1961.

Goldstein, Kenneth S. "Bowdlerization and Expurgation: Academic and Folk." *Journal of American Folklore,* 80 (1967): 374.

———. *A Guide for Field Workers in Folklore.* Hatboro, Pa.: Folklore Associates, 1964.

Goldstein, Kenneth S., and Robert Byington, eds. *Two Penny Ballads and Four Dollar Whiskey.* Hatboro, Pa.: Folklore Associates, 1966.

Green, Archie. "American Labor Lore: Its Meaning and Uses," *Industrial Relations,* 4 (1965): 51–68.

————. "Born on Picketlines, Textile Workers' Songs Are Woven into History." *Textile Labor* (April 1961): 3.

————. "Foreword." *Minstrels of the Mine Patch*, by George Korson. Hatboro, Pa.: Folklore Associates, 1964, p. iv.

————. "George Korson and Industrial Folklore." *Keystone Folklore Quarterly* 16 (1971): 53.

————. "Industrial Lore: A Bibliographic-Semantic Query." *Western Folklore* 37 (July 1978): 213–44.

————. *Only a Miner: Studies in Recorded Coal-Mining Songs.* Urbana: University of Illinois Press, 1972.

————. "Record Review: Songs and Ballads of the Bituminous Miners; Songs and Ballads of the Anthracite Miners," *Ethnomusicology* 10 (September 1966): 362.

————. "Reflexive Regionalism." *Adena* 3 (Fall 1978): 3–15.

————. "The Workers in the Dawn: Labor Lore." In *Our Living Traditions*, edited by Tristram P. Coffin. New York: Basic Books, 1968, p. 251.

Greenway, John. *American Folksongs of Protest*. Philadelphia: University of Pennsylvania Press, 1953.

————. "Foreword." *Coal Dust on the Fiddle*, by George Korson. Hatboro, Pa.: Folklore Associates, 1965.

————. "George Korson (1900–1967)." *Journal of American Folklore* 80 (1967): 343.

Guthrie, Woody. *American Folksong*. New York: Oak Publications, 1961.

Haas, Al. "The Blue Collar Worker Is Finding 'Real-Man' Image Obsolete." *Philadelphia Inquirer*, November 19, 1972, section C, 5.

Hand, Wayland. "American Occupational and Industrial Folklore: The Miner." In *Kontakte und Grenzen: Problems der Volks-, Kultur und Sozialforschung*, edited by Hans Foltin. Gottingen: Geburtstag, 1969.

————. "California Miners' Folklore: Above Ground." *California Folklore Quarterly*, 1 (1942): 25.

————. "George Korson and the Study of American Mining Lore." Address delivered before the Mid-Atlantic Conference on Folk Culture, Wilkes-Barre, Pennsylvania, April 4, 1970.

————. "George Korson and the Study of American Mining Lore." *Keystone Folklore Quarterly* 16 (1971): 65.

Handlin, Oscar. *The Uprooted*. New York: Grosset and Dunlap, 1951, p. 259.

"Hard Coal Miners' Ballads Assembled by Jerseyman in an Entertaining Book." *Newark Evening News*, August 20, 1927.

Haywood, Charles A. *A Bibliography of North American Folklore and Folksong*. New York: Dover, 1961.

Heilfurth, Gerhard. *Das Bergmannslied*. Kassel, Barenreiter-Verlag, 1954.

————. "George Korson—An Appreciation," *Keystone Folklore Quarterly* 16 (Summer 1971): 69.

Hemphill, Paul. *The Nashville Sound*. New York: Ballantine Books, 1970.

"Henry W. Shoemaker, 1882–1958," by Frank A. Hoffman. Sent in a letter from Hoffman to Korson, January 28, 1959.

Hille, Waldemar. *The People's Song Book*. New York: Boni & Gaer, 1948.

Holbrook, Stewart H. *The Age of the Moguls*. New York: Doubleday, 1953.

Howe, Irving, and Lewis Coser. *The American Communist Party: A Critical History*. New York: Da Capo Press, 1974.

Hubbard, Freeman H. "Railroaders." In *Pennsylvania Songs and Legends*, edited by George Korson. Philadelphia: University of Pennsylvania Press, 1949.

Hume, Brit. *Death and the Mines: Rebellion and Murder in the United Mine Workers*. New York: Grossman Publishers, 1971.

Inman, Raymond S., and Thomas W. Koch. *Labor in American Society*. Glenview, Ill.: Scott, Foresman, 1965.

John L. Lewis and the International Union United Mine Workers of America: The Story from 1917 to 1952. Washington, D.C.: International Executive Board of the United Mine Workers of America, 1952.

Jones, Mary Harris. *The Autobiography of Mother Jones*. Chicago: Charles H. Kerr and Co., 1925.

Keil, Charles. *Urban Blues*. Chicago: University of Chicago Press, 1966.

Konitsky, Erma, ed. *Out of the Dark: Mining Folk*. Barnesboro, Pa.: Northern Cambria High School, 1976.

———. *Out of the Dark 2: Mining Folk*. Barnesboro, Pa.: Northern Cambria High School, 1977.

Korson, George. "Anthracite Folksongs and Ballads." *Wilkes-Barre Times-Leader Evening News*, October 12, 1964.

———. *At His Side: The American Red Cross Overseas in World War II*. New York: Coward-McCann, 1945.

———. *Black Land*. Evanston, Ill.: Row, Peterson, 1941.

———. *Black Rock: Mining Folklore of the Pennsylvania Dutch*. Baltimore: Johns Hopkins Press, 1960.

———. Brochure notes to *Songs and Ballads of the Anthracite Miners*. Library of Congress AFS L 16.

———. Brochure notes to *Songs and Ballads of the Bituminous Miners*. Library of Congress AFS L 60.

———. *Coal Dust on the Fiddle*. Philadelphia: University of Pennsylvania Press, 1943. Reprinted Folklore Associates, 1965.

———. "Coal Miners." In *Pennsylvania Songs and Legends*. Philadelphia: University of Pennsylvania Press, 1949.

———. "A Communication from Folklorist George Korson." *United Mine Workers Journal*, January 15, 1965, 18.

———. "Financial Statement of 1936 Pennsylvania Folk Festival." Lewisburg, Pennsylvania: Bucknell University memorandum, 1936.

———. "Folk Festival News." *Bucknell Alumni Monthly* (February 1937): 7.

———. "A History of the United Mine Workers of America." *United Mine Workers Journal*, May 1965–July 1967.

———. "History of Wyoming Valley." *Wilkes-Barre High School Journal*, May–June 1917.

———. "How the Pennsylvania Folk Festival of Bucknell University Can Serve the State." Memorandum to Arnaud C. Marts, Acting President of Bucknell University, 1936.

———. "Indiana Speech." Lecture given at Folklore Institute of America, Indiana University, Bloomington, Indiana, Summer 1958.

———. *John L. Lewis: Young Militant Labor Leader*. Indianapolis: Bobbs-Merrill, 1970.

———. *Minstrels of the Mine Patch*. Philadelphia: University of Pennsylvania Press, 1938. Reprinted Folklore Associates, 1964.

———. " 'My Sweetheart's the Mule in the Mines': Memories of Tom and Maggie Hill." In *Two Penny Ballads and Four Dollar Whiskey*, edited by Kenneth S. Goldstein and Robert H. Byington. Hatboro, Pa.: Folklore Associates, 1966, 1.

————. "Never Underestimate an Author's Will to Live." Unpublished manuscript, George Korson Folklore Archive.

————. *Pennsylvania Folk Songs and Ballads for School, Camp, and Playground.* Lewisburg: Pennsylvania Folk Festival, 1937.

————. *Pennsylvania Songs and Legends.* Philadelphia: University of Pennsylvania, 1949. Reprinted Johns Hopkins Press, 1960.

————. "Plans for the 1937 Pennsylvania Folk Festival." Lewisburg, Pa.: Bucknell University memorandum, 1936.

————. "Rambles in Allentown." *Allentown Chronicle and News,* August 29, 1931.

————. "Rambles in Allentown." *Allentown Chronicle and News,* October 13, 1931.

————. *Songs and Ballads of the Anthracite Miner.* New York: Frederick H. Hitchcock, Grafton Press, 1927.

————. "A Stranger in Allentown." *Allentown Chronicle and News,* April 27, 1931.

Korson, George, and Marion Vallat Emrich. *The Child's Book of Folklore.* New York: Dial Press, 1947.

Korson, George, and Melvin LeMon. *The Miner Sings.* New York: J. Fischer & Bro., 1936.

"Korson's Book on Miners' Ballads Now in Schools." *Wilkes-Barre Times Leader,* October 6, 1930.

"Korson's Book on Sale Here." *Wilkes-Barre Record,* October 10, 1927.

Lantz, Herman R. *People of Coal Town.* New York: Columbia University Press, 1958.

Laws, G. Malcolm. *American Balladry from British Broadsides.* Philadelphia: American Folklore Society, 1957.

————. *Native American Balladry.* Philadelphia: American Folklore Society, 1950.

Leach, MacEdward. "The Men Who Make Folklore a Scholarly Discipline." In *Our Living Traditions,* edited by Tristram Potter Coffin. New York: Basic Books, 1968, p. 22.

Leach, MacEdward, and Henry Glassie. *A Guide for Collectors of Oral Traditions and Folk Cultural Material in Pennsylvania.* Harrisburg: Pennsylvania Historical and Museum Commission, 1968.

Lee, Howard B. *Bloodletting in Appalachia.* Morgantown: West Virginia University, 1969.

LeMon, Melvin. "Pennsylvania Anthracite Miners' Folk-Songs." Thesis, Eastman School of Music, 1941.

LeMon, Melvin, and George Korson. *The Miner Sings.* New York: J. Fischer, 1936.

Lesoravage, Alice. "Folklorist's Dream Fulfilled." *Allentown Morning Call,* October 3, 1970, 11.

Levison, Andrew. "The Working Class Majority." *The New Yorker,* September 2, 1974, p. 45.

Lewis, Arthur H. *Lament for the Molly Maguires.* New York: Harcourt, Brace & World, 1964.

Linder, Walter. "The Great Flint Sit-Down Strike Against General Motors, 1936–1937." *Progressive Labor Magazine* 5 (February/March 1967).

Lloyd, Albert Lancaster. *Come All Ye Bold Miners.* London: Lawrence & Wishart, 1952.

Lomax, Alan. *The Folk Songs of North America in the English Language.* Garden City, N.Y.: Doubleday, 1960.

Lomax, John Avery. *Adventures of a Ballad Hunter.* New York: Macmillan, 1947.
————. *Our Singing Country.* New York: Macmillan, 1941.
McCarthy, Justin. "Where Did All the 'Liberals' Go? Answer: They Went Too Far!" Editorial, *United Mine Workers Journal,* November 15, 1972, 13.
McDonald, David J. *Coal and Unionism.* Indianapolis, Ind.: Cornelius Printing Company, 1939.
Messenger, Betty. *Picking Up the Linen Threads: A Study in Industrial Folklore.* Austin: University of Texas Press, 1978.
Mikeal, Judith. "Mother Mary Jones: The Labor Movement's Impious Joan of Arc." Master's thesis, University of North Carolina, 1965.
"Miss Rosenblatt Becomes Dride *(sic)* of Geo. Korsen *(sic),*" *Morristown Jerseyman,* December 17, 1926.
Mitchell, John. *Organized Labor.* Philadelphia: American Book and Bible House, 1903.
Munn, Robert F. *The Coal Industry in America: A Bibliography and Guide to Studies.* Morgantown: West Virginia University Library, 1965.
Murray, M.A. "England as a Field for Folklore Research." *Folklore* 65 (1954): 8.
Music Division, Recording Laboratory, The Library of Congress, album cover notes to *Songs and Ballads of the Anthracite Miners,* Library of Congress AAFS L 16.
"New Book of Miners' Songs." *Pottsville Republican,* November 18, 1938.
Niles, Abbe. "Singing Miners" (review). *The Nation,* February 1, 1928.
Niles, John J. "Mountain Songs" (column). *Chicago Daily News,* March 7, 1928.
"Notes, Books, Manuscripts to King's College Library." *Wilkes-Barre Record,* September 15, 1965.
Nyden, Paul John. "Miners for Democracy: Struggle in the Coal Fields." Thesis, Columbia University, 1974.
Oliphant, J. Orin. *The Rise of Bucknell University.* New York: Appleton-Century-Crofts, 1965.
Orwell, George. *The Road to Wigan Pier.* New York: Berkley Medallion Books, 1961.
Pelling, Henry. *American Labor.* Chicago: University of Chicago Press, 1960.
Pells, Richard H. *Radical Visions and American Dreams: Culture and Social Thought in the Depression Years.* New York: Harper & Row, 1973.
Penkower, Monty Noam. *The Federal Writers' Project: A Study in Government Patronage of the Arts.* Urbana: University of Illinois Press, 1977.
Pennsylvania Folk Festival, Advertising Flyer. Jenkintown, Pa.: Beaver College Publicity Department, 1938.
Pennsylvania Folk Festival, *Program.* Lewisburg, Pa.: Bucknell University, 1936.

Pinkerton, Allan. *The Mollie Maguires and the Detectives.* New York: Dover Publications, 1973.
Pinkowski, Edward. *John Siney, the Miner's Martyr.* Philadelphia: Sunshine Press, 1963.
Pritchett, V. S. "Books in General," *The New Statesman and Nation,* May 13, 1944.
Redfield, Robert. *The Little Community and Peasant Society and Culture.* 1st Phoenix Edition. Chicago: University of Chicago Press, 1967.
Reynolds, Horace, "Book Review: *Coal Dust on the Fiddle.*" *New York Times Book Review,* July 25, 1943.
Reuss, Richard A. "American Folklore and Left-Wing Politics: 1927–1957." Thesis, Indiana University, 1971.
Rhodes, Willard. "Book Review: *Black Rock.*" *Western Folklore* 21 (October 1962): 288.

Rigdon, Dorothy. "Book Review: *Coal Dust on the Fiddle.*" *United Mine Workers Journal* 54 (June 15, 1943): 18.

Robie, Edward H. "Book Review: *Coal Dust on the Fiddle.*" *Mining and Metallurgy,* August 1943.

Rourke, Constance. Review of *Minstrels of the Mine Patch* by George Korson. *The Nation,* December 10, 1938, p. 630.

Sandburg, Carl. *The American Songbag.* New York: Harcourt, Brace, and Company, 1927.

———. "From the Notebook of Carl Sandburg" column. *Chicago Daily News,* August 11, 1928.

———. *New American Songbag.* New York: Broadcast Music, 1950.

Seltzer, Curtis. "The United Mine Workers of America and the Coal Operators: The Political Economy of Coal in Appalachia, 1950–1973." Thesis, Columbia University, 1977.

Sharp, Cecil James. *English Folk Songs from the Southern Appalachians.* London: Oxford University Press, 1932.

Shelton, Robert. "Record Review: *Songs and Ballads of the Bituminous Miners.*" *New York Times,* April 24, 1966, Section X, p. 22.

———. "The Fort Knox of Folk Song." *New York Times,* November 12, 1961.

Sherwood, John. "Machines Only Music Left in Mines, Folklorist Finds." *Washington Evening Star,* October 19, 1965, Section B, p. 1.

Shoemaker, Alfred L. *Eastertide in Pennsylvania.* Kutztown: Pennsylvania Folklife Society, 1960.

———. *The Pennsylvania Barn.* Lancaster: Pennsylvania Dutch Folklore Center, Franklin & Marshall College, 1955.

Shoemaker, Henry W. "Central Pennsylvania Legends." In *Pennsylvania Songs and Legends,* edited by George Korson. Philadelphia: University of Pennsylvania Press, 1949.

———. *Mountain Minstrelsy of Pennsylvania.* Philadelphia: Newman F. McGirr, 1931.

———. *Thirteen Hundred Old Time Words of British Continental or Aboriginal Origins Still or Recently in Use Among the Pennsylvania Mountain People.* Altoona, Pa.: Times Tribune Press, 1930.

———. *Transplants in Pennsylvania Forests.* Reading, Pa.: Reading Eagle Company, 1932.

Silver, David. Review of *Minstrels of the Mine Patch* by George Korson. *New Masses,* February 7, 1939.

Simon, Rick. "The Development of Underdevelopment: The Coal Industry and Its Effect on the West Virginia Economy, 1880–1930." Thesis, University of Pittsburgh, 1978.

Spaeth, Sigmund. "Three Volumes Brushing the Dust from Old Fashioned Songs." *Philadelphia Inquirer,* December 3, 1927.

Spargo, John W. "Book Review: *Coal Dust on the Fiddle.*" *Journal of American Folklore* 57 (1944): 91.

Stirling, Perry. *The No. Nine Mine and Other Friends.* Lansford, Pa.: Vadyak Printing, 1974.

Susman, Warren. *Culture and Commitment 1929–1945.* New York: George Braziller, 1973.

Swanson, Catherine, and Philip Nusbaum eds. "Occupational Folklore and the Folklore of Working." *Folklore Forum* 2 (1978).

Swetnam, George. "Book Review: *Black Rock.*" *Keystone Folklore Quarterly* 5 (Winter 1960): 20–22.

Tate, Cecil F. *The Search for a Method in American Studies.* Minneapolis: University of Minnesota Press, 1973.

Theiss, Lewis Edwin. "Canallers." In *Pennsylvania Songs and Legends*, edited by George Korson. Philadelphia: University of Pennsylvania Press, 1949.

———. "'Minstrels *of the Mine Patch*' Makes Contribution to State Folklore, Theiss Says of Korson's New Book." *The Bucknellian*, December 8, 1938.

Thompson, Lawrence S. "Book Review: *Black Rock.*" *Southern Folklore Quarterly* 25 (June 1961): 148–49.

Tierney, Judith. *A Description of the George Korson Folklore Archive.* Wilkes-Barre: King's College Press, 1973.

———. "The George Korson Folklore Archive." *Keystone Folklore Quarterly* 16 (1971): 109.

Trescott, Paul. "Book Review: *Black Rock.*" *Philadelphia Sunday Bulletin*, December 11, 1960, Section VB, p. 10.

Troxell, William. *Aus Pennsylfawnia.* Philadelphia: University of Pennsylvania Press, 1938.

Udall, Lee, and Joe Wilson. *Presenting Folk Culture: A Handbook on Folk Festival Organization and Management.* Washington: National Council for the Traditional Arts, 1978.

Walker, J. Herbert. "Lumberjacks and Raftsmen." In *Pennsylvania Songs and Legends*, edited by George Korson. Philadelphia: University of Pennsylvania Press, 1949.

Wallace, Paul A. *Pennsylvania: Seed of a Nation.* New York: Harper and Row, 1962.

Welsh, James C. *Songs of a Miner.* London: Herbert Jenkins, 1917.

Wheeler, Robert J. "Pike County Tall Tales." In *Pennsylvania Songs and Legends*, edited by George Korson. Philadelphia: University of Pennsylvania Press, 1949.

Wiegand, Harold J. "Book Review: *Black Rock.*" *Philadelphia Inquirer*, November 30, 1960.

Wilgus, D. K. *Anglo-American Folksong Scholarship Since 1898.* New Brunswick: Rutgers University Press, 1959.

"William S. Troxell Dies; 'Pumpernickle' Was 64." *Allentown Sunday Call Chronicle*, August 11, 1957.

Wilson, Dave. "Record Review: *Songs and Ballads of the Bituminous Miners.*" *The Broadside*, Cambridge, Mass., March 2, 1966.

Woolley, Bryan, and Ford Reid. *We Be Here When the Morning Comes.* Lexington: University Press of Kentucky, 1975.

Wyoming National Bank of Wilkes-Barre. *Wyoming Valley Landmarks* 2 (1970): 8.

Yarrow, Michael. "The Labor Process in Coal Mining: Struggle for Control." In *Case Studies on the Labor Process*, edited by Andrew Zimbalist. New York: Monthly Review Press, 1979.

Yearley, Clifton K., Jr. *Enterprise and Anthracite.* Baltimore: Johns Hopkins Press, 1961.

Yoder, Don. "Folklife." In *Our Living Traditions*, edited by Tristram P. Coffin. New York: Basic Books, 1968, p. 47.

———. "The Folklife Studies Movement." *Pennsylvania Folklife* 13 (July 1963): 43.

———. *Pennsylvania Spirituals.* Lancaster: Pennsylvania Folklife Society, 1961.

———. "Twenty-Five Years of the Folk Festival," *Pennsylvania Folklife* 23, Folk Festival Supplement (June-July 1974): 4.

Index